SAGE SERIES IN WRITTEN COMMUNICATION

Series Editors

Charles R. Cooper, *University of California, San Diego*
Linda Brodkey, *University of California, San Diego*

Editorial Advisory Board

Volumes in This Series

SPEAKING ABOUT WRITING

SPEAKING ABOUT WRITING
Reflections on Research Methodology

edited by

PETER SMAGORINSKY
University of Oklahoma

SAGE SERIES IN WRITTEN COMMUNICATION

Volume 8

P
301
.S59
1994
V.8

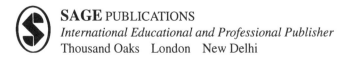

SAGE PUBLICATIONS
International Educational and Professional Publisher
Thousand Oaks   London   New Delhi

For information address:

SAGE Publications, Inc.
2455 Teller Road
Thousand Oaks, California 91320

SAGE Publications Ltd.
6 Bonhill Street
London EC2A 4PU
United Kingdom

SAGE Publications India Pvt. Ltd.
M-32 Market
Greater Kailash I
New Delhi 110 048 India

Printed in the United States of America

Library of Congress Cataloging-in-Publication Data

Speaking about writing : reflections on research methodology /
    edited by Peter Smagorinsky.
        p.   cm. — (Sage series in written communication)
    Includes bibliographical references and index.
    ISBN 0-8039-5231-7 (cl). — ISBN 0-8039-5232-5 (pb)
    1. Rhetoric.   2. Written communication.   I. Smagorinsky, Peter.
II. Series.
P301.S59   1994
302.2′244—dc20   94-3895
                                                                    CIP

94 95 96 97   10 9 8 7 6 5 4 3 2 1

Sage Production Editor: Rebecca Holland

Contents

PART III: Analysis of Collaborative Discourse

PART IV: Interviews in the Field

PART V: Counterpoint

Acknowledgments

I would like to thank a number of people who helped make this book possible. First of all, I would like to thank my contributors. Not only did they produce thoughtful essays reflecting on their work, they also provided me with feedback on various drafts of my own chapters and advice on how to develop the prospectus and resolve problems with the project. Without the many conversations I held with them over the phone and on electronic mail, I could never have put this book together.

I would also like to thank John Chiodo of the University of Oklahoma for extending department resources to recruit and maintain contact with the authors I worked with.

Thanks to Anne West, who originally encouraged this book at Sage, and to Sophy Craze for seeing the project through. My series editors, Charles Cooper and Linda Brodkey, provided valuable advice throughout the development of the book, from suggestions on how to work with authors to their ultimate critiques of the individual chapters. Thanks are due as well to Steve Witte for his foresight in suggesting Sage as a publisher.

I would also like to thank the many people who have impressed on me the importance of thinking seriously about research methodology. George Hillocks has hounded me the longest and most often on this issue, with help from Tom Trabasso, Susan Goldin-Meadow, Fred Lighthall, and Bill Pattison during the formative experience of my doctoral dissertation. There are others too numerous to mention here with whom I have discussed research methodology who are also deserving of thanks for helping me in my own thinking. I would like to extend special thanks, however, to Susan Goldman, who helped me through some early quandaries even though we'd never met.

Finally, thanks to my wife Jane and my children Alysha and David, who have put up with me throughout my development of this book and other projects. Their love and support help me endure when my ambitions and abilities sputter.

P.S.

*Dedicated with great love to
Margaret and Joseph Smagorinsky,
the original researchers*

Introduction
Potential Problems and Problematic Potentials of Using Talk About Writing as Data About Writing Process

PETER SMAGORINSKY

"This is not science!" So exclaimed a member of the audience at a panel presentation on research methodologies that focus on the collection and analysis of verbal reports in the study of writing (Greene, Higgins, Smagorinsky, & Sperling, 1992). The debate that followed this impassioned denunciation was only the latest incarnation of a methodological dispute that began in the early part of the twentieth century over the value of research methods that use the spoken word as a source of data in order to study thought processes involved in problem solving. In 1923 Lashley dismissed think-aloud studies as mere "introspection" that lacks the "chain and transit of objective measurement" (p. 352). The most that verbal data can do, its critics have maintained, is help generate hypotheses; the data are too impressionistic to verify processes, argue Nisbett and Wilson (1977).

Verbal reports in the study of writing have had a similarly difficult time finding acceptance among researchers who view them in terms of their susceptibility rather than their potential. The analysis of the spoken word in the study of writing originated in the landmark recommendation of Braddock, Lloyd-Jones, and Schoer (1963) that composition researchers should shift their study of writing from product to process. In order to study process researchers began observing writers at work, a move that necessitated the adoption and development of new approaches to study composing. Emig (1971) was the first to attempt a think-aloud methodology, although she did not provide specific details about her data collection and analysis procedures.

Meanwhile, in the field of cognitive science Newell and Simon (1972) developed *protocol analysis*, a systematic procedure for conducting think-aloud research to study general problem-solving processes. The method was adapted to the study of writing process by their Carnegie-Mellon colleagues Linda Flower and John R. Hayes in order to generate general models of writing behavior. Since the original attempts to develop composing models (Flower & Hayes, 1977, 1980a, 1980b, 1981a, 1981b, 1981c, 1984; Hayes & Flower, 1980, 1983) literacy studies have shifted their focus from strictly cognitive accounts of learning to social influences on mentation, attempting to identify the ways in which the context of learning shapes the "higher" or "sociocultural" mental processes described by Vygotsky (1978, 1986). Protocol analysis has since become only one means of using the spoken word to study writing process, with the emphasis now on developing methods that capture both social and cognitive dimensions of composing processes. Some researchers are using think-aloud protocol analysis in studies of situated writing. Others are developing or adapting methodologies that take context into account, such as in-process or post-process interviews with writers; analysis of classroom discourse; and interviews with writers reflecting on decisions, processes, and sources of knowledge.

The term that continues to surface in discussions with researchers who study verbal reports is "messy." The work is very messy indeed, and no doubt the difficulty of replication, the idiosyncratic nature of each investigation, the need to reconceive hypotheses and data analysis procedures in mid-study, and other seeming indicators of imprecision have caused great consternation among those who find the methodologies "unscientific." In eliciting the verbalized thoughts of writers, researchers are depending on a very unpredictable body of data. Conventional scientific inquiry constrains the conditions of production and focuses on the analysis of concrete products in order to provide clear, measurable results. As a result, the development and testing of hypotheses must be relatively clear. Studying the thought processes that produce concrete products, however, often requires a more tentative approach in that a researcher can only make inferences based on what people say about what they think. Due to the chimerical nature of inquiry, researchers often have little precedent to follow in conducting particular studies. Even clear guidelines (i.e., Hayes & Flower, 1983; Newell & Simon, 1972; Swarts, Flower, & Hayes, 1984) are often of little help during the conduct of unique investigations.

For my first protocol study (Smagorinsky, 1989a, 1991, 1992), for instance, I had already decided what I would study—the effects of different instructional approaches on writers' thinking—and had chosen think-aloud protocols as my means of manifesting and analyzing thought process. In planning the study, I soon realized that my knowledge of protocol analysis consisted of having read as many protocol studies as I could dig up, plus some articles debating the method's merits. From my reading I expected to be able to execute a worthwhile study. Some early piloting taught me quickly that I was undertaking a project that was immensely complex in ways I could not have foreseen, because the problematic aspects of protocol collection and analysis were not accounted for in the journal articles I'd read. Descriptions of protocol studies focused on results, not on methodological problems, and as a result I found myself uninformed as a reader of protocol research and unprepared for the great task that lay ahead.

To try to get more inside knowledge of how to collect and analyze my data, I wrote several letters to people who had conducted protocol research in a variety of fields. One respondent, Susan Goldman, advised me that:

> The nuts and bolts of protocol analysis require really "getting your head into" the data. Unfortunately, none of [the articles I've sent you] will tell you what to do. Rather, they suggest various ways I have attempted to deal with verbal reports as data, with the conditions of elicitation of those reports varying in structure.
> A few generalizations and pointers:

> - You will end up passing through your data more times than you want to count.
> - Classification schemes take at least *three* iterations before they are "right" and reliable. (First time you discover all the problems with your scheme; second time you apply a modified scheme but end up fine-tuning it; third time you actually apply the scheme, making no changes.) I usually use a 10% to 20% randomly drawn sample for reliability. Acceptable levels of agreement will also probably involve multiple passes through the data.
> - Put your data in a clear and organized form; number the protocol statements; don't trust your memory.
> - Protocol analysis doesn't get very far if you don't have any idea of what you are looking for. So be very clear on the questions you are attempting to address before you attack your data in a systematic fashion.
> - On the other hand, reading the protocols may suggest worthwhile questions. If you are not sure what you have or what questions the protocols might be able to answer then I recommend reading over several for purposes of forming questions. Then go back and decide how to attack the protocols for evidence of your "intuitive sense" of the data.

Susan's letter reassured me that my difficulty with the method was not unique, and gave me some basic procedures for handling the data. She was particularly helpful in my thinking about the coding system that I would use to analyze the transcripts; I had begun with the assumption that I could simply import a coding system from some other study, but found that these other systems had been designed to answer other questions. Her suggestions helped me realize that the answers to my questions were not available through the application of content-based coding systems developed by other researchers for the study of other problems. Rather, my analysis needed to emerge from both a theoretical anticipation of what the transcripts would reveal and insights that I would develop through repeated readings of the actual data.

As I worked on the study I developed concerns over different aspects of my research, concerns that caused me a great deal of doubt as I attempted to make sense of my pile of protocol transcripts. To what extent had the method itself shaped the data? Were some research assistants easier for some subjects to work with than others? Were some subjects "better" at yielding protocols than others? If so, how did this affect my results? Was my coding system really providing useful information, or had I developed it to help me find what I was looking for? In getting high rates of agreement, was I really establishing reliability, or had I merely succeeded in training someone to accept my politics and perspective? My uneasiness over these troubling questions led me to do a great deal of thinking about the method I'd employed and forced me to justify my work at least to my own satisfaction, a project that resulted in my first publication on the methodology (Smagorinsky, 1989b).

I found through conversations with other protocol researchers that they had experienced similar periods of doubt and concern. The idea for this book began during these discussions, particularly as the notion of verbal reports began to expand beyond the traditional uses of protocol analysis with Swanson-Owens's (this volume) development of *intervention* protocols and Rose's (1984) use of film as a stimulus for writers to discuss their process, and with the investigations into social aspects of composing such as writing conferences (Sperling, 1990) and tutorials (DiPardo, 1993). I began to understand that different researchers had encountered problems somewhat like my own, and that they would welcome the opportunity to reflect on them in this text. Anyone interested in methodological problems—particularly researchers who planned to collect and analyze verbal reports—would surely appreciate the experience of sharing these ruminations.

This book is designed to illuminate theoretical and practical problems involved in conducting research based on verbal reports, with a focus on issues that have been ignored to this point and that provide the most nettlesome impediments to researchers conducting such inquiries. The book serves two basic purposes: to continue the debate about the validity of research methods involving verbal reports, and to explicate the problems and potentials of such methodologies for the benefit of prospective researchers.

The chapters are organized according to the unit of analysis used to study writing through a verbal report. The first set of chapters looks at different aspects of conducting *think-aloud protocol analysis*. I open this section with the argument that protocol analysis, due to its origination in the information-processing paradigm, is falsely regarded as a mechanical means of investigation. It is rather, I maintain, a fundamentally "human" enterprise, subject to personal bias, interaction factors between researchers and subjects, problems of interpretation, and other aspects of human caprice. In spite of the problems caused by the vagaries of human weakness, I argue that protocol analysis nonetheless offers a unique glimpse into the workings of the human mind, and has a distinct persuasiveness due to the storytelling character of the data. Protocols can thus make an important contribution to our understanding of composing process when viewed in the context of validating research.

Stephen P. Witte and Roger D. Cherry next walk the readers through a protocol study they have conducted that examines the variability of writing process depending on writing task. Throughout their chapter they make the processes behind their decisions explicit. Witte and Cherry discuss ways in which protocol analysis can be sensitive to social and contextual issues in writing.

The first two chapters on protocol analysis present the argument that each study is unique and therefore requires the development of an appropriate coding system. In contrast, Robert J. Bracewell and Alain Breuleux present a *lexical* coding system that they argue is responsive to a coherent body of principles and procedures for treating think-aloud protocols, and is therefore not dependent on the particular assumptions of individual researchers. They argue that coding protocols according to lexical rather than study-specific, content-oriented features will result in a general, theoretically motivated methodology for integrating evidence in constructing models of writing.

The last chapter on protocol analysis presents an exploratory study on the issue of "reactivity." James F. Stratman and Liz Hamp-Lyons are concerned with the question of the extent to which a writer's process of thinking aloud actually alters the cognitive processes required to carry out the given task. They challenge the prevailing assumption that reactivity is idiosyncratic and not subject to investigation, and assert that identifying reactivity effects becomes increasingly important with the publication of each new protocol study. Their pilot study suggests that reactivity is more predictable than has previously been assumed. Stratman and Hamp-Lyons's study offers the possibility that questions about think-aloud methodologies that have previously been debated without empirical verification may in fact be amenable to systematic investigation.

The next set of chapters falls under the heading of *retrospective accounts of writing process*. Stuart Greene and Lorraine Higgins begin with an explication of *retrospective* protocols, a method that relies on a writer's report of the processes involved in composing at an earlier time. Unlike think-aloud protocol analysis, which attempts to track the linear unfolding of thought process during composing, a retrospective account relies on a writer's selective evaluations and inferences of what has occurred previously, and is necessarily a reconstruction of prior thought process. The authors argue that in spite of the pitfalls of relying on reconstructed processes, the method has a unique capacity to probe the reasons for particular decisions. In making their argument, the authors illustrate issues involved in collecting and analyzing retrospective accounts, and offer guidelines for making the data valid and reliable.

A second form of retrospective interview, *intervention* protocols, is described by Deborah Swanson-Owens and George E. Newell. Rather than eliciting a retrospective account of process after the conclusion of a composing session, this method gathers retrospective data at various points *during* a composing session. The researchers argue that the interruption of writing for the purpose of reflecting on process can serve as a supportive measure in helping writers learn about composing, and thus serves to scaffold a subject's learning during data collection. The intervention of the researcher thus becomes a part of the data as a means of instruction. The authors explicate the method, identifying the conditions that could potentially compromise its value.

Anne DiPardo describes a third type of retrospective interview, *stimulated recall*. This methodology uses some sort of stimulus to prompt recall of events from a prior time. The stimulus can be a film of a writer at work (i.e., Rose, 1984); a finished writing product that a writer can use as a stimulus to talk about a prior composing process; or in DiPardo's case, an audiotape of a conference between a student and a tutor. DiPardo discusses issues involved in selecting a stimulated recall method, and how the context of the investigation influences various decisions about the type of stimulus and the manner of the interview. She concludes that the method can enable researchers to get beneath the surface of the problems they are studying, prompting subjects to discuss processes and interactions that they otherwise might have neglected.

The next three chapters look at issues involved in *analysis of collaborative discourse*. To begin, George Hillocks identifies and discusses a problem that needlessly complicates discussions about the validity of research methodologies. Too often, research is spuriously sorted into one of two mutually exclusive categories, "quantitative" and "qualitative," with each dismissing the other as being incapable of drawing conclusions about human behavior. Hillocks argues that "quantitative" studies, while often taking the stance of being dispassionate and objective, inherently involve biased interpretation. Similarly, he makes the point that "qualitative" studies, which typically dismiss attempts to quantify behavior, invariably rely on counting instances of activity in order to arrive at their conclusions. Hillocks calls for researchers of all orientations to admit the full range of behaviors they engage in and focus on the quality of particular investigations, rather than evaluating them according to the methodology they employ.

Melanie Sperling next describes her use of discourse analysis procedures to analyze transcripts of teacher-student writing conferences. Such conferences are difficult to analyze due to the amorphous nature of the task and complex issues in objectifying the discourse; researchers of such fluid dynamics often find themselves shooting at a moving target. Yet Sperling finds that the imprecise and ambiguous nature of the task helps account for the research's theoretical appeal, highlighting the human character of the object of study. The very complexity of the research process, which she illustrates with examples from her own experience, illuminates the complexity of human interaction.

In the third chapter on discourse analysis, Elizabeth Hodges describes the sociolinguistic methods she employed to analyze classroom discourse. The study of classroom discourse, she argues, requires a theory about how language functions socially. Hodges details the sources of her sociolinguistic inquiry and discusses the drawbacks and benefits of the method. Finally, she details her own application of sociolinguistic methods in coding and analyzing classroom discourse. She argues that her coding of classroom transcripts enables her to construct maps of interaction that identify occasions when talk is both effective and ineffective in helping students achieve writing goals.

Elaine Chin next moves outside the classroom to discuss the conduct of *interviews in the field*. Drawing on methodological sources from sociology and anthropology, Chin reviews issues surrounding the study of writing in "naturalistic" settings through interviews with writers as they go about their work. She illustrates the problems with examples from her own research on faculty and master's degree students in a journalism program, focusing on the actual conduct of the interviews. The "messiness and complexity" of interviewing lead her to urge the research community to adopt the same stringent requirements for detailed reporting of interviews that are expected when using other methodologies. Otherwise the method will be open to question.

The book closes with a *counterpoint* initiated by David N. Dobrin, a vocal critic of composition research in general and protocol analysis in particular. Dobrin retains his skepticism in this chapter, arguing that the scholarly community has privileged accounts of writing that abide by the scientific principles of reliability and replicability. He argues that the lack of precision in research involving verbal reports accords such investigations no more certitude than any other type of observation, no matter how informal or unsystematic. Dobrin nonetheless finds value in verbal reports as testimonies that reveal thoughts that are otherwise difficult to share; he argues that the *stories* people tell through verbal reports "are the thing, the sine qua non of the discipline," and should be treated as significant, even without analysis through a coding system.

Robert J. Bracewell concludes the book with a response to Dobrin in which he takes issue with Dobrin's account of cognitive psychology. Dobrin argues from the standpoint of an outsider, a perspective that Bracewell feels causes Dobrin to misconstrue issues in psychological research emerging from the work of Newell and Simon. The differences articulated by Dobrin and Bracewell highlight the points of dispute that have characterized much of the controversy surrounding the systematic analysis of verbal reports in the study of writing over the past 15 years.

Taken as a whole, the chapters provide an overview of different methodologies available to researchers who desire to study composing process through verbal accounts. In discussing problems and potentials, the authors acknowledge and discuss the issues that raise questions about their work, and the prospects they see for the field in spite of the methodological problems. In doing so the authors are attempting to demystify processes of decision making that are only implied in finished reports of research.

One point that should be clarified is that a research method alone cannot account for the quality of an investigation. A researcher should not enter into a study by selecting a method first, but should be concerned with a *problem* to be studied. This book might then help researchers identify a method that, if properly conducted, could help answer the research questions. One of the most misguided debates in the field today is that which pits one method against another, as in the qualitative versus quantitative debate outlined by Hillocks in this volume. Anyone who has reviewed journal articles should know that no methodology has a lock on quality, that there are good and bad investigations conducted under the name of every research method. The questions are: What is the problem under study? What method is most appropriate for conducting the inquiry? How can the method most rigorously be applied?

My intent in putting this book together has been to extend an important debate about methodological problems. The articles published to date on the relative merits of studies employing verbal reports have tended to look at the methods in black-and-white terms. Published studies have focused on the results of difficult decision-making processes without attending to the mind-racking sessions that produced them, while articles that defend studies involving verbal reports tend to minimize the problems in their attempts to justify the methodology. On the other hand, critics of research based on verbal reports have tended to throw the baby out with the bath water, dismissing the results of protocol studies because of objections to certain aspects of the collection and analysis of the data.

One message I hope to convey through this text is that research involving verbal reports is like any other form of research in that the methodology shapes the data, and the researcher's hypotheses and theoretical framework affect the interpretation of the results. My purpose is to make the nature of these considerations more explicit so that we can identify them and then move ahead to learn from what verbal-transcript research can offer. The research cited in this book demonstrates that the potential knowledge to be mined through these methods is considerable and worthy of our attention. I hope that this book can contribute to a methodological debate that will strengthen future studies conducted along these lines.

REFERENCES

Braddock, R., Lloyd-Jones, R., & Schoer, L. (1963). *Research in written composition* (ED 003 374). Champaign, IL: National Council of Teachers of English.

DiPardo, A. (1993). *A kind of passport: A basic writing adjunct program and the challenge of student diversity* (NCTE Research Rpt. #24). Urbana, IL: National Council of Teachers of English.

Emig, J. (1971). *The composing process of twelfth graders*. Urbana, IL: National Council of Teachers of English.

Flower, L. S., & Hayes, J. R. (1977). Problem-solving strategies and the writing process. *College English, 39*, 449-461.

Flower, L. S., & Hayes, J. R. (1980a). The dynamics of composing: Making plans and juggling constraints. In L. Gregg & E. Steinberg (Eds.), *Cognitive processes in writing: An interdisciplinary approach* (pp. 31-50). Hillsdale, NJ: Lawrence Erlbaum.

Flower, L. S., & Hayes, J. R. (1980b). The cognition of discovery: Defining rhetorical problems. *College Composition and Communication, 31*, 21-32.

Flower, L. S., & Hayes, J. R.. (1981a). A cognitive process theory of writing. *College Composition and Communication, 32*, 365-387.

Flower, L. S., & Hayes, J. R. (1981b). Plans that guide the composing process. In C. H. Frederiksen & J. F. Dominic (Eds.), *Writing: The nature, development, and teaching of written communication* (pp. 39-58). Hillsdale, NJ: Lawrence Erlbaum.

Flower, L. S., & Hayes, J. R. (1981c). The pregnant pause: An inquiry into the nature of planning. *Research in the Teaching of English, 15*(3), 229-243.

Flower, L. S., & Hayes, J. R. (1984). The representation of meaning in writing. *Written Communication, 1*(1), 120-160.

Greene, S., Higgins, L., Smagorinsky, P., & Sperling, M. (1992, March). *Verbal reports in the study of writing: Problems and potentials*. Panel presentation at the annual meeting of the Conference on College Composition and Communication, Cincinnati.

Hayes, J. R., & Flower, L. (1980). Identifying the organization of writing processes. In L. Gregg & E. Steinberg (Eds.), *Cognitive processes in writing: An interdisciplinary approach* (pp. 3-30). Hillsdale, NJ: Lawrence Erlbaum.

Hayes, J. R., & Flower, L. (1983). Uncovering cognitive processes in writing: An introduction to protocol analysis. In P. Mosenthal, L. Tamor, & S. Walmsley (Eds.), *Research in writing: Principles and methods*. New York: Longman.

Lashley, K. S. (1923). The behavioristic interpretation of consciousness II. *Psychological Review, 30*, 329-252.

Newell, A., & Simon, H. A. (1972). *Human problem solving*. Englewood Cliffs, NJ: Prentice-Hall.

Nisbett, R. E., & Wilson, W.T.D. (1977). Telling more than we can know: Verbal reports on mental processes. *Psychological Review, 84*, 231-259.

Rose, M. (1984). *Writer's block: The cognitive dimension*. Carbondale: Southern Illinois University Press.

Smagorinsky, P. (1989a). *The effects of different types of knowledge on the writing process: A protocol analysis*. Unpublished doctoral dissertation, The University of Chicago.

Smagorinsky, P. (1989b). The reliability and validity of protocol analysis. *Written Communication, 6*(4), 463-479.

Smagorinsky, P. (1991). The writer's knowledge and the writing process: A protocol analysis. *Research in the Teaching of English, 25*(3), 339-364.

Smagorinsky, P. (1992). How reading model essays affects writers. In J. W. Irwin & M. A. E. Doyle (Eds.), *Reading/writing connections: Learning from research* (pp. 35-44). Newark, DE: International Reading Association.

Sperling, M. (1990). I want to talk to each of you: Collaboration and the teacher-student writing conference. *Research in the Teaching of English, 24*(3), 279-321.

Swarts, H., Flower, L. S., & Hayes, J. R. (1984). Designing protocol studies of the writing process: An introduction. In R. Beach & L. Bridwell (Eds.), *New directions in composition research*. New York: Guilford Press.

Vygotsky, L. (1978). *Mind in society: The development of higher psychological processes* (M. Cole, V. John-Steiner, S. Scribner, & E. Souberman, Eds.). Cambridge, MA: Harvard University Press.

Vygotsky, L. (1986). *Thought and language*. Cambridge: MIT Press.

Part I
Think-Aloud
Protocol Analysis

1

Think-Aloud Protocol Analysis
Beyond the Black Box

PETER SMAGORINSKY

Studying thought processes through think-aloud research methodologies has been a social science procedure since the early part of the twentieth century (i.e., Claparede, 1934; Duncker, 1926). In 1972 Newell and Simon published *Human Problem Solving,* which detailed a procedure they termed *protocol analysis* (also known as "on-line" or "concurrent" protocol analysis) for the systematic coding and analysis of thought processes during problem-solving activities. Since then researchers in a variety of fields have used think-aloud procedures to study the thought processes of people engaged in all manner of activities, from solving puzzles (Thomas, 1974) to reading poetry (Kintgen, 1983).

Social science researchers using think-aloud protocols have tended to focus on cognitive aspects of problem solving. The adaptation of the protocol analysis research method to the study of writing originally had a strong cognitivist influence, with John R. Hayes—a psychology department colleague of Herbert Simon, Allan Newell, and K. Anders Ericsson at Carnegie-Mellon University—collaborating with Linda Flower to conduct a lengthy series of studies (Flower & Hayes, 1977, 1980a, 1980b, 1981a, 1981b, 1981c, 1984; Hayes & Flower, 1980). Emig (1971) and Mischel (1974) had previously collected and analyzed verbal reports to study writing, but had done so from impressionistic observations, rather than through the rigorous segmenting and coding procedures used by researchers operating from a cognitivist paradigm.

Critics of think-aloud protocol collection and analysis have pointed to several important methodological problems that I will briefly review here. Interested readers should consult the cited sources for the elaborated arguments. The main points of contention appear to be:

1. Think-aloud data are subject to idiosyncratic interpretation and therefore, while perhaps useful in generating hypotheses, are not valid as verifications of cognitive processes (Lashley, 1923; Nisbett & Wilson, 1977).

2. Cognitivist protocol researchers, following the assumptions of their methodological antecedents, questionably assume that writing is a problem-solving task, when writing may alternatively be viewed as a stream-of-consciousness activity (Cooper & Holzman, 1983).

3. Protocols do not elicit all cognitive activity, and are therefore incomplete. These gaps in the protocol transcripts require the researcher to infer processes in order to construct a model of composing behavior, and therefore readers must trust the insights of the investigator for an understanding of the protocols' significance. The protocols themselves do not clearly reveal thought processes (Cooper & Holzman, 1983, 1985).

4. Protocols are conducted under the artificial conditions of a time-constrained session. Real writers compose while driving home, shopping, folding laundry, and so on, instead of composing only while writing. They also experience interruptions, such as phone calls and lunch, which alter their processes. Protocols do not therefore afford a true view of composing processes (Dobrin, 1986).

5. The cognitive process model does not take other factors of composing into account, such as affect, linguistic ability, and so on (Brand, 1987).

These concerns have received substantial attention and response. The most comprehensive defense of think-aloud protocols has issued from Ericsson and Simon (1979, 1980, 1984), with extensive documentation from scores of studies conducted in a variety of social science fields. I would also refer readers to the more specific defenses of think-alouds in the study of writing (Flower & Hayes, 1985; Hayes & Flower, 1983; Smagorinsky, 1989a; Steinberg, 1986; Swarts, Flower & Hayes, 1984) for a detailed understanding of the conflicting perspectives on these concerns.

In this chapter, rather than reexamining these established arguments, I will discuss problematic aspects of think-aloud protocol collection and analysis that have received little attention in the debate thus far. I will not dwell on the practical planning procedures that can help avert disaster. These might include: If collecting the protocols in a public school, make sure that the administration does not plan to conduct a fire drill, and then hope that an errant youth will not pull the alarm just for fun; test the tape recorders and change the batteries after every session; make sure that the teachers have not planned field trips on the days you bring in a brace of researchers to collect protocols (this happened to me); and so on. These nuts-and-bolts considerations do not illuminate broader research issues. My focus instead will be on problems associated with some of the more troubling aspects of the *collection, analysis,* and *interpretation* of think-aloud data. Finally, I will suggest occasions when think-aloud transcripts are appropriate data for answering particular research questions.

COLLECTION:
RESEARCHER-SUBJECT INTERACTIONS

Ideally, the researcher's role in collecting protocols is neutral. In many protocol studies, the researcher is present during the think-aloud session, acquainting the subject with procedures, giving instructions for the composing task, and then receding into the background as much as possible, speaking only on those occasions when the subject lapses into silence for more than 15 to 30 seconds, by giving a gentle, contentless prompt such as "Please remember to think aloud" or "Try to say everything that's going through your mind." Researchers should not cue particular responses by identifying specific processes or areas of content for the writer to attend to. In playing a neutral role, we assume, the researcher will not interfere with the emergence of representative writing process.

Yet more may be involved in the interaction between researcher and writer than the assumption of a neutral stance, even on those occasions when the researcher is not present during the think-aloud session. Robert Rosenthal has examined researcher effects on behavioral research and has identified a seemingly endless series of human characteristics that can affect the behavior of subjects. Among the most prominent factors is gender. Concludes Rosenthal (1966), "A good deal of research has been conducted which shows that male and female experimenters sometimes obtain significantly different data from their subjects" (p. 42). Not only that, male and female *subjects* tend to elicit different types of behavior from *researchers.* Among the findings synthesized by Rosenthal are:

1. Female subjects tend to be treated more attentively and considerately than male subjects.
2. Female researchers tend to smile more often than male researchers.
3. Male researchers tend to situate themselves closer to male subjects than do female researchers.
4. Male researchers tend to show higher levels of bodily activity than do female researchers; when the subject is a male, both male and female researchers tend

to show higher levels of bodily activity than they do when the subject is a female.

5. Female subjects rate male researchers as more friendly and as having more pleasant and expressive voices than female researchers.

6. Both male and female researchers behave more warmly towards female subjects than they do towards male subjects, with male researchers the warmer of the two.

Rosenthal (1966) also found that racial or perceived cultural factors can influence the interaction between researcher and subject. Subjects tend to give more "proper" responses to researchers of a different race or culture. For instance, white subjects in Rosenthal's research were more likely to reveal racial prejudice to a white researcher than to a black one; similarly, Gentile subjects were more likely to reveal anti-Semitic attitudes to a Gentile researcher than to one whom they perceived as Jewish. Black subjects also gave responses that were "proper" more frequently to white researchers than to black researchers.

Other characteristics that can affect the data include the researcher's age, level of anxiety, need for approval, birth order, level of hostility, authoritarianism, intelligence, dominance, relative status in the research project, warmth, acquaintance with the subject, and the type and extent of experience as a researcher. Furthermore, the room in which the study is conducted may affect not only the subject's responses but also the researcher's warmth, anxiety, and so on, thus influencing the data.

Another factor that can affect the writer's performance is the researcher's unintentional behavior based on his or her own expectations and hypotheses (Rosenthal, 1966; Rosenthal, Hall, DiMatteo, Rogers, & Archer, 1979). Through subtle cues—such as tone of voice, posture, smiling approvingly, and so on—a researcher can cue desired behaviors (cf. Smagorinsky, 1987, pp. 337-339). Cuing behavior is not necessarily intentional; Rosenthal (1966) has found that even " 'bias-wise' experimenters treated their subjects as they would have to be treated to increase the likelihood of the confirmation of the hypothesis" (p. 155).

The subjects' performance may also be a result of factors having to do with the characteristics of volunteers, an influence that researchers consistently underestimate (Rosenthal & Rosnow, 1969, 1975). Volunteer subjects strongly tend to have a higher educational level, higher occupational status, higher need for approval, higher intelligence, and lower sense of authoritarianism than nonvolunteers. They also tend to be more sociable, more arousal seeking, more unconventional, more often firstborn, and younger than nonvolunteers. These factors can bias the results of research, particularly in concert with other interactive factors.

The characteristics of the subject and personal dynamics between researcher and subject, then, may have a great deal to do with the content of the protocols. In order to account for this problem, researchers might need to train their research assistants in these interaction factors. Even with such preparation, however, "bias-wise" researchers might contribute to interactions that will shape the data.

ANALYSIS:
DEVELOPING CODING SYSTEMS

Theoretical Considerations

The coding system is the instrument that represents the import of the data. One could conceivably argue that in the hands of researchers with different assumptions and agendas, the same data could be subjected to quite different coding systems and therefore yield quite different results. This is not to say that protocols are inkblots that reflect only the researcher's own inner vision; presumably a coding system will represent a theoretical approach to the data and will be applied consistently across protocols in response to their content. Yet we can assume that researchers with different orientations would bring a different vision to the protocols. So, if not quite so amorphous as an inkblot, protocols might be analogous to a more distinct elephant perceived in different ways by researchers wearing different types of blinders. (See Hillocks, this volume, for an extended discussion of issues related to the interpretation of transcripts.)

An important task for researchers, then, is to understand and delineate their own approach to the data, and to devise a coding system that describes the processes that their theory anticipates. The relationship between theory and coding system raises an important issue for prospective protocol researchers: the difficulty of successfully importing another coding system wholesale. Surely, prior to developing a coding system a researcher should read a great number of protocol studies to examine the purpose of the studies, the theoretical underpinnings of the investigations, and the subsequent rationale for the coding systems. Unless, however, a researcher is in the rare situation of studying an identical problem from an identical perspective—for instance, in the related series of studies conducted by Durst

(1987), Langer (1986a, 1986b), Langer and Applebee (1987), Marshall (1987) and Newell (1984), which examined the level of thought in writing tasks of different types and complexity—researchers need to develop a coding system emerging from and consistent with the unique perspective they bring to the investigation. Even single researchers conducting a related series of investigations often need to modify their coding systems from study to study, to account for shifts in their increasing knowledge and their perspectives on the problem they are studying (Langer, 1989). (See Bracewell and Breuleux, this volume, for a different perspective on coding systems.)

To illustrate the considerations involved in developing a coding system from a coherent theoretical perspective, I will contrast two studies, those of Langer and Applebee (1987; cf. Durst, 1987; Langer, 1986a, 1986b; Marshall, 1987; Newell, 1984) and Smagorinsky (1989b, 1991, 1992). Langer and Applebee, having documented extensively (Applebee, 1981, 1984) the tendency of public school writing instruction to elicit elliptical forms of writing such as note-taking and short answers at the expense of more extended forms of composition, wanted to examine the types of thought processes involved in writing of different length and at different levels of student control. Thus, Applebee's observational studies justified the analysis of this problem to test the researchers' theory that when students initiate their own extended writing, their thinking is more complex and leads to greater cognitive growth than it does when tersely transcribing someone else's dicta or delivering prescribed knowledge.

The researchers therefore needed to develop a coding system that would describe hierarchical levels of thought, and develop writing prompts that would elicit data amenable to the application of the coding system. They used a coding system developed by Langer (1986a, 1986b), which she called an "Analysis of Meaning Construction," featuring reasoning operations such as generating questions, hypothesizing, citing evidence, and so on. To contrast the emergence of these operations in different tasks, they selected three school-related writing prompts to elicit data for task-related analysis: note-taking (while reading a given selection), study questions (filling in or writing a brief correct response), and essay writing (analyzing an overall problem in a given reading selection). Their data confirmed their hypotheses, enabling them to put forth an instructional agenda calling for less brief informational writing and more extended composition work.

My research (Smagorinsky, 1989b, 1991, 1992) presented me with a completely different set of problems. Langer and Applebee's research was part of a line of inquiry that had occupied them for the better part of a decade, with the intent to reform what they saw as the impoverished state of public school writing, which valued reporting brief correct answers over developing extended original insights. While I share the goals of their research, I was emerging from a different instructional perspective, due to my longtime association with George Hillocks, Jr. Hillocks's work (Hillocks, 1975, 1979, 1981, 1984, 1986a, 1986b, 1987; Hillocks, Kahn, & Johannessen, 1983) had focused on instructional methods and the types of knowledge embedded in different teaching approaches. He was critical of "traditional" instruction that relies on students' imitating exemplary model essays presented by teachers, and the most popular alternative, instruction in general composing procedures such as freewriting that proponents claim improve writing regardless of the composing task (Elbow, 1973, 1981; Murray, 1980). Hillocks has proposed instead that different writing tasks (such as comparing and contrasting two political candidates, analyzing the reasons why the Cincinnati Reds won the 1990 World Series, defining progressive education and using the definition to evaluate a political reform bill, and so on) require knowledge of different, task-specific procedures, which require instructional attention. (See Smagorinsky & Smith, 1992, for an extended review of research on composing knowledge.)

Contrasting these three instructional approaches (i.e., teaching through exemplary models, teaching through models combined with general composing procedures, and teaching through models combined with task-specific composing procedures) did not allow me to import the coding system of Langer and Applebee (1987); or of Flower and Hayes (1981c), who studied writers' pauses; or of Witte (1987), who studied the role of pre-text in composing. Rather, I was faced with the problem of developing a system that would contrast the thought processes of students who engaged in a particular task (writing extended definitions), depending on which of the three instructional approaches they had been taught through.

The coding system, which I developed with George Hillocks and modified with the help of Dorothea Anagnostopoulos, was designed to focus on the task-related thoughts of the participants. The system thus needed to identify statements related to the protocols' *content* and to the *processes* engaged in by the writers, and see if they varied according to instructional treatment. Content codes included the generation of definitional criteria, examples, contrasting examples, and so on; that is, the extent to which students talked about the substance of their definition essays. Process codes included when writers referred to their conception of the task (i.e., when they reread their composition assignment or harkened back to some aspect of the instruction), experienced a block in their thinking, made a decision to rewrite or reread, initiated a memory search, and other decisions they made about how to produce the essay. The system was designed to identify task-related thought processes depending on the type of knowledge implicit in the instruction. I hypothesized that the treatments that included procedural instruction would result in more fully developed definition essays than instruction based solely on the study of models. The protocol analysis would enable me to infer why instruction through imitation of models is insufficient, and what sorts of differences result from different procedural alternatives. Due to the unique nature of my investigation, I needed to develop a unique system for coding the transcripts.

Fine-Tuning the Coding System

Researchers do not develop coding systems in isolation, nor do they develop them whole and intact prior to their application to the data. The complete development of a coding system is recursive: A researcher first develops a rough system, then applies it to pilot data, then revises the system, then applies it again, and so on. One helpful procedure is to go through this process with the co-rater who will eventually provide a reliability measure for the researcher's coding decisions. This method not only helps teach the co-rater the system, but also encourages the discussion of the system's strengths and weaknesses with an intelligent and knowledgeable co-worker. When researcher and co-rater can work through several protocols together with few disputes about the quality of the system or the manner of its application, then they should be prepared for a run at reliability.

The intensive review of the data will help modify the coding system, and will also help researchers reconsider their hypotheses. Often, the data simply do not produce what the researcher anticipates. For instance, I predicted that students in both of the procedural treatments would exhibit fewer instances of writing block (statements such as "This is a hard topic to write on," or "I'm really stuck here"); and, when blocked, employ a procedure to reinitiate composing, such as conducting a memory search ("I need to think of an example of someone who's a friend"). The data did not support this hypothesis well, primarily because in the General Procedures treatment, students rarely experienced a block in either their pretest or posttest protocols.

Similarly, hypotheses often develop through the application of the coding system. For instance, I had predicted that students learning composing procedures would make significantly greater gains in their generation of criteria than students studying only models. I found, however, that most students in all treatments generated *fewer* criteria in the posttests than in the pretests. Careful study of the data revealed that on their posttests, students tended to compose more deliberately and purposefully, concentrating on relating criteria to supportive examples instead of on simply generating more criteria. In applying the system, therefore, I revised my hypotheses to predict which treatments would improve this purposeful composing to the greatest extent, abandoning the more simplistic notion that studying the protocols would involve counting up categorical instances of processes or content utterance and noting differences in the frequency of the counts. What was more compelling was the *relationship* between categories in the protocols and how these relationships differed from treatment to treatment. Therefore, researchers are faced with the paradox that, while their hypotheses determine the coding system, often their hypotheses emerge from or are shaped by the application of the system.

INTERPRETATION:
ANALYZING DATA AND REPORTING RESULTS

In most cases protocol studies present the researcher with difficult choices in the interpretation of the data, particularly when the protocols are part of an experimental design and we are looking for contrasts between treatments or conditions. In exceptional cases (such as the Langer and Applebee study and the Witte and Cherry study described in this volume) the sample sizes are large enough to make statistical comparisons with no less difficulty than one would in normal experimental studies. Most protocol studies, however, are not so generously funded and must rely on far fewer participants from whom to draw their results, forcing the researcher to choose a medium for presenting the data.

Even with my small sample (six subjects in each of three treatments) certain measures showed large enough differences to support a statistical comparison using ANOVAs. When I submitted an article version of the study for publication, I received two completely different responses to my statistical approach. One reviewer suggested that I focus on the statistical comparisons in interpreting the results. The other reviewer found the statistics unconvincing because in the reviewer's judgment I should, rather than belaboring small numbers, present a much condensed version of the results in descriptive form, focusing on gain scores and then noting places where the other counts had clear explanatory power, suggestions that the reviewer felt would make this a more theoretically interesting piece and less a statistical exercise.

The reviewers' disagreement over the most effective way to treat the results suggests that we have no clearly established means of reporting protocol data. Undoubtedly each reviewer was reflecting a personal bias in suggesting ways to treat the data. The first reviewer might have been an exponent of the experimental paradigm and endorsed its conventions, and the second might have regarded any controlled study as a statistical exercise. Protocol research, however, faces researchers with problems that go beyond merely adhering to methodological biases. The data challenge the notion that research is either qualitative or quantitative and force the investigator to consider new ways of reporting data that are neither statistical exercises nor descriptions of differences that may only be apparent.

In that my study was part of an experimental design and intended to contrast effects of instructional treatments, I chose to stay within the conventions of experimental research and report significant results between treatments. However, simply presenting the tables would not have been very convincing, and would not have taken advantage of the particular strengths of protocol data, that is, *their capacity for telling stories*. I therefore moved the statistics into the background and let examples from the transcripts tell the story of how different treatments affected the thought processes of students as they composed. I chose to focus on particularly revealing segments from the protocols and then gave a statistical context that showed how the segment illustrated a tendency in the data as a whole. Used in this manner, perhaps it did not matter whether I used descriptive statistics or reported results of ANOVAs, although my editors' recommendation that parametric tests are usually more powerful would support the use of statistical tests when they are possible. Most important in my presentation of the data was that readers could understand clearly changes in process that students experienced, and could see connections between instructional emphases and writing process by following the thoughts captured by the protocol. The vivid illustration of thought process provided by protocols gives the method a unique power in demonstrating why people perform as they do. While perhaps only a glimpse into the way a writer thinks at a particular moment, dependent on a number of contextual variables, the story told by protocols—particularly when placed in the context of strong statistical evidence—gives a ring of truth to research findings not available through strictly quantitative analyses.

RESEARCH PROBLEMS
POTENTIALLY INVOLVING PROTOCOL ANALYSIS

As I noted in the introduction to this volume, research should be conducted to investigate problems and questions, not to employ methodologies. The question under consideration at this point is: Given the array of methodologies available to researchers, what sorts of problems and questions are best investigated by protocol analysis? The obvious and general answer is, research that intends to study composing process. Yet composing process is a vast area of study. In this volume alone, researchers look at aspects of composing that do not necessarily involve putting pen to paper: writing conferences (Sperling), classroom discussions (Hodges), tutorials (DiPardo), the physical and social context of composing (Chin), and small group discussions (Hillocks). Even studying the thoughts of writers in the physical act of writing can vary, in terms of both method (see Greene & Higgins; DiPardo; Swanson-Owens & Newell, this volume, for analyses of methods involving retrospective accounts) and focus (as in the contrast between my own work and that of Langer and Applebee, reviewed previously). With the view of composing extending well beyond an actual writing session, both in terms of time and in terms of the social and cultural influences on writers, for what types of investigations is a think-aloud account of thought processes a valuable source of information about writing?

Protocol research in the current era of sociocultural studies will probably be different from the prototype investigations of Flower and Hayes. With attention shifting to the context of writing, we will probably see less need for the generation of general models of writing process determined from think-alouds conducted in isolated sessions, and a greater focus on the processes involved in "real time" writing. Protocol collection will probably become more situated in "authentic" composing situations, or at least as authentic as a situation can get when a person thinks aloud while writing with a tape recorder running nearby. As Brodkey (1987) argues, "writing is best understood as a set of observable human practices . . . and any attempt to study writing, even writing as literature, must entail situating writers and writing practices within a social, psycholgoical, historical, and political context" (p. 80).

I will give one example of a possible use for protocol analysis in research situated in an authentic context. (See Bracewell & Breuleux; Witte & Cherry, this volume, for others.) The example comes from a study for which I am currently collecting data. I will illustrate how the method emerges from my interest in a composing problem that springs from my experiences as a teacher (14 years as a high school English teacher) and from the line of research inquiry that originated in my dissertation and has extended through other projects. The problem I am investigating concerns knowledge transfer (cf. Smagorinsky & Smith, 1992), particularly the extent to which learners transfer knowledge across domains. As explained earlier, my dissertation looked into the effects of general and task-specific instruction on students' ability to write definitions, a genre with distinctive traits. In schools teachers often assume that students who receive instruction in one domain can apply it to another; in other words, history teachers often say that students "learn to write" in English class, and therefore the composing knowledge learned in English will transfer to the different disciplines regardless of the unique characteristics of particular genres they learn in English (literary analysis, personal experience narratives) and those they produce in other subjects (lab reports, newspaper stories, "the research paper"). I wanted to investigate the extent to which the knowledge about writing that students learn in English class is appropriate and transferrable to the particular demands of teachers and conventions in other disciplines.

Protocol analysis seemed a good means of investigating this problem, allowing me see what sorts of knowledge students consciously drew on when composing in different areas. I selected classes from a local high school from which to recruit students to participate in the project, getting a total of 10 volunteers from two classes to agree to contribute protocols. My request was quite demanding, for rather than conducting single protocol sessions under "lab" conditions (i.e., summoning a student to an isolated location to conduct a protocol session at an assigned time), I issued portable cassette tape recorders to them so that they could provide a protocol wherever and whenever they found an opportunity to write and think aloud (cf. Walvoord & McCarthy, 1990). Their English teachers were very cooperative and agreed to excuse the students whenever they asked to go to a conference room to compose aloud. One of the teachers ran a "writing workshop" class in which students could work on personal writing or writing for other classes, so the opportunity existed to capture the writers thinking aloud across a variety of domains, including personal writing.

The initial data collection met with mixed success and also suggested the need to collect other sources of data. Of the original 10 students, 8 dropped out of the study—not surprising, given the demands of participation. The 2 who remained contributed extensive data, however, so case studies are possible. During the course of the study, it became apparent that the protocols were only one possible source of information. I began to schedule classroom observations and interviews with the teachers, not only the English teachers but also other teachers from whom the students took courses. I also decided that the students could provide additional data with interviews stimulated by a portfolio of their writing, and that the portfolios themselves (including their writing from one quarter of the school year) should also be included in the data analysis. The text-based interviews were structured to get students to talk about the range of texts they had composed and the extent to which the writing of one text had influenced the writing of another. (See Chin, this volume, for an analysis of the use of interviews in writing research.) In addition to providing corroboration of findings, the triangulation of data has helped to alleviate the problem of choosing between methods, allowing me instead to employ a range of complementary means of appropriate investigation.

I am presently collecting data of a similar type from a second set of students, so I cannot report results of the inquiry at this time. I explain this project primarily to illustrate one instance where protocol analysis can be adapted for the study of situated writing, particularly when complemented by other sources of data. Used in this way, protocol analysis removes the researcher from immediate contact with the writer, potentially diminishing many of the researcher-subject interaction problems described by Rosenthal.At the same time the collection of data in the manner I have described is clearly problematic. Most students in the study dropped out, and those who remained to participate can hardly be called representative of the average teenager in that they agreed to walk around with a tape recorder for a few months and think aloud whenever they composed (they were encouraged to regard as "composing" any thoughts that led to, happened during, or followed from writing). Undoubtedly they also possessed many of the traits described by Rosenthal as being characteristic of volunteer subjects. Generalizing from the data will therefore be quite tentative.

Yet the data will allow for an exploration into the extent to which writers—albeit an uncharacteristic set of writers—transfer knowledge from genre to genre, and domain to domain. In this instance, protocol analysis can provide a tool for generating hypotheses and preliminary data about a problem that has to this point prompted much speculation yet little empirical data.

CONCLUSION

Protocol analysis is often considered as a key to the mysteries residing within the black box of the writer's mind, an instrument that will reveal the cognitive mechanisms and processes that drive composing. I propose that protocol analysis is above all a fundamentally *human* methodology, eliciting a sample of the thoughts that go through writers' minds, through a medium that can affect their behavior and which may be indeterminably complex due to interactions between the writer and researcher; and subjecting the data to the interpretations of people with biases, agendas, assumptions, and weaknesses. These human factors have caused some critics to question the validity of protocol findings.

The critics have made good points, and protocol researchers need to respond to the problems by modifying procedures to make the conditions more conducive to eliciting representative process. While retaining the human qualities of the method, then, researchers need to control as much as possible for human caprice. Researchers need to consider the effects of the protocol conditions themselves on the emergence of process, and attempt to neutralize as much as possible variations in data due to cultural and gender-related interactions between researcher and subject. The human factor, however, also lends a very particular power to protocol research. The human quality revealed through protocols gives the data a unique soul and spirit as they illustrate ways in which writers think in the act of composing, an essence that animates our understanding of thinking and learning.

Given the potentially mercurial nature of the data, protocols require a context in order to be accorded validity. The context can come from other protocols collected in the same study, or from related research conducted by other scholars. Protocol researchers need to guard against generalizing from data that may only reflect a process occurring at a particular time and under particular conditions. Due to the small samples that protocol researchers typically work with, we might modestly claim that most such investigations are exploratory rather than conclusive. Even so, the broader the context a researcher can provide for interpretation, the more compelling and persuasive the results will be to the educational community.

When researchers are attentive to the potential problems caused by the procedure and take steps to control and account for them, think-aloud protocol collection and analysis can be a remarkably illuminating research methodology. Often represented as a mechanical procedure conducted by automatons on information-processing subjects, it is in fact an essentially human experience, fraught with the potential for mishap through personal flaws and vagaries and the fragility of social interactions, and dogged throughout by agonizing decision making at every level. Researchers who understand the magnitude of their task and account for the potential perils to the greatest extent possible can provide a rich source of data that, when seen in the context of validating research, can provide a unique and important view of composing process.

REFERENCES

Applebee, A. (1981). *Writing in the secondary school*. Urbana, IL: National Council of Teachers of English.

Applebee, A. (1984). *Contexts for learning to write*. Norwood, NJ: Ablex.

Brand, A. (1987). The why of cognition: Emotion and the writing process. *College Composition and Communication, 38*(4), 436-443.

Brodkey, L. (1987). *Academic writing as social practice*. Philadelphia: Temple University Press.

Claparede, E. (1934). Genese de l'hypotheses [Genesis of the hypotheses]. *Archives de Psychologie, 24*, 1-155.

Cooper, M., & Holzman, M. (1983). Talking about protocols. *College Composition and Communication, 34*, 284-293.

Cooper, M., & Holzman, M. (1985). Reply to Linda Flower and John R. Hayes. *College Composition and Communication, 36*(1), 97-100.

Dobrin, D. (1986). Protocols once more. *College English, 48*(97), 713-726.

Duncker, K. (1926). A qualitative (experimental and theoretical) study of productive thinking (solving of comprehensible problems). *Pedagogical Seminar, 33*, 642-708.

Durst, R. K. (1987). Cognitive and linguistic demands of analytic writing. *Research in the Teaching of English, 21*(4), 347-376.

Elbow, P. (1973). *Writing without teachers*. New York: Oxford University Press.

Elbow, P. (1981). *Writing with power: Techniques for mastering the writing process*. New York: Oxford University Press.

Emig, J. (1971). *The composing processes of twelfth graders*. Urbana, IL: National Council of Teachers of English.

Ericsson, K. A., & Simon, H. A. (1979). *Thinking-aloud protocols as data: Effects of verbalization* (C.I.P. Working Paper No. 397).

Ericsson, K. A., & Simon, H. A. (1980). Verbal reports as data. *Psychological Review, 87*(3), 215-251.

Ericsson, K. A., & Simon, H. A. (1984). *Protocol analysis: Verbal reports as data*. Cambridge: MIT Press.

Flower, L. S., & Hayes, J. R. (1977). Problem-solving strategies and the writing process. *College English, 39*, 449-461.

Flower, L. S., & Hayes, J. R. (1980a). The dynamics of composing: Making plans and juggling constraints. In L. Gregg & E. Steinberg (Eds.), *Cognitive processes in writing: An interdisciplinary approach* (pp. 31-50). Hillsdale, NJ: Lawrence Erlbaum.

Flower, L. S., & Hayes, J. R. (1980b). The cognition of discovery: Defining rhetorical problems. *College Composition and Communication, 31*, 21-32.

Flower, L. S., & Hayes, J. R. (1981a). The cognitive process theory of writing. *College Composition and Communication, 32*, 365-387.

Flower, L. S., & Hayes, J. R. (1981b). Plans that guide the composing process. In C. H. Frederiksen & J. F. Dominic (Eds.), *Writing: The nature, development, and teaching of written communication* (pp. 39-58). Hillsdale, NJ: Lawrence Erlbaum.

Flower, L. S., & Hayes, J. R. (1981c). The pregnant pause: An inquiry into the nature of planning. *Research in the Teaching of English, 15*(3), 229-243.

Flower, L. S., & Hayes, J. R. (1984). The representation of meaning in writing. *Written Communication, 1*(1), 120-160.

Flower, L. S., & Hayes, J. R. (1985). Response to Marilyn Cooper and Michael Holzman, "Talking about protocols." *College Composition and Communication, 36*(1), 94-97.

Hayes, J. R., & Flower, L. S. (1980). Identifying the organization or writing processes. In L. Gregg & E. Steinberg (Eds.), *Cognitive processes in writing: An interdisciplinary approach* (pp. 3-30). Hillsdale, NJ: Lawrence Erlbaum.

Hayes, J. R., & Flower, L. S. (1983). Uncovering cognitive processes in writing: An introduction to protocol analysis. In P. Mosenthal, L. Tamor, & S. Walmsley (Eds.), *Research in writing: Principles and methods*. New York: Longman.

Hillocks, G. (1975). *Observing and writing*. Urbana, IL: National Council of Teachers of English.

Hillocks, G. (1979). The effects of observational activities on student writing. *Research in the Teaching of English, 13,* 23-35.

Hillocks, G. (1981). The response of college freshmen to three modes of instruction. *American Journal of Education, 89,* 373-395.

Hillocks, G. (1984). What works in teaching composition: A meta-analysis of experimental treatment studies. *American Journal of Education, 93*(1), 133-170.

Hillocks, G. (1986a). *Research on written composition*. Urbana, IL: NCRE and ERIC/RCS.

Hillocks, G. (1986b). The writer's knowledge: Theory, research, and implications for practice. In A. R. Petrosky & D. Bartholomae (Eds.), *The teaching of writing* (pp. 71-94). Chicago: University of Chicago Press: The National Society for the Study of Education.

Hillocks, G. (1987, May). Synthesis of research in teaching writing. *Educational Leadership*.

Hillocks, G., Kahn, E., & Johannessen, L. (1983). Teaching defining strategies as a mode of inquiry: Some effects on student writing. *Research in the Teaching of Writing, 17,* 275-284.

Kintgen, E. R. (1983). *The perception of poetry*. Bloomington: Indiana University Press.

Langer, J. (1986a). Learning through writing: Study skills in the content areas. *Journal of Reading, 29*(4), 100-406.

Langer, J. (1986b). *Children reading and writing: Structures and strategies*. Norwood, NJ: Ablex.

Langer, J. (1989). Paper presented at the annual meeting of the Research Assembly of the National Council of Teachers of English, Chicago.

Langer, J., & Applebee, A. (1987). *How writing shapes thinking: A study of teaching and learning*. Urbana, IL: National Council of Teachers of English.

Lashley, K. S. (1923). The behavioristic interpretation of consciousness II. *Psychological Review, 30,* 329-353.

Marshall, J. D. (1987). The effects of writing on students' understanding of literary texts. *Research in the Teaching of English, 21*(1), 30-63.

Mischel, T. (1974). A case study of a twelfth grade writer. *Research in the Teaching of English, 8,* 303-314.

Murray, D. (1980). Writing as process. In T. R. Donovan & V. W. McClelland (Eds.), *Eight approaches to teaching composition*. Urbana, IL: National Council of Teachers of English.

Newell, A., & Simon, H. A. (1972). *Human problem solving*. Englewood Cliffs, NJ: Prentice-Hall.

Newell, G. E. (1984). Learning from writing in two content areas: A case study/protocol analysis. *Research in the Teaching of English, 18*(3), 265-287.

Nisbett, R. E., & Wilson, W.T.D. (1977). Telling more than we can know: Verbal reports on mental processes. *Psychological Review, 84,* 231-259.

Rosenthal, R. (1966). *Experimenter effects in behavioral research*. New York: Appleton-Century-Crofts.

Rosenthal, R., Hall, J. A., DiMatteo, M. R., Rogers, P. L., & Archer, D. (1979). *Sensitivity to nonverbal communication: The PONS test*. Baltimore: The Johns Hopkins University Press.

Rosenthal, R., & Rosnow, R. L. (1969). The volunteer subject. In R. Rosenthal & R. L. Rosnow (Eds.), *Artifact in behavioral research*. New York: Academic Press.

Rosenthal, R., & Rosnow, R. L. (1975). *The volunteer subject*. New York: John Wiley.

Smagorinsky, P. (1987). Graves revisited: A look at the methods and conclusions of the New Hampshire study. *Written Communication, 4*(4), 331-342.

Smagorinsky, P. (1989a). The reliability and validity of protocol analysis. *Written Communication, 6*(4), 463-479.

Smagorinsky, P. (1989b). *The effects of different types of knowledge on the writing process: A protocol analysis*. Unpublished doctoral dissertation, The University of Chicago.

Smagorinsky, P. (1991). The writer's knowledge and the writing process: A protocol analysis. *Research in the Teaching of English, 25*(3), 339-364.

Smagorinsky, P. (1992). How reading models affects writers. In J. Irwin & M. A. Doyle (Eds.), *Research making reading/writing connections* (pp. 160-178). International Reading Association.

Smagorinsky, P., & Smith, M. W. (1992). The nature of knowledge in composition and literary understanding: The question of specificity. *Review of Educational Research, 62*(3), 279-305.

Steinberg, E. (1986). Protocols, retrospective reports, and the stream of consciousness. *College English, 48*(7), 697-704.

Swarts, H., Flower, L., & Hayes, J. R. (1984). Designing protocol studies of the writing process: An introduction. In R. Beach & L. Bridwell (Eds.), *New directions in composition research*. New York: Guilford Press.

Thomas, J. C. (1974). An analysis of behavious in the Hobbits-Orcs problem. *Cognitive Psychology, 6,* 257-269.

Walvoord, B. E., & McCarthy, L. P. (1990). *Thinking and writing in college: A naturalistic study of students in four disciplines*. Urbana, IL: National Council of Teachers of English.

Witte, S. P. (1987). Pre-text and composing. *College Composition and Communication, 38*(4), 397-425.

2

Think-Aloud Protocols, Protocol Analysis, and Research Design
An Exploration of the Influence of Writing Tasks on Writing Processes

STEPHEN P. WITTE
ROGER D. CHERRY

More than two decades have now passed since think-aloud data (e.g., Emig, 1971) were first used in writing research and well over a decade since they began to figure prominently in it. In one sense, their use during the late 1960s and early 1970s as data for studying composing was inspired by Braddock, Lloyd-Jones, and Schoer's (1963) conclusion that before 1960, research had yielded no useful answers to the question, "What is involved in the act of writing?" (p. 53). Since their early use, think-aloud protocols have provided a means of studying the ways in which writers orchestrate

AUTHORS' NOTE: Initial funding for the research reported in the present chapter was provided by the U.S. Department of Education through FIPSE Grant G008005896. The views expressed in the present chapter are not necessarily those of the U.S. Department of Education, and the authors assume full responsibility for those views. The authors would like to thank a number of people who have contributed, at a number of different stages and in a number of different ways, to the research reported herein: Bob Bayley, Bob Bracewell, Bob Calfee, Elaine Chin, John Daly, David Elias, Jennifer Flach, Linda Flower, Sarah Freedman, Ed Haertle, Dick Hayes, David Jolliffe, Jim Kinneavy, Dick Larson, Gary Lichtenstein, Erika Lindemann, Paul Meyer, Tom Miller, Marty Nystrand, Mike Rose, Anna Skinner, Nancy Spivey, Deborah Swanson, Mary Trachsel, Chris Vander Ark, and Keith Walters. Most particularly, the authors would like to thank the 40 students who participated in the study: Without them, nothing would have been possible.

what came to be viewed as underlying cognitive processes. And the history of writing research during the thirty years following the publication of *Research in Written Composition* lends strong support to the contention that think-aloud protocols and cognitive process theory have been crucial in calling attention to "the act of writing."

Central to that effort was, of course, the work of Flower and Hayes (e.g., Flower & Hayes, 1977, 1980a, 1980b, 1981a, 1981b, 1981c, 1984; Hayes & Flower, 1980) during the late 1970s and early 1980s. As is well known, Flower and Hayes's protocol-based studies of "the act of writing" were greatly influenced by Newell and Simon (1972), whose work on problem solving is widely regarded as seminal—if not canonical—in cognitive psychology. In the early work of Flower and Hayes, think-aloud protocols and cognitive psychology converged in a theory of composing (Flower & Hayes, 1981a; Hayes & Flower, 1980) that did much to establish a common vocabulary (though certainly not always a common sense) among researchers, textbook writers, and teachers for talking about composing (cf. Scardamalia & Bereiter, 1986). Moreover, their work was of a piece in many ways with the interests and emphases of other researchers of the same period (see, for example, Beaugrande, 1984; Bereiter & Scardamalia, 1987; Bracewell, Fredriksen, & Fredriksen, 1982; Faigley & Witte, 1981; Fredriksen, 1977; Kintsch & Van Dijk, 1978; Tierney & Pearson, 1983).

In spite of a number of sensible defenses of protocols as data in process-tracing studies (e.g., Ericsson & Simon, 1980, 1984; Flower & Hayes, 1981a; Steinberg, 1986; Witte, 1987; Witte, Nakadate, & Cherry, 1992), think-aloud protocols have always been to some extent controversial in composing research (cf. Cooper & Holzman, 1989; Dobrin, 1986). They are often regarded as more laced with problems than imbued with potential for understanding the complex riddle that is composing. Moreover, the problems that some perceive with protocols as data appear to be exacerbated by the difficulty researchers have in specifying the interpretive methods used to analyze think-aloud data, and the perceived problems appear to be compounded by a tendency among some to downplay the role of cognition in writing. Yet the developments in writing research over the decade or so since Hayes and Flower's protocol-based cognitive theory of composing was first published demonstrate how clearly influential that line of research has been in calling attention to what may be "involved in the act of writing."

An important dimension of that influence can be seen in the fact that Flower and Hayes's early work not only provided a touchstone for many who were concerned with the role of cognition in writing but also functioned as a springboard for alternative conceptualizations of composing and composing processes. For example, Bizzell's (1982) influential essay on discourse communities begins as a critique of Flower and Hayes's conceptualization of composing as a cognitive process. So, too, does Bartholomae's (1985) insightful analysis of the university as a complex community that student writers must learn to negotiate. Moreover, Faigley (1986), in his attempt to set out some bases for a social theory of writing, begins by pointing to what he sees as the limitations of cognitive theory generally and of Flower and Hayes's cognitive process theory of composing specifically. Similarly, Nystrand (1986) urges the efficacy of his social interactive theory of reciprocity by opposing it to the cognitive process theory of Flower and Hayes. Although such social theories of writing are not themselves devoid of problems (cf. Witte, 1992), the apparent need of some who would articulate a social perspective on writing to begin with critiques of Flower and Hayes's cognitive perspective provides ample testimony to the influence of that body of work. It would appear that the cognitive perspective—regardless of whatever limitations may now seem to be associated with it and with the data and the methodologies typically employed—provided at least one important prerequisite for the identification of a "kairotic moment" (cf. Kinneavy, 1986; Miller, 1992)—a temporal, intellectual, and social space—that permitted important developments in our understanding of writing and how it gets done.

Beyond its influence as a sort of "negative example," Flower and Hayes's cognitive theory of writing—in concert with a current and growing interest in "situated cognition" (cf. Brown, Collins, & Duguid, 1989)—appears to have played a critical role in the development of a social-cognitive approach to writing. Applied to the study of "acts of writing," this perspective recognizes that although language is fundamentally social in nature, one of the things people do when they write is manipulate and reflect on symbols. In such acts, cognition must certainly play a major role because while symbols may be socially constructed or constituted, people can neither reflect upon nor manipulate those symbols without recourse to cognition (cf. Witte, 1992; Witte & Elias, 1988). As it does generally for research from a problem-solving perspective, the invocation of the symbolic aspects of writing justifies a cognitive approach. Although reasons might be advanced for dissolving boundaries between the social and the cognitive altogether, as Brandt (1992) does on the basis of her analyses of protocol data, a number of researchers (e.g., Daiute & Dalton, 1988; Geisler, 1991; Hull & Rose, 1989) now talk about social-cognitive theories of writing, while others readily acknowledge that protocol data and thinking processes are situated in particular contexts (e.g., Bracewell & Breuleux, 1989; Breuleux, 1988; Fredriksen, Bracewell, Breuleux, & Renaud, 1990; Smagorinsky, 1991; Witte, 1987; Witte & Cherry, 1986); and Flower and Hayes's own work seems to have consistently moved in a direction that makes cognitive processes appear more and more dependent on specific situations or contexts for writing (see, for example, Flower, 1989; Flower, Stein, Ackerman, Kantz, McCormick, & Peck, 1990; Flower, Schriver, Carey, Haas, & Hayes, 1992).

Regardless of how critical some have been of studying composing through analyses of protocol data, such research has contributed significantly to how writing is presently understood, even if it has provided only a contrast to more "acceptable" approaches—none of which, we should point out, requires any less "meaning construction" on the part of the researcher or leads to any greater certainty with regard to conclusions drawn. Certainly, protocols demand interpretation. But so do all other forms of data, whether verbal or nonverbal: Data, after all, never mean in and of themselves (Witte, Nakadate, & Cherry, 1992; see also Hillocks, this volume, for an elaboration). Clearly, protocol data and the methods of analyzing them miss some of what is important in writing. But just as clearly, other data used in writing research and the interpretive frameworks applied to them also fall short of representing writing in its entirety. Writing entails more than simply managing underlying thinking processes, something that some cognitive psychologists concerned with writing have acknowledged all along (e.g., Bracewell, Fredriksen, & Fredriksen, 1982). But writing clearly entails thinking; and thinking during writing, however it may be focused or directed, certainly plays an important role in mediating between individual intention and action.

Fully mindful of the limitations both of think-aloud protocols as data and of interpretations of them, we report in the present chapter on a study that explored two questions that required us to face directly several methodological and substantive issues not faced in previous studies employing think-aloud data to understand writing processes. Through the study, we sought answers to the questions of whether and (if so) how composing processes of college freshmen might differ for different types of writing tasks and for comparable writing tasks of the same type. Even though it depends on analyses of think-aloud protocols, the study appears to have something important to say about composing to those who adopt either a strictly cognitive or a strictly social perspective on writing as well as to those who prefer to see composing from a social-cognitive perspective.

A PROTOCOL STUDY
OF THE DEMANDS OF WRITING TASKS

To investigate whether and how composing processes of college students might differ across writing tasks of the same type and across writing tasks of different types, we:

1. constructed, evaluated, and tested two "comparable" expository writing tasks (or "prompts" or "assignments") and two "comparable" persuasive writing tasks (See Appendix for the four writing tasks used),
2. collected think-aloud protocols from four comparable groups of college freshmen, each of which wrote in response to one of the four writing tasks,
3. analyzed the think-aloud protocols according to a coding scheme that accommodated three major composing processes and a number of subprocesses whose operations were seen as embedded within the three major processes, and
4. compared the results of our analyses of the four sets of protocols to determine whether composing processes differed across the two types of writing tasks (i.e., expository and persuasive) and whether they differed across "comparable" writing tasks representing the same task type (e.g., the two persuasive prompts or tasks).

Development and Testing of the Four Writing Tasks

Types of Writing Tasks

The notion of "types of writing tasks" can be defined in various ways (e.g., subject matter, genre, structure of the prompt). However, we chose to define "types" in terms of the global purpose the elicited written text is supposed to serve. We chose two types of writing tasks, one to elicit written discourse whose dominant purpose was *to inform* or *to explain* and a second to elicit written discourse whose dominant purpose was *to persuade*.

In defining "type," we appealed to the taxonomy set out in Kinneavy's *A Theory of Discourse* (1980). Although Kinneavy recognizes that the aims or purposes of written discourse always overlap to some degree in practice and that, accordingly, there is no pure type of discourse, he argues that in all cases one purpose or aim will dominate. In insisting that all discourse represents a purposeful response to a communication situation, Kinneavy offers positions that are basically of a piece with those of such theorists as Malinowski (1946), Morris (1946), Jakobson (1960), Halliday (1973, 1978), and Britton (Britton, Burgess, Martin, McLeod, & Rosen, 1975). We believed that our research would be more ecologically valid if we used writing tasks calling for particular aims of discourse rather than modes. To some extent basing our choice of types on a national survey of college writing programs (Witte, Meyer, Miller, & Faigley, 1981), we opted to elicit types of writing we knew to be regularly taught and produced in a large number of college writing courses nationwide.

Comparability of Writing Tasks Within Task Types

With the help of a number of fellow researchers and teachers, we identified, constructed, or rewrote a total of 10 writing tasks, 5 for each of the two task types. Through a series of evaluative procedures involving both qualitative and quantitative methods, these 10 tasks were reduced to the 4—2 for each task type—that were used in the present study.[1]

Because we intended to investigate composing processes across task types as well as across tasks of the same type, we needed to know whether the different task types resulted in writing performances (in terms of perceived quality of written products) that differed significantly from each other. This question was important because we wanted some evidence that differences in composing processes, if such were identified, could not be attributed to systematic differences in difficulty across task types. Accordingly, we conducted a one-way analysis of variance in which summed holistic scores for each of the four tasks were treated as the dependent variable and the tasks were treated as the independent variable. This analysis indicated that the mean scores on the four tasks—the four tasks included in the Appendix of this chapter—were not significantly different from one another: $F(3,98) = .0023$, $p = .9998$. These results gave us some confidence that whatever differences in composing processes might be observed could not be attributed to general differences in task difficulty or to general differences in the ability of college freshmen to perform on the different tasks specified.[2]

Subjects and Data Collection

Think-aloud protocols were collected from 40 subjects, nearly all of whom were first-semester college freshmen (3 were second-semester freshmen). All were enrolled in their first course in college composition, a course designed for "regular" (as opposed to "provisional" or "advanced") fresh-men; SAT Verbal scores for the 40 students ranged from 410 to 530 (Median = 470). The students all participated voluntarily. They were told that they would be participating in a study of how college freshmen write in response to different writing tasks, that their participation would involve their making an appointment for a 90-minute session with one of the investigators, and that they would be providing a think-aloud protocol as they wrote an essay much like the ones they wrote for in-class assignments in their composition classes. They were promised, and given, an informal tutorial session based on what their think-aloud protocols and texts generally revealed about their composing processes.[3]

Writing topics were randomly assigned to the subjects. Thirteen copies of each of the four writing tasks were printed on 52 separate sheets. These sheets were shuffled, and each subject wrote in response to the task that happened to be at the top of the stack when he or she came to the protocol session. The first 10 protocols collected for each of the four writing tasks were used, thus creating four equal groups of subjects whose assignment to the individual groups was entirely random.

After reading the writing task, each student was instructed to "say aloud everything that comes into your mind as you write the essay." Once the actual think-aloud sessions began, the investigator intervened only if a subject stopped talking for more than 4 seconds, at which time the subject was reminded to "keep talking." The individual protocol sessions were audiotaped.

The Protocol Data

The sessions yielded data in the form of think-aloud protocols and written texts. The protocols were transcribed from the audiotapes and divided into "thought units." To illustrate the general nature of the think-aloud protocol data, we include in Figure 2.1 a brief section from one of the protocols produced in response to the "education" task (see Appendix). The underlined portion of the protocol (see Unit 41) designates written text produced by the writer, and each series of three dots indicates a discernable pause in the writer's verbalization.

The data collected during the protocol sessions are described in Table 2.1 and Table 2.2. Of the comparisons suggested by Table 2.1 and Table 2.2—whether across the two task types (*expository* and *persuasive*) or across the two tasks within each task type (the "education" and "sports" tasks

(30) Well okay ... let's do a ... (31) what's gonna be the thesis on
this? ... (32) how about the educational system? (33) ... the educational system in America has ... uh ... transformed itself from ... a
... (34) golly ... a ... a ... (35) god that doesn't make any kind of
sense ... (36) the educational system in America ... (37) no ... (38)
during the past thirty years ... the American public education system
has been influenced and ... a ... a ... changed in ... a ... myriad of
ways ... a ... a number of ways ... a lotta ways ... (39) during the
past thirty years the American education system has been influenced and changed in ... a ... a number of ways ... (40) ... um ... okay
... (41) During the past thirty years, the American education system
has been influenced and changed ... a ... ways ... tremendously. (42)
... um ... okay ... now that's what we're gonna be working off of ...

Figure 2.1. Example Section of a Think-Aloud Protocol

NOTE: Numbers in parentheses designate coded "thought units" in the protocol; a series of three dots
indicates a discernable pause in the protocol; underlining designates transcribed text.

TABLE 2.1: Protocol Session Data by Task Type

Task Type/ Protocol Session Data	Expository (N = 20)	Persuasive (N = 20)
Average Length (in Minutes) of Protocols	59.2	56.2
Standard Deviation	7.4	8.0
Average Number of Codings in Protocols	273.0	283.1
Standard Deviation	77.7	88.2
Average Length (in Words) of Texts	360.1	268.0
Standard Deviation	96.3	72.6

TABLE 2.2: Protocol Session Data by Prompt Within Task Type

Prompt Within Task Type/ Protocol Session Data	Expository (N = 20)		Persuasive (N = 20)	
	Education (N = 10)	Sports (N = 10)	Cheating (N = 10)	Hiring (N = 10)
Average Length (in Minutes) of Protocols	59.6	58.8	57.8	54.6
Standard Deviation	7.7	7.6	8.3	7.7
Average Number of Codings in Protocols	225.7	320.0	260.0	275.9
Standard Deviation	64.2	60.1	74.4	73.8
Average Length (in Words) of Texts	360.9	359.4	307.0	259.1
Standard Deviation	97.0	100.7	90.0	84.0

Coding Categories	Coding Subcategories
Planning	Generating Ideas: Content that is either writing task/prompt dependent or writing task/prompt independent content
	Goal Setting: Content, procedural, rhetorical, and structural goals
	Organizing: Operating from structural goals
Translating	Outcomes in the forms of transcribed notes, un-transcribed pre-text, and transcribed text
Reviewing	Rereading the Task (i.e., the writing assignment)
	Evaluating: Task/prompt, pre-text, content goals, procedural goals, rhetorical goals, and structural goals
	Revising: Pre-text, text, content goals, procedural goals, rhetorical goals, and structural goals

Figure 2.2. Categories and Subcategories of Protocol Coding Scheme

within the *expository* task type, and the "cheating" and "hiring" tasks within the *persuasive* task type)—only two are statistically significant: The 20 expository texts are significantly longer than the 20 persuasive texts ($F[1,38] = 6.98$, $p = .012$), and the total amount of composing activity in the 10 "sports" protocols is significantly larger than that in the 10 "education" protocols ($F[1,18] = 11.18$, $p = .003$). The amounts of "composing activity" are designated in the two tables as "average number of codings in protocols."

Coding of the Protocol Data

Each of the thought units in the protocol data was coded according to a scheme based on Flower and Hayes's (1981a) cognitive process model of composing. Figure 2.2 lists the principal categories and subcategories used in our analyses of the think-aloud protocols. The principal difference between our scheme and the one implied by the Flower and Hayes model is

Planning Subcategories	Examples From the Protocols*
Generating Ideas	... he gave Charlie his notes ...//... when I was a kid all girls were told to get teaching cerificates ... because it was wonderful job security ...
Setting Content Goals	... why do I like sports ...
Setting Procedural Goals	... I'm just going to have to write some notes down ...
Setting Rhetorical Goals	... I have to persuade the committee to vote for the less experienced woman ...
Setting Structural Goals	... now I need about three in-between main-point paragraphs ...
Organizing	... I'll start off with number six ... and say that ... we should hire Ms. X ...

Figure 2.3. Planning Subcategories with Examples from the Protocols

*More than one coding subcategory can be applied to some examples.

that ours is somewhat more specific, particularly with regard to outcomes of some processes (e.g., generating ideas, goal-setting, and translating). We think our coding scheme permits a more detailed account of some aspects of what may be involved in the act of writing than has been offered to date.

Figure 2.3 provides examples of the three *Planning* subcategories—*generating ideas, goal-setting,* and *organizing.* The first, *generating ideas,* itself consists of two subcategories—generating content ideas that are traceable to the writing task (or assignment) and generating content ideas that apparently originate in the writer's long-term memory.

The second major planning category, *goal-setting,* refers to the different types of goals writers produce during composing. As Figure 2.3 indicates, we identified four subcategories of goals—content, procedural, rhetorical, and structural. *Content goals* refer to plans for generating ideas or content. Some of these goals are global in nature, such as the one given in Figure 2.3. Other content goals—such as "I gotta come up with a good example here"—are much more local in nature. *Procedural goals* typically tell the writer what to do next; less frequently, procedural goals specify a multilayered plan for approaching the whole writing task. The example provided in

Figure 2.3 is of the former type, specifying what the writer should do next. Like content and procedural goals, *rhetorical goals* can be either global or local in their application, or somewhere in between. Rhetorical goals generally set out relationships among the various components of the well-known communication triangle and its enclosed area—writer, reader, content, and text. The example given in Figure 2.3 is a rhetorical goal of the global type because it informs or directs production of the whole text in terms of a perceived communication environment. Other rhetorical goals—such as one writer's decision to eliminate his own redundant use of the word *society* because readers would perceive the redundancy as "stupid"—are much more local in character and application. *Structural goals* may in some sense be subordinate to content and rhetorical goals, but in another sense they are distinct from them. Structural goals refer primarily to the writer's projections of needed textual elements or components, as in the example in Figure 2.3, which falls somewhere between a global and a local goal.

In applying our coding scheme, we found that goal statements sometimes needed to be double-coded because a given thought unit may reflect more than one type of goal. Consider the example of the structural goal given in Figure 2.3. This thought unit not only specifies structural elements of the discourse the writer intends to produce but also couches that goal in terms of what the writer intends to do next. Accordingly, this thought unit was double-coded as embedding both a structural goal and a procedural goal.

Organizing, the third major planning category specified in Figure 2.3, refers to a writer's deliberate attempts to arrange information already present either in the writer's mind or on paper. This "arranging" process is illustrated by the example in Figure 2.3. In that case, the writer is looking over a set of "notes" she wrote and is rearranging them by altering the order in which she had written them on paper. To a large extent, organizing occurs as a consequence of acting on rhetorical and structural goals; and to a large extent, organizing is pervasive, though usually implicit, throughout composing. Only those thought units—such as the one in Figure 2.3—that explicitly signaled organizing activity were coded as such. Accordingly, we believe that although think-aloud protocols never capture everything that goes on during composing, organizing is particularly underrepresented in our coding of the protocols. The problem we faced was developing consistent ways of coding non-explicit organizing activity, a problem we were never able to solve satisfactorily.

Our second major category of composing processes is *Translating,* which in our scheme consists of three subcategories that are distinguished on the basis of outcomes—written notes, memorial pre-text, and written text.

Translating Subcategories	Examples From the Protocols*
Written Notes	... O.K. ... teach patience ... learn to work to-gether ... learn about competition ...
Memorial Pre-Text	... during the past thirty years ... the American public education system has been influenced and ... a ... a ... changed in ... a ... myriad ... a ... a ... number of ways ... a lotta ways ... during the past thirty years the American education system has been influenced and changed in ... a ... a number of ways
Written Text	... um ... okay ... <u>During the past thirty years</u>, <u>the American education system has been influenced and changed</u> ... a ... ways ... <u>tremendously.</u>

Figure 2.4. Translating Subcategories with Examples from the Protocols

*More than one coding subcategory can be applied to some examples.

These three subcategories, or outcomes of translating, are illustrated in Figure 2.4.

At its most general level, translating refers to the process of attempting to express ideas in or through language. The subcategory of *written text* refers to text the writer has transcribed on paper as part of the current draft of the text in progress, what Flower and Hayes call the "text produced so far." Unlike thought units that we coded as "notes," those coded as "written text" seem to be intended by the writer as integral components of a text that readers could read and make sense of as connected text. Thought units coded as written text might consist of transcribed parts of sentences or transcribed whole sentences, depending on whether translating (and, in this case, transcribing) had been interrupted by other processes of composing (e.g., formulating additional content or procedural goals in the middle of transcribing a sentence).

In our coding scheme, the *notes* subcategory refers only to those thought units wherein the writer actually transcribes notes, which are written in visible language on paper but do not (usually) meet the syntactic require-ments for sentences and which never meet the requirements of different genres for connectivity among sentences. Notes usually specify goals of one or more types. In the case of the example in Figure 2.4, the writer has simply translated into print-linguistic form three major ideas she intends to develop in the course of her essay. As notes, these translated (and transcribed) ideas serve principally to remind the writer of goals (e.g., content goals) he or she is either simultaneously formulating or has previously set.

Of course, not all writers transcribe notes to remind themselves of their goals or to construct those goals, and not all of our writers did, although enough did to justify including the subcategory in our coding scheme. Such written notes and the translating process in general serve to remind us that the major processes of composing are not necessarily as distinct as our coding scheme and theoretical discussions of those processes make them out to be. When writers transcribe notes (and not all do), they seem to be using language in one or more of three ways. First, they may be using written language as a vehicle for expressing ideas in order to add stability or permanence to their mental representations of intended meaning, which representations might not be stored in memory in conventional forms of language at all (cf. Witte, 1992). Second, they might be using written language as a springboard for subsequent planning and subsequent translating. That is to say, they might be using language as a heuristic. Third, they might be simply moving along a continuum of meaning representations that are increasingly closer to formal written prose (cf. Flower & Hayes, 1984). Thus, transcribed notes can be seen as an outcome of planning as well as a basis for additional planning.

Perhaps the least familiar translating subcategory is that of *pre-text,* a writer's mental representation of "text" prior to transcription. Witte (1985, 1987) regards the notion of pre-text as critical to our understanding of translating because of its relation to other composing processes, particularly planning. Like transcribed notes and transcribed text, memorial pre-text is an outcome of planning, can serve itself as a "plan" or a template to guide either subsequent planning or subsequent translating, and can function as a "plan" or a template for transcribing text.

Figure 2.4 includes one example of how pre-text can function during composing. An examination of the writer's transcribed text (the underlined portion at the bottom of Figure 2.4) in the context of the preceding thought units (labeled as "memorial pre-text" in Figure 2.4) shows how transcribed (written) text can be influenced by a memorial pre-text. The portion of the protocol that precedes the writer's transcription shows the writer in the process of translating a "mental" or "memorial" version of the sentence she subsequently transcribes as written text.

To be sure, the writer's memorial pre-text often emerges in the protocol only after some struggle, and parts of that pre-text are sometimes revised in the process of translating it. This suggests that other composing subprocesses (in this case, revising) can both interrupt the translation of pre-text and operate or act on pre-text, just as those subprocesses can interrupt transcriptions of written text and act on the writer's written "text produced so far." Although translating pre-text is not a feature in all 40 of the think-aloud protocols, our examination of the protocols indicated that translating memorial or mental pre-text occurs frequently enough in the 40 protocols and figures importantly enough in some protocols that we had to include it as a separate translating subcategory.

Our third major category of composing processes is *Reviewing,* which includes a number of subcategories distinguished according to the particular phenomenon acted upon. Examples of these subcategories are set out in Figure 2.5. Although in coding the protocols we distinguished between *evaluating* and *revising* for several of the reviewing subcategories listed in Figure 2.5, for the purposes of the present study we have collapsed *evaluating* and *revising* data for each of the subcategories of reviewing. As Figure 2.5 indicates, reviewing was coded primarily in terms of goal-setting, as set out in Figure 2.3, and in terms of translating outcomes, as specified in Figure 2.4. Accordingly, the reviewing subcategories in Figure 2.5 do not map perfectly onto the planning and translating activities illustrated in Figures 2.3 and 2.4.

For example, as Figure 2.5 shows, our coding scheme provides for no reviewing subcategory for ideas the writer may have generated (see Figure 2.3). One reason that such a subcategory does not appear in our coding scheme is that in developing the coding scheme, we discovered that deliberately evaluating or revising ideas was always embedded within some other activity of composing, such as evaluating or revising content goals, pre-text, or text. Separating the evaluation and revision of ideas from these superordinate processes proved to be a task that we could not manage consistently. A second reason is that when "changes" in the writer's ideas occurred apart from or independent of these superordinate processes, those changes seemed to occur because the ideas were no longer salient in the writer's working memory. In those cases, the writer seemed simply to have "forgotten" that he or she had previously generated an idea. We did not code such "dropped" ideas because we could not attribute them to any particular cognitive activity that was not already accounted for in the superordinate processes identified above.

Figure 2.5 is also notable because it does not list written notes as objects of the review process. Apart from the fact that such notes do not undergo a great deal of evaluation and revision, when they are evaluated and revised, the writer is quite obviously focusing on those written notes not as written notes per se but as written reminders of different types of goals. Accord-

Reviewing Subcategories	Examples From the Protocols*
Reviewing Prompt	... what's it called ... a disciplinary faculty ... a faculty committee ...//... you've gotta be kidding ...
Reviewing Pre-Text	... she has the education and the qualifications ... her resume ... on her resume ... no ... I don't need to bring that up ... she has the qualifications we want ... and her education shows ... shows her potential ... O.K ...
Reviewing Text	... O.K. ... a ... let's see ... looking at this paragraph again ... uh ... it's fair to the employees of the company ... //... We're gonna change that last sentence to "my job to hire a successor ..."
Reviewing Content Goals	... um ... body building ... I don't know ... body building is not important ...
Reviewing Rhetorical Goals	[in response to a subject's prior rhetorical goal] ... I guess telling them what they already know won't convince them ...
Reviewing Structural Goals	... that won't work ... I think point three should come before two ...
Reviewing Procedural Goals	[as the subject is in the process of transcribing] ... no ... that won't get me anywhere ...

Figure 2.5. Reviewing Subcategories with Examples from the Protocols

*More than one subcategory can be applied to some examples.

ingly, when written notes were evaluated or revised, we coded those activities in some other way. In addition, some written notes suffer the same fate as some generated ideas: The writer forgets about them and subsequently never directs any conscious attention to them. It would, of course, be interesting to look at both generated ideas and written notes that simply "drop out" of the writer's working memory or active goal network. Apart from the difficulties of developing a reliable way of coding such "dropouts," accounting for them was judged to be quite beyond the scope of the present investigation.

Another difference between the subcategories specified in Figures 2.3 and 2.4, on the one hand, and in Figure 2.5, on the other hand, has to do with the appearance in Figure 2.5 of the writing task (i.e., assignment sheet or writing prompt) as an object of the reviewing process. Thought units coded as either "reading/reviewing the prompt" or as "evaluating the prompt" (none of the subjects undertook a revision of the prompt) always occurred after the subject had read the prompt once, and those thought units most generally appeared at the beginning of the protocol. Because some subjects "evaluated the prompt," we thought it necessary for our coding scheme to be sensitive to those differences across subjects.

Another lack of parallelism between the subcategories specified in Figure 2.5 and those specified in Figures 2.3 and 2.4 has to do with evaluating and revising goals. In Figure 2.5, evaluating and revising are collapsed within the four types of goals that can serve as objects of reviewing—content goals, procedural goals, rhetorical goals, and structural goals. We had three principal reasons for collapsing across these two identifiable subprocesses. First, there are—in comparison to the total number of thought units coded—relatively few instances of evaluating or revising goals; collapsing across the categories seemed, therefore, the expedient thing to do. Second and more important, only very infrequently were goals evaluated and not also revised. In the vast majority of occurrences, the writers did not engage in explicit evaluations of goals unless they already had inferred from the direction their writing had taken that their goals needed to be altered. Evaluation, therefore, usually took the form of specifying the inadequacy of the goal and led usually to revision. In determining how to code the thought units placed in these subcategories, we distinguished between revising goals and elaborating goals. Elaborations served to make global goals more specific and were coded as goal statements on the grounds that such elaborations represented the same goal but at a lower level of specificity. Revisions, on the other hand, involved replacing one goal with another.

A final lack of parallelism between Figures 2.3 and 2.4 and Figure 2.5 is seen in the absence—with regard to Figure 2.5—of *organizing* as an object of reviewing. The reason for this omission is easily explained: Both organizing and reviewing are themselves processes, and while it is possible for one to interrupt the other, it is not possible for one to act on the other. The reviewing process may act on goals that drive the organizing process, and it may act on the organization of something, such as text or pre-text. Accordingly, in our coding scheme, the relationship between reviewing and organizing had to be captured through the other coding subcategories listed in Figure 2.5. Those subcategories are, predictably, "evaluating" and "revising pre-text," "evaluating" and "revising text," and "evaluating" and "revising structural goals." To the extent that reviewing operates on "organizing," it operates on either plans for organizing or on the outcomes of organizing. Our coding scheme merely reflects that situation.

Analyses of the Protocol Data

The coding scheme we have described was used to analyze the 40 transcribed think-aloud protocols. Each protocol was coded separately by two people, one of whom coded all forty of the protocols. To compute interrater reliabilities, 15 thought units from each of the 40 protocols were randomly selected, and the two coders' codings of those 15 units were compared.

Although coding reliability was computed for only a limited number of the total thought units coded, all of the differences between the two coders of each protocol were resolved by mutual consent in conference. Most of the coding differences between coders can be grouped under three headings—failure of one coder to apply all of the necessary subcategories to a given thought unit, failure to distinguish between generating ideas and translating pre-text, or failure to code instances of revision of written text or pre-text.

Although there were divergent codings of other types, these three major classes cover the vast majority (more than 79%) of them. Some divergence was expected because coding think-aloud protocols is a complex task that demands high levels of concentration over extended periods of time. The task involves careful readings of a transcribed verbal artifact whose parts cohere in different ways than, say, an essay in *The Atlantic Monthly*. It involves sometimes constructing rather substantial inferences because the verbal data available can never be regarded as a "complete" data set. And it involves categorizing (and thereby interpreting) limited data about complex and interactive thinking processes according to an a priori coding scheme that, because of the static nature of all classification schemes, can never capture all the complexity of composing itself. Because the coding scheme we used captures some of that complexity, we could justify using the results of that coding in our study of the effects on composing of types of writing tasks and of different tasks within task types.

TABLE 2.3: Means (in "Thought Units") and Statistical Results for
Composing Variables by Task Type

Task Types/ Composing Variables	Expository (N = 20)	Persuasive (N = 20)
Generating Ideas*	97.5	75.3
Setting Content Goals*	20.7	9.7
Setting Procedural Goals	11.9	11.6
Setting Rhetorical Goals*	9.4	20.3
Setting Structural Goals	7.1	8.9
Organizing	3.2	3.9
Total Planning	**149.6**	**129.7**
Translating Pre-Text*	7.9	22.9
Translating Notes*	2.0	6.5
Translating Text*	53.4	38.9
Total Translating	**63.2**	**68.2**
Reviewing Prompt	5.4	5.7
Reviewing Pre-Text*	5.1	15.9
Reviewing Text	38.6	30.2
Reviewing Content Goals	6.9	5.7
Reviewing Procedural Goals*	1.0	3.8
Reviewing Rhetorical Goals*	1.8	4.8
Reviewing Structural Goals*	1.8	4.1
Total Reviewing	**60.3**	**70.1**
Total Composing Activity	**272.1**	**268.0**

*Significant univariate tests following a MANOVA ($F[16,23] = 9.02$, $p < .001$) in which the 16 composing activity variables were treated as the dependent variable set.

Accordingly, the protocol data were probed to explore the following: (a) In what ways are composing processes that are prompted by "noncomparable" writing tasks alike or different? and (b) In what ways are composing processes that are prompted by "comparable" writing tasks alike or different? Table 2.3 and Table 2.4 present the mean number of instances per protocol for the sixteen composing variables identified in Figures 2.3, 2.4, and 2.5. Table 2.3 lists the comparisons of the protocols across the two task types (*expository* and *persuasive*); Table 2.4 lists (a) the comparisons of the "education" and "sports" protocols and (b) the comparisons of the "cheating" and "hiring" protocols.

TABLE 2.4: Means (in "Thought Units") and Statistical Results for Composing Variables by Task Within Type

Task Types/ Composing Variables/	Expository (N = 20)		Persuasive (N = 20)	
	Education (N = 10)	Sports (N = 10)	Cheating (N = 10)	Hiring (N = 10)
+Generating Ideas	84.2[a]	110.7[a]	65.4	85.2
+Setting Content Goals	19.2	22.1	9.3	10.0
+Setting Procedural Goals	5.8[a]	17.9[a]	11.1	12.0
Setting Rhetorical Goals	6.4	12.4	19.4	21.1
Setting Structural Goals	6.0	8.1	11.3	6.4
Organizing	2.3	4.0	3.6	4.1
Total Planning	**123.9[S]**	**175.2[S]**	**120.6**	**138.8**
+Translating Pre-Text	6.7	9.0	15.9	29.9
+Translating Notes	1.4	2.6	3.2[b]	9.7[b]
+Translating Text	47.2[a]	59.5[a]	46.6[b]	31.1[b]
Total Translating	**53.3[S]**	**71.1[S]**	**65.7**	**70.7**
+Reviewing Prompt	7.0	3.7	5.2	6.2
Reviewing Pre-Text	4.2	6.0	9.9	21.8
+Reviewing text	24.9[a]	52.2[a]	42.6[b]	17.8[b]
+Reviewing Content Goals	8.3	5.4	7.1	4.3
+Reviewing Procedural Goals	1.1	0.9	3.6	4.0
+Reviewing Rhetorical Goals	0.4[a]	3.2[a]	3.3	6.2
Reviewing Structural Goals	1.0	2.6	2.0	6.1
Total Reviewing	**46.5[S]**	**74.0[S]**	**73.7**	**66.4**
Total Composing Activity	**225.5[S]**	**320.3[S]**	**260.0**	**275.9**

NOTES: S: Significantly different means as indicated through simple F-tests.
+: Discriminant variable set in a four-task discriminant analysis: Wilks's λ = .0068; χ^2 (33 df) = 157.44, $p < .0001$.
a: Significant univariate tests following a MANOVA ($F[11,8] = 5.74$, $p = .01$) in which the 11 variables (+) from the four-task discriminant analysis were used as the dependent variable set to compare the two groups of expository protocols.
b: Significant univariate tests following a MANOVA ($F[11,8] = 11.60$, $p = .001$) in which the 11 variables (+) from the four-task discriminant analysis were used as the dependent variable set to compare the two groups of persuasive protocols.

Results: Question 1

To investigate whether writing processes differ in response to "noncomparable" tasks, we pooled the protocol data for the two groups of 10 subjects each who responded to the two "comparable" expository tasks (the "education" and "sports" tasks), and we pooled the protocol data for the two groups of 10 subjects each who responded to the two "comparable" persuasive tasks (the "cheating" and "hiring" tasks). The composing processes of the two resulting groups of 20 writers each were compared along the three major process categories—planning, translating, and reviewing. As Table 2.3 shows, the differences in the total amounts of planning, translating, and reviewing between the 20 expository and 20 persuasive protocols proved not to be statistically significant.

A second analysis, however, showed significant differences between the expository and persuasive protocols. For this second analysis, the individual process variables for which means are reported in Table 2.3 were used as a dependent variable set in a multivariate analysis of variance (MANOVA). The result of this analysis was significant beyond the .001-level ($F[16,23] = 9.02$), which means that the probability is less than 1 in 1,000 that the differences between the 20 expository and 20 persuasive protocols are attributable to chance. The highly significant MANOVA suggests that writing processes vary in important ways across the two types of tasks—expository and persuasive.

The specific ways in which the two groups differ are indicated in Table 2.3 by the composing variables that are marked with an asterick. Each variable so marked indicates a statistically significant univariate test. Table 2.3 indicates that the 20 expository writers did significantly more generating of ideas, setting of content goals, and translating written text. Table 2.3 also indicates that the 20 persuasive writers did significantly more setting of rhetorical goals, translating pre-text and notes, and reviewing pre-text, procedural goals, rhetorical goals, and structural goals.

Results: Question 2

To explore whether writing processes differ across comparable writing tasks, we conducted two multivariate analyses of variance (MANOVAs), one on the data for the expository protocols and one on the data for the persuasive protocols. Table 2.4 shows that differences in the total amounts of planning, translating, and reviewing between the 10 "cheating" protocols and the 10 "hiring" protocols are not statistically significant. For the 10 "education" and 10 "sports" protocols, however, the total amounts of planning ($F[1,18] = 13.07$, $p = .002$), translating ($F[1,18] = 4.40$, $p = .05$), and

TABLE 2.5: Matrix Comparing Composing Across the Four Sets of Protocols in Terms of an 11-Variable Discriminant Set

Protocol Groups	Education (N = 10)	Sports (N = 10)	Cheating (N = 10)
Sports (N = 10)	F = 5.45 p = .0002		
Cheating (N = 10)	F = 7.00 p < .0001	F = 6.79 p < .0001	
Hiring (N = 10)	F = 24.63 p < .0001	F = 26.64 p < .0001	F = 14.86 p < .0001

reviewing ($F[1,18] = 7.33$, $p = .014$) do differ significantly. Each of these differences is designated with an uppercase S in Table 2.4.

We also conducted a discriminant analysis (see Table 2.5) to determine which of the 16 composing process variables listed in Figures 2.3, 2.4, and 2.5 best distinguished among the sets of protocols associated with the four writing tasks. That four-task discriminant analysis identified 11 process variables (marked with "+" signs in Table 2.4) that—in concert with one another—were able to distinguish among the four sets of protocols. As indicated in the note appearing below Table 2.4, that discriminant analysis was significant beyond the .0001-level.

Using the 11-variable discriminant set (i.e., the variables identified with a "+" sign in Table 2.4) as a dependent variable set in two multivariate analyses of variance (MANOVAs), we then compared, first, the "education" and the "sports" protocols and, second, the "cheating" and the "hiring" protocols. The first MANOVA revealed that the differences between the "sports" and "education" protocols on the 11 variables identified in the discriminant analysis are significant at the .01-level. Univariate tests revealed that the "sports" protocols exhibit significantly larger amounts (marked with lowercase a's in Table 2.4) of generating ideas, setting procedural goals, translating written text, reviewing written text, and reviewing rhetorical goals. These significant differences were not expected because of the care taken to establish the "comparability" of the two expository tasks and because neither the mean word lengths of the two sets of rough drafts nor the mean lengths of the protocols (in minutes) differ significantly (see Table 2.2). The multivariate analysis (MANOVA) for the two sets of persuasive protocols is also statistically significant, at the .001-level, as indicated by the note at the bottom of Table 2.4. The univariate F-tests revealed that the "cheating" and "hiring" protocols differ most significantly with respect to translating notes and written text and reviewing written text, as designated by the lowercase b's in Table 2.4.

The results of these analyses indicate that for the 40 college freshmen we studied, composing differed not only across the two types of tasks but also across the four individual writing tasks. Apparently, the four tasks led writers to employ composing processes in different ways, even though the two tasks within each task type were previously found to be "comparable" in terms of the form and language of the tasks themselves, in terms of type of writing elicited, in terms of the holistic quality of the writing elicited, and in terms of the four tasks eliciting the "best" writing from the "best" students and the "poorest" writing from the "poorest" students.

Discussion

Expository Versus Persuasive Tasks

The multivariate and the univariate tests suggest that the two groups of 20 writers orchestrated the processes of composing in very different ways. Generally speaking, the composing of the expository writers appeared to be more driven by a concern for the "what" of discourse than by a concern for the "how" of discourse, whereas the reverse is true for the persuasive writers.

The significantly larger means associated with the 20 persuasive protocols can be attributed to a more pronounced concern among those writers for "how" the text being written could be made to satisfy the rhetorical situation specified in the two persuasive writing tasks. The persuasive writers not only formulated more rhetorical goals and more frequently revised their rhetorical and their structural goals, but they also did so in advance of translating written text. The persuasive writers' rhetorical goals—which specify relationships among writer, audience, position adopted, and projected written text—appear, in turn, related to the significantly larger number of notes and memorial pre-texts. The pre-texts of the persuasive writers are especially noteworthy because they are not only more frequent but also more extensive and more frequently evaluated and revised in light of their function as precursors to written text. Both memorial pre-texts and written notes are intermediate linguistic representations of intended meaning; pre-texts and notes are at one and the same time outcomes of planning and plans themselves. The persuasive writers' concerns for producing written texts that would satisfy the demands of the rhetorical situations specified in the writing tasks appear to lead both to more planning in advance of translating written text and to more global planning of written text.

In contrast to the persuasive writers, the expository writers planned and produced written text in a very different way. Their protocols evidence much less advance planning and much less global planning in terms of rhetorical effect. Global and advance planning in the 20 expository protocols were pretty much limited to specifying a "general idea" (sometimes even a "thesis") and one or two "main points" subsumed under that general idea. Generating ideas *and* translating written text then began almost immediately and usually occurred simultaneously. Through an associative and iterative process of discovering "what" to write by writing, translated written text typically became a springboard for translating additional written text. These differences in planning and translating carried over into the reviewing subcategories as well. Although the two groups did not differ significantly with respect to the total amounts of evaluating and revising written text (activities collapsed in the "reviewing text" subcategory), the two groups did review written text in different ways. Whereas the persuasive writers tended to review written text in order to evaluate its rhetorical effectiveness, the expository writers tended to review written text in order to discover what to write next. Review of written text was often followed immediately by the formulation of additional content goals; then the associative and iterative process of simultaneously generating ideas and translating text began again.

To understand why these two composing patterns resulted, we must examine the two sets of writing tasks. The expository tasks and the persuasive tasks differ in the degree to which and in the manner by which they circumscribe composing itself. Consider the two expository tasks. Both frame their topics historically, make some fairly broad assertions about those topics, and then direct the writer to "discuss" the "role" of education or sports "in American society." The two persuasive tasks, which exhibit more of a narrative frame, are quite different. The use of "time" as a framing element in the persuasive tasks is much more task-specific than it is in the expository tasks. The narrative frame in the persuasive prompts is complete with characters, actions, settings, and conflict—elements altogether absent from the expository tasks. Moreover, the writer is assigned a major role in the situation circumscribed by the narrative. In addition, all of the narrative information presented in the persuasive tasks is directly relevant to the writer's identification of the issue that must be addressed, to the "opinion" the writer must form, and to the "statement" the writer is directed to produce. In short, the expository tasks seem to present writers primarily with "content" problems, and the persuasive tasks appear to present writers primarily with "rhetorical" problems. These different problems, in turn, appear to result in different composing patterns, one largely focused on discovering the "what" of written discourse and the other on discovering the "how" of written discourse.

In briefly outlining these two patterns of composing, we are not suggesting that one pattern is to be preferred to the other. Nor are we suggesting that one type of writing task is necessarily better than the other. The claim we want to make is that the two ways of orchestrating the processes of composing are directly attributable to differences between the two types of tasks—the expository and the persuasive. The protocol analysis highlights these differences and allows us to see patterns that might otherwise have been missed. Whether the differences in composing are attributable to differences between expository and persuasive writing or to differences in the amounts and kinds of information provided in the tasks themselves is not known because these two important variables were not controlled in the first analysis. Some control was, however, exerted over those variables in the second and third analyses.

The Expository Tasks:
"Sports" Versus "Education"

Composing differences in response to the "education" and "sports" tasks appear largely attributable to the different demands the two tasks made on the writers' knowledge of the two topics. In general, the writers who responded to the "sports" task displayed a greater knowledge of "sports" than their counterparts displayed of "education." Even writers who were not sports enthusiasts had no difficulty generating ideas; in fact, they frequently generated more ideas than they could incorporate into their written texts, which often resulted in a "generate and drop" pattern of composing. In contrast, the "education" writers tended to use almost every idea they could generate.

Related to the "generate and drop" pattern among the "sports" writers was a second pattern, which might be called the "single-idea" pattern of translating written text. This second pattern helps explain the significant differences in setting procedural goals, in translating written text, in reviewing written text, and in reviewing procedural goals. Compared to the "education" protocols, the "sports" protocols exhibited a much larger number of thought units in which a single idea or piece of content information was generated, transcribed, and then reviewed as a springboard for discovering additional ideas.

In contrast, the "generating ideas-translating written text" sequences in the "education" protocols tended to be more sustained, exhibiting a substantially larger number of individual ideas before transcribing written text was interrupted by the reviewing process. In the "education" protocols, reviewing text usually occurred at the boundaries of transcribed clauses, whereas in the "sports" protocols reviewing occurred much more frequently within clauses. In both cases, reviewing was tied to the boundaries of transcribed written text. Compared to the "education" writers, the "sports" writers seemed to have available more individual pieces of information, but it was information that appeared not to be very well organized in memory, at least not well organized according to "the role of sports in American society." These apparent differences in the amount of available information and in the organization of that information appear to make composing a different task for the "sports" writers than it was for the "education" writers.

The Persuasive Tasks: "Cheating" Versus "Hiring"

In the "hiring" protocols, as compared to the "cheating" protocols, the significantly larger number of translating notes and the significantly smaller amount of reviewing written text seems to be of a piece with the "hiring" writers' tendency to generate more ideas, to translate more pre-text, and to review pre-text more frequently—variables that all approached statistical significance. In concert, these five composing variables suggest that the "hiring" writers operated along something of a continuum of composing activity linking ideational content to increasingly more linguistically constrained planning—from idea generation, to notes, to pre-text, to pre-textual reviewing, to transcribing written text. The fewer thought units involving translation of written text in the "hiring" protocols thus seem to be a function of the writers' prior planning (in the form of notes, pre-text, and pre-textual reviewing), which allowed them to sustain transcription over longer stretches of written text.

As in the case of the "education" and the "sports" protocols, composing differences across the two persuasive tasks are probably attributable to the different demands of the two writing tasks. These different demands seem to be reflected in the extent to which the two groups of persuasive writers were able to rely on personal experience in developing their essays. The "hiring" writers seemed to rely much less on their personal knowledge of hiring practices than the "cheating" writers relied on their personal knowledge of cheating. This phenomenon is altogether understandable because college freshmen are likely to have a larger store of personal and general knowledge of cheating practices than of hiring practices. As a possible consequence of having greater topic knowledge, the writers who responded to the "cheating" task seemed to be more concerned about integrating their own topic knowledge with the topic information supplied in the writing task. Accordingly, transcribing written text seemed to be more frequently interrupted by review of written text as the "cheating" writers repeatedly checked the integration of the two bodies of "cheating" knowledge—their personal knowledge and the knowledge derived from the task itself.

SOME AFTER WORDS

In the present chapter, we have explored two questions—whether composing differs across tasks of different types and whether composing differs across comparable tasks of the same type. Both questions are, it seems to us, extremely important ones if Braddock, Lloyd-Jones, and Schoer's question of 30 years ago—"What is involved in the act of writing?" (1963, p. 53)— still has meaning today. Although we may now know more of what such an answer might entail than we did three decades ago, *the* answer to the question, if indeed there is such a beast, seems yet a long way off. Our own view (cf. Witte, 1987, 1992; Witte, Nakadate, & Cherry, 1992) is that Braddock, Lloyd-Jones, and Schoer's question is so complex that it demands exploration through the application of different theoretical (or, interpretive) frameworks, the study of many types of data, and the use of different methodologies. In an age when knowledge (and, mutatis mutandis, truth or Truth) is widely regarded—and rightfully so—as indeterminate, such pluralism in research seems to us necessary.

In exploring the two questions that form the center of the present chapter, we invoked frameworks associated with discourse theory and cognitive psychology, studied several different types of verbal data—for example, the various writing tasks (i.e., assignments), students' written texts, written and oral comments about the tasks, interviews with teachers, think-aloud protocols—and employed both qualitative and quantitative research methods.

But our exploration was not exhaustive on any front: No research study ever is. We simply couldn't cover, as it were, all the bases. The ones we did cover, however, seem to support the contention that writing generally and composing processes particularly are very much tied to situations, even when our knowledge of the situation is limited both to knowledge of certain very general characteristics of the writers studied and to knowledge of the particular tasks to which those writers responded. Such findings imply that neither teaching nor assessing writing should be conceptualized in terms of some "generic" notion of writing, that research which employs writing tasks to explore dimensions of what is involved in the act of writing cannot ignore the possibility that results have limited generalizability because they are task specific, and that research that focuses on particular situations cannot ignore the possibility that those findings lack generalizability as well. Situations are, indeed, variable. Although our findings suggest that theoretical models of composing should probably not be constructed on the basis of data on performances elicited by a single writing task (or two or three or four), our findings also suggest that our modification and use of the Flower and Hayes (1981a) cognitive process model of composing is sensitive to at least some variability in composing processes that can be attributed to the four particular writing tasks we used in the present study. Finally, it should be noted that the study we have reported strongly suggests that in concert think-aloud protocols, protocol analysis, and research designed to explore specific questions can be used to further our understanding of some of what "social context" in writing might entail.

NOTES

1. Because we were interested in knowing whether our initial 10 tasks would, in fact, be perceived as representing our two task types, we printed each of the 10 tasks on separate sheets and distributed a randomly ordered set of the 10 tasks to each of 74 people representing three different groups of experts: (a) experienced college composition teachers; (b) advanced English Education undergraduates who had completed their practice teaching in high schools and graduate students who had previously taught in high schools; and (c) students enrolled in freshman writing courses. None of the 74 experts had been involved in constructing any of the tasks. These three groups were then asked to sort, on the basis of perceived differences (excluding differences in subject matter or content), the 10 writing tasks into "piles or groups of comparable writing tasks." After they had sorted the tasks into piles, we asked each person to write a brief statement setting out his or her "reasons for placing the 10 tasks into the [selected] piles or groups." The data that resulted from this procedure gave us a basis for eliminating four problematic

writing tasks (two expository and two persuasive), which the 74 experts could not consistently sort. Given the 74 brief statements that explained the experts' reasons for their groupings, the procedure also gave us a way of tentatively confirming our assumptions about the relationship of the remaining six tasks to our two hypothesized task types.

We then arranged for the remaining six writing tasks—three expository and three persuasive—to be tested as in-class, graded writing assignments in two freshman composition classes each. Based on previous institutional research, we were willing to assume that none of the 12 classes was significantly different from any of the others in terms of the students' SAT or their ECT (English Composition Test) scores. In each of the classes, one of the tasks was distributed at the beginning of a 50-minute class period, and the students were allowed 45 minutes to produce an essay, which was subsequently graded by the classroom teacher as one of the in-class writing assignments required for the course.

Before the teachers graded the essays, we photocopied them. We removed the names of students from the photocopies in preparation for holistic rating sessions, read texts produced in 6 of the 12 classes to develop a sense of the range of performance on each of the six tasks, and selected for training papers sample texts that we believed would likely fall into the four holistic scoring categories we intended to use in the holistic scoring sessions. Subsequently, we trained three pairs of experienced raters to score holistically the written texts from the other 6 classes, one group of 23 to 27 student texts for each of the six tasks. Each set of texts was scored separately, and each text was scored only twice. No attempt was made to adjudicate divergent scores, largely because doing so would have produced reliability estimates that would either have obscured potential problems with the writing tasks themselves or with the texts based on them. On the basis of our findings, we concluded that student writing performance (as indicated by the perceived quality of their written products) could be reliably scored according to and distributed across the four available scoring categories for two of the expository tasks and two of the persuasive tasks.

To gather further evidence on whether the three tasks within each task type yielded comparable performances in terms of perceived quality of the written products, we conducted two one-way analyses of variance, with summed holistic scores serving as the dependent variable and task within task type as the independent variable. The results for neither analysis were statistically significant, although they approached significance and thereby suggested that in concert the three tasks of each type might lead to mean scores that were significantly different (for the expository tasks, $F[2,78] = 1.65$, $p = .19$; for the persuasive tasks, $F[2,69] = 1.06$, $p = .35$).

A priori contrasts involving different pairs of tasks within the expository set indicated that one task elicited writing that tended to differ in quality from that elicited by the other two tasks in the set. A priori contrasts for the set of three persuasive tasks revealed a similar pattern. Using these analyses, we concluded that two of the expository tasks and two of the persuasive tasks elicited, from the college freshmen, writing of nearly identical perceived overall quality.

2. These findings, however, did not provide answers to questions that bear on the suitability of the writing tasks to the population of college freshmen we studied: Are the "best" texts (i.e., those given the highest holistic scores) written by the "best" students in the writing classes? and Are the "poorest" texts written by the "poorest" students? To answer these questions, we randomly selected eight holistically scored papers for each of the six writing tasks for which we had asked teachers to collect writing samples. We matched those papers with the teachers' graded versions, and we examined with the

individual teachers the students' grades on previous writing assignments during the semester.

Four teachers indicated that the tasks they had administered elicited texts that conformed to their general expectations, not only for the eight randomly selected "sample" students but also for the remaining students in their classes. These teachers reported that the writing tasks elicited the best writing (in terms of grades awarded) from their "best" students and the poorest writing from their "poorest" students. The same general pattern held for the other two teachers, but they observed that their students as a group did not perform as well as expected, given those students' performances on previous writing assignments during the semester. These latter two teachers had administered, respectively, the expository and the persuasive tasks that had yielded the lowest scoring reliability estimates and that were shown by t-tests to be the most unlike the other two tasks of the same task type. These tasks also elicited the writing samples that the raters had the most difficulty placing in the highest holistic scoring category.

Given the results of these evaluative procedures, we concluded that the two expository and the two persuasive tasks included in the Appendix to this chapter were suitable for our study of composing processes within and across different types of writing tasks.

3. Data collection took place during the fourth and fifth weeks of three different semesters after the students had completed two or three graded essays in their composition courses. The protocol sessions were scheduled at the students' convenience. Ninety minutes were allotted for each session because the investigators' previous experience suggested that talking aloud while writing on a "45-minute" writing assignment would take longer than 45 minutes. In most cases, it did, but none of the protocols runs longer than 72 minutes.

The individual protocol sessions began with a brief review of the general nature of the study and a restatement of what the subject was expected to do, after which the investigator answered any questions the subject might have had. Next, the subject was encouraged to provide a "practice think-aloud protocol" as he or she solved either a "matchstick problem" or a "letter problem." These 2-to-3-minute problem-solving exercises served to demonstrate to the subjects that they could in fact provide think-aloud protocols as they engaged in a complex activity and that they could do so without altering the outcomes of that activity; and those exercises seemed to reduce most of the anxieties the subjects had about thinking aloud while they wrote.

APPENDIX

Writing Tasks Used in the Study

Education Prompt
(Expository Task)

For the Founding Fathers of this country, education was seen as a way to insure that the nation's youth would learn to make the informed decisions necessary for this country's democratic institutions to survive. Paradoxically, however, until after World War II, education was not readily accessible to many people in this country, particularly higher education.

At the present time, higher education appears accessible to many of the people to whom it was denied in the past. Accordingly, during the past thirty years, the number of junior and community colleges has increased dramatically, and enrollment in four-year colleges and universities has steadily increased.

Obviously, people in modern America value education, in part because it allows them to change their lives and in part because it gives them access to things they would not otherwise have.

Write an essay in which you discuss the role of education in American society. (from Witte, Cherry, Meyer, & Skinner, 1985)

Sports Prompt
(Expository Task)

Sports have always been popular in America, but they are even more popular now than in the past. Not only are more people attending sporting events, but more people now participate in sports, whether team sports or individual sports, than ever before.

Whether or not one is an avid sports fan, sports are ever-present in modern America. Some television channels now carry nothing but coverage of sporting events; the sports section in most newspapers is one of the largest; even network newscasts report on sporting events. Each year, hundreds of new handball courts, tennis courts, swimming pools, and baseball fields are constructed to accommodate the needs of growing numbers of sports enthusiasts. In fact, one writer recently argued that sports is so important that if sports were suddenly outlawed, the United States' economy would crumble. Obviously, Americans value sports very highly and for a number of different reasons.

Write an essay in which you discuss the role of sports in American society. (from Witte, Cherry, Meyer, & Skinner, 1985)

Cheating Prompt
(Persuasive Task)

Charlie had had trouble with zoology all semester, and now that the final was approaching, he began to get desperate. One day he approached his friend Jack and suggested that the two attempt to exchange answers during the test.

Not wanting to offend Charlie, Jack never explicitly refused to cooperate with Charlie in the scheme. Jack was decidedly uneasy about it, however, and attempted to compromise by offering Charlie his class notes to use in preparing for the test.

During the test, Charlie was caught using a set of class notes and automatically failed both the test and the course. When the professor examined the notes Charlie had used during the test, he discovered that they belonged to Jack. As a result of the discovery, the professor also failed Jack, claiming that he too had cheated on the test.

Jack felt that he was innocent and appealed to the Faculty Disciplinary Committee, which is responsible for deciding appeals in cases involving academic cheating. In preliminary discussions about the case, some Committee members have said that they think Jack is guilty of collaboration for lending his notes to Charlie. They say that Jack should have suspected what Charlie was going to do, and, in any case, Jack was responsible for how his notes were used. Other members of the Committee believe that Jack is innocent because he had no control over how his notes were used.

You are the student member of the Faculty Disciplinary Committee. The Chair of the Committee has asked you to prepare a written statement on whether Jack is innocent or guilty. Your statement will be distributed to the members of the Committee in advance of a meeting to discuss the issue. Try to persuade the faculty members on the Committee of your opinion. (A somewhat different version of this prompt appears in Faigley, Cherry, Jolliffe, & Skinner, 1985, pp. 130-131.)

Hiring Prompt (Persuasive Task)

At the place where you work, a woman has just quit her job, leaving vacant the company's only executive position ever held by a female. The Board of Directors has stated its preference that a woman replace her in order to conform to Affirmative Action guidelines. As a member of the Hiring Committee, it is your job to help choose a successor to the post.

The only woman who has applied for the job is competent and meets the written qualifications for the job, but she is less experienced than both of the two men she is competing with. Members of the Hiring Committee disagree about what should be done. Some say hiring a woman is absolutely necessary for breaking employment discrimination; others say hiring a less experienced person would be foolish as well as unfair to those working under the new executive.

To have a full hearing of all views on this critical issue, the Chairperson of the Hiring Committee has asked each member to prepare a carefully written statement to be distributed in advance of a meeting to discuss the issue. Write a statement that represents your position on the matter, making it as logical and persuasive as possible. Your writing task is to persuade the Committee to vote on the job candidates in accordance with your view. (Adapted from Cooper, Cherry, Copley, Fleischer, Pollard, & Sartisky, 1984)

REFERENCES

Bartholomae, D. (1985). Inventing the university. In M. Rose (Ed.), *When a writer can't write: Studies in writer's block and other composing-process problems* (pp. 134-165). New York: Guilford Press.

Beaugrande, R. de. (1984). *Text production: Toward a science of composition.* Norwood, NJ: Ablex.

Bereiter, C., & Scardamalia, M. (1987). *The psychology of written composition.* Hillsdale, NJ: Lawrence Erlbaum.

Bizzell, P. (1982). Cognition, convention, and certainty: What we need to know about writing. *Pre/Text, 3,* 213-243.

Bracewell, R. J., & Breuleux, A. (1989). *Le diagnostic cognitif dans la rédaction* [Cognitive diagnosis in writing]. In G. Denhiere & S. Baudet (Eds.), *Questions de Logopédie, 21: Le Diagnostic du Functionment cognitif dans la Comprehension de textes* (pp. 18-28). Braine-le-Comte, Belgium: Union Professionelle des logopèdes francophones.

Bracewell, R. J., Fredriksen, C. H., & Fredriksen, J.D. (1982). Cognitive processes in composing and comprehending discourse. *Educational Psychologist, 17,* 146-164.

Braddock, R., Lloyd-Jones, R., & Schoer, L. (1963). *Research in written composition.* Champaign, IL: National Council of Teachers of English.

Brandt, D. (1992). The cognitive as the social: An ethnomethodological approach to writing process research. *Written Communication, 9,* 315-355.

Breuleux, A. (1988). The analysis of writers' think aloud protocols: Developing a principled coding scheme for ill-structured tasks. In G. Denhiere & J. P. Rossi (Eds.), *Texts and text processing* (pp. 333-362). Amsterdam: North-Holland.

Britton, J., Burgess, T., Martin, N., McLeod, A., & Rosen, H. (1975). *The development of writing abilities (11-18).* London: Macmillan Education.

Brown, J. S., Collins, A., & Duguid, P. (1989). Situated cognition and the culture of learning. *Educational Researcher, 18*(1), 32-42.

Cooper, C. R., Cherry, R., Copley, B., Fleischer, S., Pollard, R., & Sartisky, M. (1984). Studying the writing abilities of a university freshman class: Strategies from a case study. In R. Beach & L. S. Bridwell (Eds.), *New directions in writing research* (pp. 19-52). New York: Guilford Press.

Cooper, M. M., & Holzman, M. (1989). *Writing as social action.* Portsmouth, NH: Boynton/Cook.

Daiute, C., & Dalton, B. (1988). "Let's brighten it up a bit": Collaboration and cognition in writing. In B. A. Rafoth & D. L. Rubin (Eds.), *The social construction of written communication* (pp. 249-269). Norwood, NJ: Ablex.

Dobrin, D. N. (1986). Protocols once more. *College English, 48,* 713-725.

Emig, J. (1971). *The composing processes of twelfth graders.* Urbana, IL: National Council of Teachers of English.

Ericsson, K. A., & Simon, H. A. (1980). Verbal reports as data. *Psychological Review, 87,* 215-251.

Ericsson, K. A., & Simon, H. A. (1984). *Protocol analysis: Verbal reports as data.* Cambridge: MIT Press.

Faigley, L. (1986). Competing theories of process: A critique and a proposal. *College English, 48,* 527-542.

Faigley, L., Cherry, R. D., Jolliffe, D., & Skinner, A. M. (1985). *Assessing writers' knowledge and processes of composing*. Norwood, NJ: Ablex.

Faigley, L., & Witte, S. P. (1981). Analyzing revision. *College Composition and Communication, 32,* 400-414.

Flower, L. (1989). Cognition, context, and theory building. *College Composition and Communication, 40,* 282-311.

Flower, L., & Hayes, J. R. (1977). Problem-solving strategies and the writing process. *College English, 39,* 449-461.

Flower, L., & Hayes, J. R. (1980a). The cognition of discovery: Defining a rhetorical problem. *College Composition and Communication, 31,* 21-32.

Flower, L., & Hayes, J. R. (1980b). The dynamics of composing: Making plans and juggling constraints. In L. W. Gregg & E. R. Steinberg (Eds.), *Cognitive processes in writing* (pp. 31-50). Hillsdale, NJ: Lawrence Erlbaum.

Flower, L., & Hayes, J. R. (1981a). A cognitive process theory of writing. *College Composition and Communication, 32,* 365-387.

Flower, L., & Hayes, J. R. (1981b). Plans that guide the composing process. In C. H. Frederiksen & J. F. Dominic (Eds.), *Writing: The nature, development, and teaching of written communication* (Vol. 2, pp. 39-58). Hillsdale, NJ: Lawrence Erlbaum.

Flower, L., & Hayes, J. R. (1981c). The pregnant pause: An inquiry into the nature of planning. *Research in the Teaching of English, 15,* 229-243.

Flower, L., & Hayes, J. R. (1984). Images, plans, and prose: The representation of meaning in writing. *Written Communication, 1,* 120-160.

Flower, L., Schriver, K., Carey, L., Haas, C., & Hayes, J. R. (1992). Planning in writing: The cognition of a constructive process. In S. P. Witte, N. Nakadate, & R. D. Cherry (Eds.), *A rhetoric of doing: Essays on written discourse in honor of James L. Kinneavy* (pp. 181-243). Carbondale: Southern Illinois University Press.

Flower, L., Stein, V., Ackerman, J., Kantz, M.J., McCormick, K., & Peck, W.C. (1990). *Reading to write: Exploring a social and cognitive process*. New York: Oxford University Press.

Fredriksen, C. H. (1977). Structure and process in discourse production and comprehension. In M. A. Just & P. A. Carpenter (Eds.), *Cognitive processes in comprehension* (pp. 313-322). Hillsdale, NJ: Lawrence Erlbaum.

Fredriksen, C. H., Bracewell, R. J., Breuleux, A., & Renaud, A. (1990). The cognitive representation and processing of discourse: Function and dysfunction. In Y. Joanette & H. H. Brownell (Eds.), *Discourse ability and brain damage: Theoretical and empirical perspectives* (pp. 67-110). New York: Springer-Verlag.

Geisler, C. (1991). Toward a sociocognitive model of literacy: Constructing mental models in a philosophical conversation. In C. Bazerman & J. Paradis (Eds.), *Textual dynamics of the professions: Historical and contemporary studies of writing in professional communities* (pp. 171-190). Madison: University of Wisconsin Press.

Halliday, M.A.K. (1973). *Explorations in the functions of language*. London: Edward Arnold.

Halliday, M.A.K. (1978). *Language as social semiotic: The social interpretation of language and meaning*. Baltimore, MD: University Park Press.

Hayes, J. R., & Flower, L. (1980). Identifying the organization of writing processes. In L. W. Gregg & E. R. Steinberg (Eds.), *Cognitive processes in writing* (pp. 3-30). Hillsdale, NJ: Lawrence Erlbaum.

Hull, G., & Rose, M. (1989). Rethinking remediation: Toward a socio-cognitive understanding of problematic reading and writing. *Written Communication, 6,* 139-154.

Jakobson, R. (1960). Linguistic and poetics. In T. A. Sebeok (Ed.), *Style in language* (pp. 350-377). New York: John Wiley.

Kinneavy, J. L. (1980). *A theory of discourse: The aims of discourse.* New York: Norton. (Original work published 1971)

Kinneavy, J. L. (1986). *Kairos,* A neglected concept in classical rhetoric. In J. D. Moss (Ed.), *Rhetoric and praxis: The contributions of classical rhetoric to practical reasoning* (pp. 79-105). Washington, DC: Catholic University of America Press.

Kintsch, W., & Van Dijk, T. A. (1978). Towards a model of discourse comprehension and production. *Psychological Review, 85,* 363-394.

Malinowski, B. (1946). The problem of meaning in primitive languages. In C. K. Ogden & I. A. Richards, *The meaning of meaning: A study of the influence of language upon thought and of the science of symbolism* (8th ed., Supp. 1, pp. 296-336). New York: Harcourt, Brace & World. (Original work published 1923)

Miller, C. (1992). *Kairos* and the rhetoric of science. In S. P. Witte, N. Nakadate, & R. D. Cherry (Eds.), *A rhetoric of doing: Essays on written discourse in honor of James L. Kinneavy* (pp. 310-327). Carbondale: Southern Illinois University Press.

Morris, C. (1946). *Signs, language, and behavior.* New York: Braziller.

Newell, A., & Simon, H. J. (1972). *Human problem solving.* Englewood Cliffs, NJ: Prentice-Hall.

Nystrand, M. (1986). *The structure of written communication: Studies in reciprocity between writers and readers.* Orlando, FL: Academic Press.

Scardamalia, M., & Bereiter, C. (1986). Research on written composition. In M. C. Wittrock (Ed.), *Handbook of research on teaching* (3rd ed., pp. 778-803). New York: Macmillan.

Smagorinsky, P. (1991). The writer's knowledge and the writing process: A protocol analysis. *Research in the Teaching of English, 23,* 339-364.

Steinberg, E. R. (1986). Protocols, retrospective reports, and the stream of consciousness. *College English, 48,* 697-704.

Tierney, R. J., & Pearson, P. D. (1983). Toward a composing model of reading. *Language Arts, 60,* 568-580.

Witte, S. P. (1985). Revising, composition theory, and research design. In S. W. Freedman (Ed.), *The acquisition of written language: Revision and response* (pp. 250-284). Norwood, NJ: Ablex.

Witte, S. P. (1987). Pre-text and composing. *College Composition and Communication, 38,* 397-425.

Witte, S. P. (1992). Context, text, intertext: Toward a constructivist semiotic of writing. *Written Communication, 9,* 237-308.

Witte, S. P., & Cherry, R. D. (1986). Writing processes and written products in composition research. In C. R. Cooper & S. Greenbaum (Eds.), *Studying writing: Linguistic approaches* (pp. 112-153). Beverly Hills, CA: Sage.

Witte, S. P., Cherry, R. D., Meyer, P. R., & Skinner, A. M. (1985). *An evaluation of DCCCD's "the write course".* Austin, TX: Information Transfer Services for the Center for Telecommunications and the Annenberg Foundation.

Witte, S. P., & Elias, D. (1988). Review of Martin Nystrand's *The structure of written communication: Studies in reciprocity between writers and readers. Style, 22,* 670-676.

Witte, S. P., Meyer, P. R., Miller, T. P., & Faigley, L. (1981). *A national survey of college and university writing program directors* (Writing Program Assessment Project Technical Report No. 2; FIPSE Grant G008005896). Austin: University of Texas.

Witte, S. P., Nakadate, N., & Cherry, R. D. (1992). Introduction. In S. P. Witte, N. Nakadate, & R. D. Cherry (Eds.), *A rhetoric of doing: Essays in written discourse in honor of James L. Kinneavy* (pp. 1-52). Carbondale: Southern Illinois University Press.

3

Substance and Romance in Analyzing Think-Aloud Protocols

ROBERT J. BRACEWELL
ALAIN BREULEUX

The use of think-aloud protocols as a source of evidence about the nature of cognition has a long and controversial history, both for what we can call laboratory types of tasks, such as the Tower of Hanoi, and for more naturally occurring tasks, such as writing (see, e.g., Cooper & Holtzman, 1983; Nisbett & Wilson, 1977; for criticisms). By and large these criticisms have been answered for both laboratory and natural tasks, particularly with respect to the assumptions and constraints that apply to the use of think-aloud protocols as evidence (see, e.g., Ericsson & Simon, 1984; Smagorinsky, 1989; Steinberg, 1986). Although this response has validated think-aloud evidence, it has of necessity been directed outward to meet the criticisms made against the procedure. Less attention has been given to a more inwardly directed activity, namely, the development of a coherent body of principles and procedures for treating the content of think-aloud protocols. The result of this bias has been a proliferation of different coding schemes for protocols, in which the coding categories and the specification of content that stand as instances of a category have been dependent on the assumptions of the researchers who develop a particular scheme. For the treatment of protocols taken from laboratory tasks, this proliferation does not present a serious problem. But for the coding of protocols from more complex tasks it does, for reasons outlined below concerning the frequently ill-structured nature of such tasks.

AUTHORS' NOTE: Preparation of this manuscript was supported by the Fonds pour la Formation de Chercheurs et l'Aide à la Recherche, Québec, Le Centre francophone de recherche en informatisation des organisations, Québec, and the Social Sciences and Humanities Research Council of Canada. We thank Michael L. Hoover for his comments on an earlier draft of the chapter and his guidance concerning lexical semantics.

55

The *substance* that we refer to in the title of this chapter concerns the possibility of uniting different coding schemes through the application of theories of the semantic structure of discourse to think-aloud protocols. This is not to say that various schemes will be replaced by our approach; rather, this approach promises to provide a more principled basis for the development of coding schemes, and a procedure for mapping among the categories of different schemes. We shall illustrate the development of one such coding scheme that we have been applying to protocols taken from newspaper journalists.

The *romance* that we refer to in the title addresses a more subjective problem in the treatment of think-aloud protocols, although one that is potentially as fatal to their use as the relative absence of an objective basis for the development of coding schemes. The problem is that of the general ennui that accompanies the presentation and use of coding schemes for think-aloud protocols. This is of course understandable—why should one get excited about or have confidence in yet another coding scheme when (a) each scheme is complex, difficult to master, and laborious to apply; (b) coding categories arise largely in an ad hoc manner from consideration of the protocol rather than from a rational analysis of the cognitive processes required for the task; and (c) the relationship among different schemes is unclear, and therefore a choice of one over another must be made as much on intuition as principle? Our hope is to rekindle interest in the development, choice, and use of coding schemes by showing the potential of analyzing the detailed semantic structure of think-aloud protocols, a potential that ranges from showing the benefits of incorporating lexical semantics into the analysis to realizing the linking of communicative strategies with specific syntactic structures. Our experience with this approach is that the more one examines the structure of a protocol, the more one sees about the skill of writing. But the question of romance in science depends on whether the story spun out by the analyst can be given a principled basis.

Our general approach to writing is to treat the activity as a problem-solving task.[1] Thus we are interested in determining the operations and objects used by the writer in producing a text. A major feature of most writing tasks, however, is that the problem itself is not usually fully defined beforehand (Bracewell & Breuleux, 1989); rather, the process of problem definition is in part carried out through the activity of text production as the writer organizes, reorganizes, and elaborates knowledge in the course of writing. In the terminology of problem-solving research, tasks such as text production are both *ill-structured* (at least initially) and *knowledge-rich* (Simon, 1978).

The dynamic characteristic of the writing task poses a serious challenge for researchers who wish to develop comprehensive and detailed models for writing. In the standard problem-solving approach one would first carry out a task analysis to achieve a preliminary specification of the operations and objects relevant to doing a task. But such a tactic is not very informative for the task of writing, primarily because the writer constructs and modifies the task itself in the course of the activity (Breuleux, 1991). Thus a model for writing must allow the implementation of text production strategies, and in addition task definition strategies.

To deal with this challenge we present a methodological approach in which the coding categories for operations and objects are defined independently of the evolving task definition. We call this methodology *Task Independent Coding,* or TIC for short. In applying this method, following Witte (1987), we treat both the think-aloud protocols and what is written as texts. We code these texts using Frederiksen's (1975, 1986) theory of propositional representations for natural language, a procedure that yields a detailed description of the semantic structure of both think-aloud and written text. We then code the protocols for the writer's strategic operations (such as planning), knowledge transformation operations, and language operations. We specify criteria for recognizing instances of these operations in terms of specific propositional and lexical structures. Recognition of operations occurs in two ways: (a) directly in terms of identifying propositional structures that meet the criteria for an operation, and (b) indirectly via a comparison of differences in semantic and lexical structure that occur within and between think-aloud and written texts. The semantic description also allows us to define criteria for identifying the objects, or knowledge, that the writer uses in producing the text, both content considered for inclusion in (or deletion from) the eventual text, and language knowledge used for presenting content knowledge. Content knowledge is usually recognized indirectly in terms of the semantic structures that are nested within (i.e., scoped by) structures that define strategic operations. Language knowledge is recognized directly in terms of specific semantic and syntactic structures. The outcome of this coding process is a detailed representation of the actions and knowledge that the writer uses in constructing a text.

The TIC method has three principal advantages. The first lies in the *unified treatment* of both think-aloud and written text. The use of a single coherent method of analysis permits comparison of structures across think-aloud and written texts, and hence allows us to make inferences concerning the relationships among strategic operations, writing operations, and knowledge structures. The second advantage lies in the *precision* achieved by specifying coding for operations and content in terms of semantic structures. This specification makes coding assumptions more explicit and reduces the subjectivity of categorizing a verbalization as an instance of an operation or knowledge structure (Ericsson & Simon, 1984, p. 270). In particular, the approach allows us to distinguish between interpretive and identification actions in carrying out the coding. It is desirable to minimize interpretation in coding; and in any case, one would want to know which coding activities involve interpretation (Breuleux, 1990). The third advantage lies in the *detail* of the coding, which allows us to identify specific instances of strategies such as planning and then to determine whether and how the strategies are successfully implemented in the think-aloud or written text. We illustrate the application of the approach for a protocol collected from an expert journalist as he wrote copy for his publication.

DESCRIPTION OF PROCEDURES

Preliminaries: Protocol Sources, Transcription, and Integration

Application of our method depends upon the collection of think-aloud verbalizations and written text from writers. We use audiotape to record think-aloud verbalizations and videotape to record written text. The audiotrack of the videotape also records the think-aloud and provides a backup copy of the verbalizations. Our practice has been to collect protocols in as realistic a situation as possible; thus for the journalism protocols, the think-alouds and written texts were taken in the offices of the newspaper as journalists were inputting copy that they were submitting to their editors for publication. Typically journalists wrote for 35 to 60 minutes with the researcher present, ending the session with a break for coffee or a meal, or the initiation of another task such as collecting information from the wire service.

The audiotapes of think-aloud verbalizations are transcribed according to standard transcription conventions. These conventions have been adopted to ensure that we obtain a sequential record that is as accurate as possible of the lexical and syntactic structures of the think aloud. Only a rough record is obtained for intonation patterns of the verbalizations. Written text produced by the writers is transcribed from the videotape record, and includes deletions and revisions of the text. The transcription conventions are presented in Table 3.1.

TABLE 3.1: Transcription Conventions

Mark	Significance	Example
.	Period: Used with utterances having normal (falling) intonation	I'll start that now.
?	Question mark: Used with interrogative (rising) intonation	what word am I looking for?
!	Exclamation point: Used with exclamatory (sharp rise at end of word) intonation	this is confusing!
!xxx!	Bracketing exclamation points: Used with utterances that are stressed with loudness or highly pitched	they don't quite insist on having them !abandon! it.
::	Colon(s): Used to indicate prolongation of syllables	the prospects seem to b::e uh seem to be dim
...	Multiple periods: Used to indicate pause by speaker, each period counts 1 second	that gives uh ... the reader a ... little bit of an overview
xxx-	Hyphen: Used for utterances that are cut off or unfinished	if he starts saying outrageous- or did I use the word outrageous up there already?
xxx-,	Hyphen plus comma: Used for utterences that are revised in the course of production	Reagan's been saying that he ex-, he would hope that at least they would have plans for another meeting
((xxx))	Double parentheses: Used where transcription may not be accurate	to ((cold))-, to uh u::m...
xxx	Bracketing asterisks: Used for all comments made by transcriber	*typing resumes.* From all reports *typing sounds* pessimism.. would appear to be the um.. the-
<xxx>	Angle brackets: Used where utterance is being read by subject	<at next week's summit in Geneva between Gorbachev and Reagan>
{xxx}	Curly brackets: Used where subject writes or types utterance	{The ou::tstanding question in world affai::rs today is...}
^XXX^	Cap brackets: Used when subject types and does not utter typed information	^For the Americans...^

The text of the think-aloud and written transcripts are next segmented into clauses, with each clause being numbered in sequence. This segmentation is carried out primarily to facilitate the subsequent semantic analysis of the transcripts, since it allows the coder to work on one clause at a time in coding the detailed semantic structure expressed by the writer. Currently we base our segmentation procedure on Winograd's (1983, Appendix B) phrase structure grammar, obtaining segments that consist of clauses with finite verbs and also adjunct clauses containing nonfinite verbals such as participles.

The segmented think-aloud and written transcripts are then integrated to obtain a single record that reflects the sequence of language production during the writing session. An example of such a sequence, which we shall use for illustrative purposes in the rest of this chapter, is presented in Table 3.2.

Semantic Analysis

We are using Frederiksen's (1975, 1986) theory of propositional representation as a basis for coding the detailed semantic structure of transcripts. The basic unit of this theory is the concept-relation-concept triple: Concepts are defined as objects, actions, or properties; relations among concepts are defined as case relations (e.g., AGENT, RESULT) or as logical relations (e.g., CONDITION, CATEGORY). A propositional representation in its simplest form consists of a single concept-relation-concept unit. For example, "I think" expresses the unit *think*-AGENT-*I* where *think* and *I* are concepts, and AGENT is the relation between them.

Two aspects of Frederiksen's theory merit further comment. The first concerns the ways in which concept-relation-concept units can be related. In most instances propositional representations are more complex than the simple concept-relation-concept unit presented above. One form of complexity consists of a concept that is related to a number of other concepts. For example, in "Speech created thought" the concept *create* is related both to *speech* and to *thought*: *speech*-AGENT-*create*-RESULT-*thought*. Another form of complexity consists of treating a propositional representation as if it were a single concept in a concept-relation-concept unit. For example, "I think, therefore I am" expresses two simple units: (a) *think*-AGENT-*I*, and (b) *am*(=*exist*)-PATIENT-*I*. These two units in turn are related by a CONDITION relation, which is expressed by the word "therefore." These two enhancements, multiple relations for a concept and embedding a proposition in a concept slot, allow us to deal with the complexity of semantic structures that one finds in think-aloud transcripts from tasks such as the present one.

TABLE 3.2: Excerpt From Journalist (GM1) Integrated Transcript

Segment #	Transcription
1	I'll be writing an article on the uh.. the prospects uh for success or failure at next week's.. summit meeting between uh Gorbachev and Reagan.
2	And I'll start that now. Okay.
3	Okay first sentence. *Hits keyboard four times.*
4	{The um.. *Presses keyboard seven times* overridi::ng *presses keyboard repeatedly while talking* questi::on in world affairs *continues to press keyboard rapidly* toda::y is what.. uh will.. happen at next week's Geneva S::ummit between U.S. President Re::agan and Soviet Leade::r Mikhail Gorbachev. *Typing sounds.*} Th::e...
1	**The overriding question in world affairs today is what will happen at next week's Geneva Summit between U.S. President Reagan and Soviet Leader Mikhail Gorbachev.**
5	*Experimenter* ((*unintelligible*))
6	*Subject* Um.. um.. certainly th-, for the-, the prospects seem to b::e uh seem to be dim uh if-,
7	((??)) if one reads everything in the newspapers and listens to the various uh.. uh.. um musings of the two leaders involved the propaganda explosions and so on um.. the um-...
8 to 22	*Task talk with experimenter*
21	First what I want to get down here is the uh-, in terms of a general introduction is uh um.. what the prospects are
22	and then explain.. why they are that way u::h.
23	looking at the problem of summits generally first
24	and then focusing on the American side
25	and then Soviet side or vice versa. Um...
26	So I should say some introductory-, introductory remarks now about my views of..-, of what will happen next week um. ..
27	{*Typing resumes.* From all reports *typing sounds*.. pessimism.. would appear to be} um.. the-
28	*typing ceases* what word am I looking for?
29	The um um um.. {predominant *typing resumes* sentiment}
30	one could say..
31	{going into the meetings} um...
2	**From all reports pessimism would appear to be the predominant sentiment going into the meetings.**
32	{If we listen.. to the U.S. side..}
3	**If we listen to the U.S. side,**
33	{it appears that they are fearful.. um.. of creati::ng um.. over-expectations.. um...*typing stops*}
4	**it appears that they are fearful of creating over-expectations**
34 to 43	*Task talk with experimenter*

(Continued)

TABLE 3.2: (Continued)

Segment #	Transcription
44	\<It appears that they are fearful of-, of creating over-expectations\> um..
45	{and.. *typing resumes* therefore.. um um.. have had.. the president himself and various aides.. um telling.. everyone concerned.. uh.. not to expect.. too much.} *Typing ceases.*
5	**and therefore have had the president himself and various aides telling everyone concerned not to expect too much.**
46	Well they say you-, in fact they say uh don't even expect a uh-, a joint communique uh..
47	so I should mark that in um. ..
48	{*Typing resumes.* They are going so far as to sa::y that one should not.. even expect a joint..} *typing ceases*-,,
49	oh I got that all in uh capital letters
50	now I must shift it down.
51	*Typing resumes.* A joint {communique from meeting.} *Typing ceases.*..
6	**They are going so far as to say that one should not even expect a joint communique from the meeting.**

NOTE: xxx = think-aloud transcript, **xxx** = written transcript

The second aspect concerns the theory's comprehensive coverage of semantic relations. As mentioned above, relations between concepts are divided into two general classes, case relations and logical relations. The case relations such as AGENT specify the roles that object concepts can take on in relation to actions. A list of these, together with definitions and examples, is presented in Table 3.3. The logical relations are of two types, basic and derived.[2] The basic types consist of dependency relations such as CONDITION and AND (or union). A list of these, together with definitions and examples, is presented in Table 3.4. Derived logical relations take on a number of forms, including comparisons of concepts; tense and modal relations for actions; quantitative relations; and temporal, locative, categorical and part relations (collectively called "identifying" relations by Frederiksen). The common feature of these derived relations is that they specify a relation among concepts with respect to a particular property concept. For example, a PAST tense relation on an action is derived from an ORDER relation between the time property of the action and the present. A list of the derived relations, together with definitions and examples, is presented in Tables 3.5, 3.6, 3.7, and 3.8. As is indicated by the extent of Tables 3.3

TABLE 3.3: Case Relations

Relation	Definition	Example
AGENT	concept is the immediate cause of an action	"I'll write an article" write-AGENT-I
PATIENT	concept is a participant in an action	"We saw the light" see-PATIENT-we
OBJECT	concept is affected by an action	"I'll revise the piece" revise-OBJECT-piece
RECIPIENT	action "transfers" a concept to another concept	"She gave the article to the editor" give-RECIPIENT-editor
INSTRUMENT	concept is used to carry out an action	"He wrote the piece on the computer" write-INSTRUMENT-computer
SOURCE	concept precedes an action	"We took the bulletin from the wire service" take-SOURCE-wire service
RESULT	concept produced by an action	"He made the paper plane" make-RESULT-plane
THEME	symbolic concept produced by an action	"She wrote the story" write-THEME-story
GOAL	action is directed towards a future concept	"We rewrote the piece for submission" rewrite-GOAL-submission

SOURCE: Adapted from Frederiksen (1975, 1986)

through 3.8, this development of semantic relations provides a comprehensive coverage of the relations to be found in natural language productions, including think-aloud transcripts.

Although Frederiksen's theory deals in principle with the complexity and range of semantic relations found in natural language, application of the theory as a coding system to identify the concepts and relations verbalized by the writer in the course of producing the text is not straightforward. First, the coder must be well versed in the semantic categorizations of the theory; and it also helps to be familiar with the work of Chafe (1970), Fillmore

TABLE 3.4: Dependency Logical Relations

Relation	Definition	Example
IF	Material implication: Relation contraposes (e.g., valid inferences are if p then q, and if not-p then not-q)	"If the number is 4, then it is even" IF [4] [*even*]
CONDITION	Reduced set of implications, may not contrapose	"If rain threatens, I take my umbrella" CONDITION [*rain threat*] [*take umbrella*]
CAUSE	Reduced set of implications, never contraposes	"Absence makes the heart grow fonder" CAUSE [*absence*] [*heart grow fonder*]
AND	Specifies a union of concepts	". . . for the oracle will say both yes and no" AND [*yes*] [*no*]
OR-EXCLUSIVE	Specifies one concept from among a set of concepts	". . . success or failure at next week's summit" OR-EXCLUSIVE [*success*] [*failure*]
OR-ALTERNATIVE	Specifies one or more concepts from among a set of concepts	"increase dietary fiber by eating bran or fruit" OR-ALTERNATIVE [*bran*] [*fruit*]

SOURCE: Adapted from Frederiksen (1975, 1986)

(1968), and Leech (1970). Second, in addition to the theory, some of our coding decisions make use of the context of previous clauses, particularly their syntactic structure, when coding in order to complete propositional structures. Both propositional coding and the use of context are illustrated

TABLE 3.5: Derived Logical Relations: Algebraic Relations

Relation	Definition	Example
EQUIVALENCE	Specifies concepts having the same value of a property	"One word is as bad as the other" EQUIVALENCE [*one word*] [*other*]
ORDER	Specifies concepts that differ in the value of a property, and orders the concepts with respect to the value	"This version reads better than the previous one" ORDER [*this version*] [*previous one*]
PROXIMITY	Specifies concepts with similar values of a property	"Birnham Wood is near Dunsinane" PROXIMITY [*Burnam Wood*] [*Dunsinane*]

SOURCE: Adapted from Frederiksen (1975, 1986)

in Table 3.9, which presents the propositional coding for part of the transcript presented in Table 3.2.

The use of context can be seen in segments 21 to 24 of the Table. In these segments, the actions of propositions 21.2 *get down,* 22.1 *explain,* 23.1 *look at,* 24.1 *focus on,* and 25.1 *focus on* have all been coded as having an AGENT relation with *I* (that is, the writer) even though the relationship does not appear explicitly in the think-aloud verbalization. We have added this AGENT relation in the propositional coding because of the syntactic structure of the segments in which the actions appear as verb or verbal constituents. In the syntactic structures, the AGENT relation of the action with the writer has been elided. Usually in the protocols such ellipsis occurs in order to realize a well-formed surface structure (e.g., *get down* as an infinitive complement of *want*). At other times the ellipsis occurs in order to eliminate what would be a redundant noun or verb (e.g., see the coding for segment 7 of Table 3.9).

The propositional coding of the think-aloud and the written text gives us what is essentially a database of the semantic structures produced by the writer. We then use this base of semantic structures to code strategic and

TABLE 3.6: Derived Logical Relations: Tense and Modality Relations

Relation	Definition	Example
Tense		
PAST	Temporal relation in which concept occurs before the present	"I returned" *return*-TENSE:PAST
PRESENT	Temporal relation in which concept occurs at a time equivalent with the present	"I return" *return*-TENSE:PRESENT
FUTURE	Temporal relation in which concept occurs after the present	"I shall return" *return*-TENSE:FUTURE
Modality		
QUALIFIED	Unstated conditions exist that imply a concept	"I may return" *return*-MODALITY:QUAL
NECESSITY	Unstated conditions exist that make a concept a necessity	"I must return" MODALITY:MUST
ABILITY	Unstated conditions exist that will lead to a concept	"I can return" MODALITY:CAN

SOURCE: Adapted from Frederiksen (1975, 1986)

writing operations and conceptual and language objects that have been applied by the writer in the course of composing.

Coding of Operations and Objects

To code the writer's operations we first define criteria for recognizing operations in terms of configurations of semantic, conceptual, and syntactic structures. We also define criteria for coding the relationship among operations in terms of semantic and conceptual structures. Given these criteria, we recognize specific instances of operations and relations in the writer's

TABLE 3.7: Derived Logical Relations for Quantification

Relation	Definition	Example
UNIVERSAL	Specifies all concepts that belong to a set of concepts	"All of the people" *people*-UNIVERSAL
NULL	Specifies no concepts belong to a set	"None of the people" *people*-NULL
NUMBER	Specifies a count for concepts	"Three-score years" *years*-NUMBER-*three-score*
DEGREE	Specifies extent for concepts that are not countable	"some of the time" *time*-DEGREE-*some*
DEFINITE	Specifies a particular concept or concepts from among a set of concepts	"We, the people of . . ." *people*-DEFINITE
INDEFINITE	Specifies a concept or concepts from among a set without identifying it or them uniquely	"some of the people" *people*-INDEFINITE

SOURCE: Adapted from Frederiksen (1975, 1986)

protocol in two ways: (a) directly by a match of semantic or syntactic structure in the protocol with the defined criteria, and (b) indirectly by differences in the semantic structures for a particular concept that occurs at two points in the protocol.

The objects that the writer has operated on are coded directly from the protocol, and consist of the non-operation semantic structures, concepts, and syntactic structures that the writer produces in both the think-aloud protocol and the written text. The major issue in coding content is defining a level of abstraction for categorizing the content. For example, the writer produces a text by typing letters on a keyboard, so in some sense the writer is treating letters as objects. However, this very fine level of object definition is not likely to be informative for a model of text production. The appropriate level of abstraction is constrained both by the strategic operations themselves and by the overt actions of the writer. First, strategic

TABLE 3.8: Derived Logical Relations for Identifying Relations

Relation	Definition	Example
CATEGORY	Specifies that a concept is a member of a class of concepts	"summit meeting" *meeting*-CATEGORY-*summit*
THEME	Specifies that a concept is a member of a class of symbolic concepts	"article on the summit meeting" *article*-THEME-*summit meeting*
IDENTITY	Specifies that a set of one class of concepts has the same members as another class	" 'To be or not to be' is the question" *'to be or not to be'*-IDENTITY-*question*
ATTRIBUTE	Specifies a relation between a concept and a property concept	"This is alright" *this*-ATTRIBUTE-*alright*
PART	Specifies that a concept is a constituent of another concept	"Now for the conclusion of the piece" *piece*-PART-*conclusion*
LOCATION	Specifies where a concept is with respect to another concept	". . . meeting in Geneva" *meeting*-LOCATION-*Geneva*
TEMPORAL	Specifies a temporal property for a concept	". . . meeting next week" *meeting*-TEMPORAL-*next week*

SOURCE: Adapted from Frederiksen (1975, 1986)

operations scope sets of propositions through case relations and identifying relations (see below). We treat these sets as objects manipulated by the writer. Second, the sequence of operations and overt action serves to segment performance and thereby gives us clues concerning the objects the writer has been working with. For example, typing tends to occur in clausal

TABLE 3.9: Propositional Analysis of Excerpt From Journalist (GM1) Integrated Transcript

Segment Number	Transcription	
1	I'll be writing an article on the uh.. the prospects uh for success or failure at next week's.. summit meeting between uh Gorbachev and Reagan.	
	1.1 *write*	AGENT: I, THEME: *article*, TENSE:FUTURE
	1.2 *article*	THEME: *1.3, 1.4*
	1.3 *meet*	AGENT: *Gorbachev, Reagan*, RESULT: *success*, CATEGORY: *summit*, TEMPORAL: *next week*
	1.4 *meet*	AGENT: *Gorbachev, Reagan*, RESULT: *failure*, CATEGORY: *summit*, TEMPORAL: *next week*
	1.5 OR:EXCLUSIVE	[*1.3*] [*1.4*]
	1.6 CONDITION	[*prospects*] [*1.5*]
2	And I'll start that now. Okay.	
	2.1 *that *=write**	AGENT: *I*, PART: *start*
	2.2 *2.1*	ATTRIBUTE: *okay*
3	Okay first sentence. *Hits keyboard four times.*	
	3.1 *elided*	ATTRIBUTE: *okay*
	3.2 EQUIVALENCE	[*first sentence*] [**segment 4**]
4	{The um.. overridi::ng *presses keyboard repeatedly while talking* questi::on in world affairs toda::y is what.. uh will.. happen at next week's Geneva S::ummit between U.S. President Re::agan and Soviet Leade::r Mikhail Gorbachev.} *Typing sounds.* Th::e...	
	4.1 *see analysis for **written segment 1***	
1	**The overriding question in world affairs today is what will happen at next week's Geneva Summit between U.S. President Reagan and Soviet leader Mikhail Gorbachev.**	
	1.1 IDENTITY	[*1.2 *question...**] [*1.4 *what will happen...**]
	1.2 *question*	ATTRIBUTE: **importance(elided)**, DEGREE: *overriding*, TEMPORAL: *today*
	1.3 *question*	CATEGORY: *world affairs*

(Continued)

TABLE 3.9: (Continued)

Segment Number	Transcription	
1.4	happen	RESULT: what, LOCATION: Geneva, TEMPORAL: next week, TENSE:FUTURE
1.5	summit	AGENT: Reagan, Gorbachev
1.6	ORDER:CATEGORY	[Mikhail] [Gorbachev]
1.7	EQUIVALENCE	[U.S. President] [Reagan]
1.8	EQUIVALENCE	[Soviet Leader] [Gorbachev]
1.9	ORDER:TEMPORAL	[1.2 *question*] [1.4 *what will happen..*]

5   *Experimenter* ((*unintelligible*))

6   *Subject* Um.. um.. certainly
th-, for the-, the prospects
seem to b::e uh seem to be
dim uh if-, +

| 6.1 | CONDITION | [prospects] [*success-elided*] |
| 6.2 | 6.1 | DEGREE: dim, MODALITY:QUALIFIED: seem, MODALITY:ROOT: certainly |

7   ((??)) if one reads everything in the newspapers and listens to the various
uh.. uh.. um musings of the two leaders involved the propaganda
explosions and so on um.. the um-...

7.1	read	AGENT: one, OBJECT: everything, SOURCE: newpapers
7.2	listen to	AGENT: one, OBJECT: musings, SOURCE: leaders
7.3	listen to *elided*	AGENT: one, OBJECT: propaganda explosions
7.4	CONDITION	[7.1, 7.2, 7.3] [6.2 *prospects dim*]

8 to 22   *Task talk with experimenter*

21   First what I want to get down here is the uh-, in terms of a general
introduction is uh um.. what the prospects are

| 21.1 | want | AGENT: I, THEME: 21.2, 22.1, 23.1, 24.1, 25.1 *syntax*, TEMPORAL: first |
| 21.2 | get down | AGENT: I *elided*, THEME: prospects, LOCATION: here |

TABLE 3.9: (Continued)

Segment Number	Transcription	
	21.3 *introduction*	ATTRIBUTE: *general*
	21.4 EQUIVALENT	[*prospects*] [*21.3*]
22	and then explain.. why they are that way u::h	
	22.1 *explain*	AGENT: *I *elided**, THEME: *22.2*
	22.2 CONDITION	[*why*] [*they *prospects**]
	22.3 *why*	PART: *23.1, 24.1, 25.1*
	22.4 ORDER:TEMPORAL	[*21.2*] [*22.1*]
23	looking at the problem of summits generally first	
	23.1 *look at*	AGENT: *I *elided**, THEME: *problem*, CATEGORY: *general*, TEMPORAL: *first*
	23.2 *summit*	PART: *problem*
24	and then focusing on the American side	
	24.1 *focus on*	AGENT: *I *elided**, THEME: *American side*
	24.2 ORDER:TEMPORAL	[*23.1*] [*24.1*]
25	and then Soviet side or vice versa. Um...	
	25.1 *focus on *elided**	AGENT: *I *elided**, THEME: *Soviet side*
	25.2 ORDER:TEMPORAL	[*24.1*] [*25.1*]
	25.3 ORDER:TEMPORAL	[*25.1*] [*24.1*] **vice versa**
	25.4 OR:EXCLUSIVE	[*25.2*] [*25.3*]
26	So I should say some introductory-, introductory remarks now about my views of..-, of what will happen next week um ..	
	26.1 *say*	AGENT: *I*, THEME: *remarks*, TEMPORAL: *now*, MODALITY:MUST: *should*
	26.2 *remarks*	CATEGORY: *introductory*, THEME: *26.3*
	26.3 *views*	AGENT: *I*, THEME: *26.4*
	26.4 *happen*	RESULT: *what*, TEMPORAL: *next week*, TENSE:FUTURE
27	{*Typing resumes.* From all reports *typing sounds*.. pessimism.. would appear to be the} um.. the-	

(Continued)

TABLE 3.9: (Continued)

Segment Number	Transcription	
	27.1 *see analysis for **written segment 2***	
28	*typing ceases* what word am I looking for?	
	28.1 *look for*	AGENT: *I*, GOAL: *word*
29	{The um um um.. predominant *typing resumes* sentiment}	
	29.1 *see analysis for **written segment 2***	
30	one could say..	
	30.1 *say*	AGENT: *one,* MODALITY:CAN: *could,* TENSE:PAST
31	{going into the meetings} um...	
	31.1 *see analysis for **written segment 2***	
2	**From all reports pessimism would appear to be the predominant sentiment going into the meetings.**	
	2.1 *reports*	THEME: *2.2,* UNIVERSAL
	2.2 IDENTITY	[*pessimism*] [*2.3*] MODALITY:QUALITATIVE: *would appear*
	2.3 *sentiment*	DEGREE: *predominant*
	2.4 ORDER:TEMPORAL	[*2.2 *pessimism . . .*] [*meetings*] *going into*

NOTES: xxx = think-aloud transcript, **xxx** = written transcript; concepts are coded in *italics*, relations in UPPER CASE

or clause constituent bursts (see segments 27 through 31 of Table 3.9), which suggests that the writer is manipulating clause and constituent structures at the syntactic level.

Strategic Operations

The principal strategic operations that we code have to do with planning and with evaluations of the implementation of plans (i.e., with whether the text that is written does in fact realize the plan). The semantic criteria defining these operations have been developed by Breuleux (1990, 1991).

The basic unit of a plan is a goal. A goal is defined to have the characteristics of *intentionality* of the writer, and *future* or *potential* action. This definition allows us to identify semantic structures in the protocol that meet these characteristics. An evaluation operation is defined as a *psychological attribute* that is predicated of a concept. A list of these structures that constitute criteria for goal operations and evaluations is presented in Table 3.10.

The objects to which the writer assigns goal status are contained in THEME relations with the actions that constitute part of the goal. That is, the content that is to be realized consists of the concept(s) linked to the goal action by a THEME case relation. Thus in Table 3.9 propositions 1.2 through 1.6 of segment 1 make up the content of the initial goal that the writer has expressed in the protocol.

Breuleux (1991) defines a *plan* as a set of related goals; so we are also interested in defining criteria for operations that link a goal to other goals that we have identified from the semantic structure of the protocol. These relationships among goals are defined by specific semantic relational structures. The principal ones are temporal order of goals (see for example the semantic structures for segments 21 and 22 of Table 3.9) and hierarchical relations among goals as indicated by THEME and PART relations (see for example the semantic structures for segments 22 through 25 of Table 3.9).

A summary of the goal, planning, and evaluation operations that can be coded given these criteria is presented in Table 3.11. (Table 3.11 also presents knowledge operations and language operations that are discussed below.) The outcome of this type of goal analysis is that we are able to identify directly the process of planning in which the writer engages, and the actual plan that is constructed to help write the article. For example, the plan that the writer verbalized in Table 3.9 is presented in graphical form in Figure 3.1. At this point one can begin to see the heuristic value of representing the detailed semantic structure of the protocol: The analysis of this structure reveals the content of goal operations and the structure of that content. This allows us to track the content of these strategic operations through reinstatement and transformation operations in the protocol and to determine finally whether and in what form the content is realized in text.

Knowledge Operations

The coding of knowledge operations is in some instances quite straightforward and in other instances demands serious detective work. The straight-

TABLE 3.10: Semantic Structures That Realize Goals and Evaluations

Characteristic	Semantic Structure	Example
Goals:		
Intentionality	Volitional lexical identifier (with first person agent relation)	"what I want to get down here"
		I-AGENT-*want*
	First person agent relation (with action marked as future or potential)	"I'll be writing an article . . ."
		I-AGENT-*write*-TENSE:FUTURE
Future action	Action temporally marked as future (with first person agent relation)	"I'm going to reread this"
		I- AGENT-*reread* -TENSE:FUTURE
Potential action	Action modally marked as qualified, necessary, or ability (with first person agent relation)	"I should say . . ."
		I-AGENT-*say* -MODALITY:MUST
	Disjunction relation between actions (with first person agent relation)	"either I drop the show or I drop Reagan"
		[*drop show*]-OR-EXCLUSIVE-[*drop Reagan*]
	Goal case relation (with first person agent relation)	"What is the word I'm looking for?"
		I-AGENT-*look for*-GOAL-*word*
Evaluation:	Psychological attribute relation with a concept	"I'll start that now. Okay"
		[*start*] -ATTRIBUTE-*okay*

SOURCE: Adapted from Breuleux (1991)

TABLE 3.11: Strategic, Knowledge, and Language Operations

Strategic Operations	Knowledge Operations	Language Operations
S1. General goal operations:	K1. Simple operations:	L1. Rhetorical operations:

Set goal
Reinstate goal
Delete goal
	Retrieve content
	   from memory
	Reinstate content
	Delete content
		Select propositions for
		   adjunct topic
		Select propositions for
		   subject topic
		Select propositions for
		   comment

S2. Evaluation operation:		
Evaluate	K2. Complex operations:	Select rhetorical frame structure
	Reduce content Expand content	
S3. Planning operations:		L2. Syntactic operations:

Set coordinate relation
Set subordinate relation
Set alternative relation
Move goal structure
Reinstate goal structure
		Generate constituent
		   structure
		Generate clause
		   structure
		Reinstate constituent
		   structure

SOURCE: Adapted from Bracewell & Breuleux (1990)

forward instances, where we can directly identify operations, are of two types. The first is where the writer produces new information. We treat such instances as evidence for the retrieval of information from memory, with the novelty of the information defining the criteria for a retrieval operation. These instances are revealed in the semantic structure of the protocol by the presence of propositions containing concepts not seen before, and the coding consists of a direct match of such propositions with the novelty criterion. The second type is where the writer reintroduces previously produced information into the protocol. At this detailed level of coding the semantic structure, the duplication of propositional structure is not very frequent; rather, the repetition of concepts is usually accompanied by some alteration in the propositional structure that relates the repeated concept with other concepts.

The more challenging (and more interesting) instances are those where we suspect that the writer has transformed knowledge already introduced

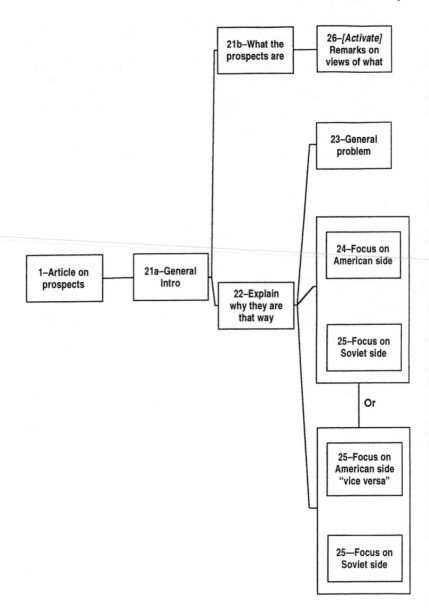

Figure 3.1. Plan Structure for Segments 1 to 25 (Levels of Subordination Indicated Left to Right, Temporal Sequence Indicated Top to Bottom)

previously in the protocol. Such transformation operations either reduce or expand prior content in the protocol. Coding a transformation operation necessarily involves making an inference based upon differences of semantic structure between two places in the protocol for the same concept(s). The issue is how to define criteria that differentiate transformation operations from memory retrieval and reinstating operations. Criteria for coding transformations that involve deletions or expansions between propositional structures are easier to specify. Such changes include modifications in case semantic structure and in identifying concepts. Both deletion and expansion operations are illustrated in the differences between the propositions of segment 1 of the think aloud and segment 1 of the written protocol: A deletion operation transforms ". . . summit meeting between . . ." to ". . . summit between . . ."; an expansion operation transforms ". . . Gorbachev and Reagan" to ". . . U.S. President Reagan and Soviet Leader Mikhail Gorbachev" (see Table 3.9). These knowledge transformation operations are illustrated in Figure 3.2.

Most difficult to specify are criteria for a transformation that reduces a propositional structure to a single concept, or expands a concept into a propositional structure. Unlike the transformations between propositional structures described immediately above, we cannot use the context of the larger propositional structure to circumscribe the difference seen with the smaller structure. The definition of criteria for either expansion of a concept or reduction to a concept depends on an analysis of the internal structure of a concept. Such analyses for this work are at a preliminary stage; however, we think the initial development is sufficiently promising that it is worth presenting in illustrative form. Our analysis of conceptual structures draws on research being conducted in lexical semantics (Pinker, 1989), and particularly on the structure of verbs. For example, Gleitman and Gleitman (1992) present an analysis of a class of verbs that specify the transfer of an object from a source to a recipient. Such verbs cover the transfer of both concrete and symbolic objects (e.g., *give* versus *explain*). One of the characteristics of these verbs is that they differ according to whether a potential agent relation must be paired with the source or the recipient of the action: Compare *give,* where the source and agent are paired, with *accept*, where the recipient and agent are paired. We are making use of the well-specified structure of such verbs to define criteria for the coding of these radical transformation operations. At a general level, the criteria are based on a match between an expressed propositional structure and a concept that has a corresponding internal relational structure.

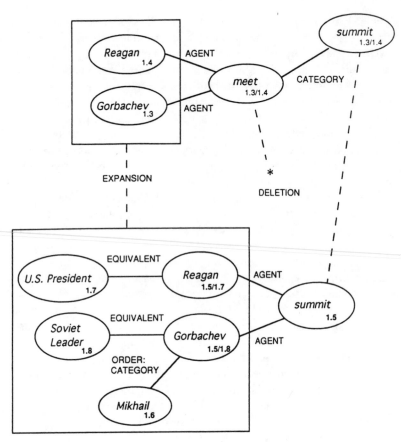

Figure 3.2. Expansion and Deletion Operations on Propositional Structures

An illustrative use of this type of criterion is seen in the relation between the content expressed in think-aloud segment 7 of Table 3.9 and that expressed in written segment 2. Intuitively from reading the segments, one recognizes that the content of think-aloud segment 7 has been reduced to "all reports" in written segment 2. The issue for coding is what criteria justify this intuitive judgement that a knowledge reduction transformation occurred? Notice that all the action concepts in the two segments (*reads, listens,* and *report*) consist of symbolic transfer verbs of the type outlined above. In the case of the actions in segment 7 (*reads* and *listens*) the agent relation is paired with the recipient relation, while for the action of segment

2 (*report*) the agent relation is paired with the source relation. Thus the criteria for coding a knowledge transformation operation across these two segments consist of the similarity in relational structures of the actions.[3] This similarity is illustrated in Figure 3.3. Once again, we can see the heuristic value of this level of detail in the analysis—with the transformation documented, the issue becomes that of accounting for why such a radical reduction in content occurred. Such an account involves consideration of language operations.

Language Operations

Language operations are by far the easiest type of operation to code since the outcome of the operation is seen in the surface structure of the text itself. Once again, however, one is faced with the problem of defining an appropriate level of abstraction for coding the operations. The most obvious level, that of constituent structures (e.g., noun phrases, verb phrases, and so forth) is too detailed a level to be useful in itself. What is required is a level of abstraction that allows us to continue tracking content initially expressed in terms of a goal, or retrieved from memory, or transformed in structure. At the same time the level should allow us to deal with language operations that serve to create a textual surface structure. Given these conditions, the appropriate level for defining language operations is in terms of the constituent structures that realize topic and comment structures across clauses.

Our list of language operations was presented in Table 3.11. These comprise two types of operations. First, there are operations that produce structures that serve a rhetorical function, namely topic/comment operations and rhetorical frame operations. Criteria for the coding of topic/comment operations come from Halliday (1985, pp. 38-64) where major constituents that come before the major verb phrase of a clause are defined as topics, and the verb phrase and following constituents are defined as comment.[4] Topic structures are of two types: (a) constituents in the position of subject of the verb, and (b) fronted adjunct constituents such as prepositional phrases, adverbs, and subordinate clauses. We treat the presence of such structures in the text as evidence for operations that select propositions to be realized in these surface structures. In addition we posit an operation of selecting a rhetorical frame structure. These are structures that are similar to Grimes's (1975) rhetorical predicates. Rhetorical frames bring together propositional structures so that they can be realized in a surface structure that meets pragmatic goals of memorability or interestingness. We define criteria for

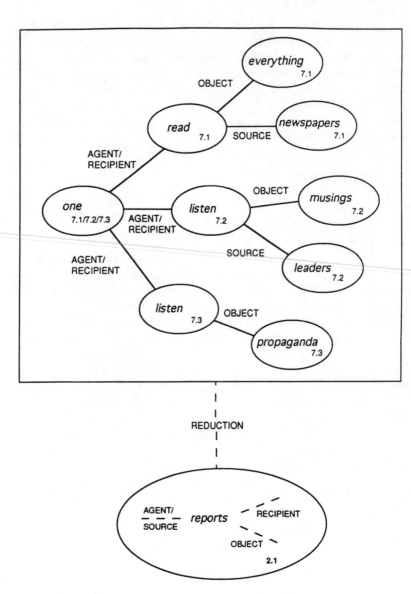

Figure 3.3. Radical Reduction of Propositional Structures to Concept (Numbers on Concepts Indicate Proposition Numbers in Table 3.9)

the coding of two such frame operations. The identity frame operation is revealed by an IDENTITY relation between propositional structures, and is realized in a surface structure in which two definite noun phrases are linked by a copula verb. We think this structure is used by writers to enhance the memorability of their text (see illustration below). The counterindicative conditional operation is revealed by a special form of CONDITIONAL relation between propositional structures in which the consequent term of the relation is unexpected or counterintuitive. The surface structure realizations of this frame include concessive subordinators (e.g., although, while) and adversative coordinators (e.g., but, however). We think these structures are used by writers to enhance readers' interest in the text. Second, there are operations that generate syntactic structures. We have defined these only in sufficient detail to support the topic/comment and rhetorical frame operations outlined above.

An Illustrative Synthesis

At the beginning of this chapter we claimed that the TIC method constitutes a unified approach that allows us to identify the goals of the writer and the content of these goals, and then to analyze how content is transformed and expressed in the manner that it is. We can gain some closure on the promise of this approach by examining further what the coding of written segment 2 reveals about the writer's processes.[5] The syntactic structure of the segment consists of a fronted (and therefore topicalized) prepositional phrase followed by a noun phrase-copula-noun phrase clause. An appreciation of the significance of this surface structure, and our analysis of how it came about, can be obtained by referring to Table 3.12. This table presents the time sequence of writing and think-aloud for the production of written segment 2, a summary of the propositional structures, and the operations coded from these structures. Writing begins at segment 27 with the prepositional phrase *From all reports*. The topicalization of this content provides the reason for the radical reduction in content from think-aloud segment 7: This content is placed in topical position because it indicates that sources exist for the gloomy assessment about the outcome of the summit meeting. But the content of think-aloud segment 2 cannot be simply reinstated in the written text. To do so would produce a complex and lengthy adjunct topic that would interfere with the reader's uptake of the following main clause

TABLE 3.12: Excerpt From Protocol GM1

Think-Aloud Segments	Propositional Summary		Operations (from Table 3.11)
27. From all reports* ()	reports	THEME: pessimism . . .	• L1: Select adjunct topic • K2: Reduce content (from propositions 7.1 to 7.4) • L2: Generate constituent structure
pessimism	IDENT	[pessimism] [*empty*];	• L1: Select rhetorical frame • L1: Select subject topic • K2: Reduce content (from propositions 6.1 and 6.2) • L2: Generate constituent structure
would appear to be the um () the-	MOD(QUAL);		• K1: Reinstate content (from proposition 6.2) • L1: Select comment • L2: Generate constituent structure
28. what word am I looking for?			• S1: Set goal
29. the um um um () **predominant sentiment**	sentiment IDENT	DEG: pre-dominant; [pessimism] [sentiment];	• K1: Retrieve content • L1: Select comment • L2: Generate constituent structure
30. one could say ()			• S2: Evaluate
31. **going into the meetings** um ().	ORD(TEM)	["pessimism . ."] ["meetings"] *going into*;	• K2: Reduce content (from written propositions 1.5 and 1.8) • L1: Select comment • L2: Generate constituent structure

SOURCE: Adapted from Bracewell & Breuleux (1990)
NOTE: **boldface** indicates written text

(Yngve, 1960). For the content to appear in this position, it must be reduced. In addition, the reduction is required to ensure the prominence of the following main clause, which is an identity frame structure. Selection of this structure, which requires an initial noun phrase, forces a reduction in content of propositional structures of think-aloud segment 6 (i.e., *dim prospects*) to the noun *pessimism*. The modal nature of this evaluation is reinstated in the copula component of the frame from segment 6. But then the writer gets into trouble: The identity frame requires a second noun phrase to complete it, but no appropriate content is at hand (. . . *would appear to be the um the-,*). Hence, the writer exercises a goal operation (segment 28) to retrieve and write content (*predominant sentiment*) that completes the identity structure.[6] He then evaluates this production (segment 30), and finishes the written segment with reduced content on the time relation between the assessment and the meeting (. . . *going into the meetings*). Thus, we begin to see for this instance how rhetorical (and ultimately communicative) considerations shape the expression of content in text.

Discussion

The Task Independent Coding methodology that we have presented in this chapter provides a comprehensive and unified treatment at a detailed level of the semantic structure of verbal information provided by the writer. Moreover, the coding categories of the method are defined independently of the specific task definition constructed in a particular protocol. As our application of the TIC method to the protocol presented in Table 3.2 illustrates, the outcome is a database of the operations and content manipulated by the writer, particularly with respect to planning operations and knowledge transformations that fit content with rhetorical structures.

A number of characteristics of the TIC method merit further comment. We deal below with three of these: (a) its role with respect to theory, (b) the perspective gained on coding for a complex task like writing, and (c) implications concerning protocols as trace data for writing processes.

Role With Respect to Theory

As a database, an important function of the TIC method is that it reveals phenomena that stimulate the development of theoretical constructs and serve as evidence against which to test theories. Two examples illustrate this role for the coding. First, the frequency in which radical knowledge transformation operations co-occur with language operations differs greatly across writer expertise. For our expert writer such co-occurrences are three times more frequent than for beginning journalists (Bracewell & Breuleux, 1990). Such data help us to define expertise in writing in a direct manner in terms of theorizing about specific processes and strategies that differentiate expert from less-expert writers. Second, in his dissertation research with journalism students, Breuleux (1990) found that the depth of planning operations never exceeded three levels for a planning episode within a think-aloud protocol before planning was interrupted by other processes such as writing or rereading (even though the plan constructed over the length of the protocol could reach many levels in depth). We find a similar pattern with our expert journalist. In fact one such episode has been presented in Figure 3.1 for segments 21 through 26. Such a consistent pattern across expertise suggests a structural characteristic of the strategic system that controls writing operations. Further this structural characteristic is consistent with the situated nature of planning in writing. That is, the generation and relation of goals are never very far removed from knowledge and language operations and the content they act upon.

Perspective on Complexity

The comprehensiveness of the TIC method provides a context for discussing the challenge of dealing with the complexity of writing. In general, the complexity of methods for coding protocols does not match the complexity of the writing task itself, yielding a radical oversimplification in the methodologies. This issue of complexity bears on both the writer's task and the coding procedure that is applied to the writer's protocols. The TIC method provides an articulation of both these aspects of complexity. With regard to the complexity of writing, the comprehensiveness and detail of our coding are consequences of the variability and multiple levels of representation that characterize writing. With regard to the complexity of coding, we think that complexity is always in the head of the coder, and that our coding scheme, insofar as it is comprehensive, is only making this complexity explicit. This articulation reveals why the "labor intensive" character of coding is no longer an issue. It is now necessary, and possible, to understand clearly the nature of the labor.

We want to argue that the articulation realized by the TIC method is a first step toward an approach in which the researcher adjusts the grain of the coding appropriately for the requirements of the research question. For some questions detailed coding of a few protocols will be required; for others a coarser coding of many protocols will be required. By way of example, two dissertation projects in our laboratory are examining the developmental patterns in students' use of high-level semantic structures (or "frames"; see Frederiksen, 1986) in their compositions (Crammond, in preparation; Senecal, in preparation). In order to code for frame use, we have developed a more coarse-grained analysis that codes individual frame-units (procedures, events, and descriptions) and the relations among them (Senecal, Crammond, & Bracewell, 1991). This coding system is linked to the more detailed approach, however, in that each of the units is defined in terms of specific propositional structures. Moreover, procedurally such a linkage allows us to fall back on the more detailed coding system when faced with coding problems in order to modify the coarser system in a principled manner. This example illustrates the sense of our claim, in the beginning of the chapter, that the approach offers the possibility of uniting different coding schemes.

Further, given the potential complexity of coding, an important challenge that writing researchers are currently facing when using protocols is the development of tools for managing the complexity of protocols and the complexity of the coding procedures that are applied to them. The development of such tools will also facilitate the documentation and communication of coding methods. This has obvious implications for training researchers and graduate students, since the quality of learning a coding procedure depends to a large extent on the availability of instructional communication material. The TIC method can serve as a basis for identifying the direction for this development—namely, toward tools for realizing multiple and coordinated dynamic representations.

Protocols as Trace Data

In treating think-aloud protocols we are dealing with a trace of the writing process, and in general one has reservations about how accurately such trace data map the writing process. Two aspects of the TIC method address these reservations. The first concerns the detailed and comprehensive coding of protocol structure. The fine-grained analysis allows us to code directly for basic composing operations, such as setting a goal; and further, the comparison of differences across semantic structures allows us to make inferences concerning operations not directly revealed in verbalizations. We have confidence that we are obtaining a record that does reflect writing activity. Second, in process research on writing one is always working with trace data in the sense that there is no direct access to cognitive processes.[7] Thus such a reservation applies to any verbalization associated with the writing process, whether think aloud, retrospective report, response to a question, or the written text itself.

What the TIC method demonstrates is that it is possible to integrate two different protocols (the think-aloud and the text) in order to code the operations and content that the writer operates upon. Because of the independence of the coding criteria from specific task characteristics, the method can be applied to code any set of related verbalizations. Thus the method provides a means of triangulating on the activity of the writer to evaluate such questions as whether the think-aloud procedure itself biases the activity. More generally, the TIC method provides an operational basis for Witte's proposal (1992) for a constructive semiotic that can bring together the cognitive and social perspectives on writing. An additional consequence is that the potential for integrating different related verbalizations raises the issue of how to determine whether a set of verbalizations is related. The prospect of this issue points to the need for evidence concerning the writer's strategic operations, especially goals and and evaluations, and the content of these operations. As the above method demonstrates, the most direct evidence for these phenomena comes from the analysis of think-aloud protocols.

NOTES

1. Dobrin (1986) presents a critique of treating writing as problem solving (pp. 717-723). Unfortunately, he does not critique either Simon (1978, pp. 284-287) or Newell (1980, pp. 712-717), where many of the issues he raises are considered.

2. Theorists have not been notably systematic in their specification of semantic concepts and relationships. This bias is quite understandable given that the principal purpose of such semantic treatments is to characterize the wide variety of semantic structures found in natural language, rather than specifying the semantics of a narrow domain on the basis of a minimum of assumptions (see Beaugrande, 1980, pp. 60-77; and Leech, 1970, pp. 6-17; for further discussion). Moreover, in principle one could derive Frederiksen's propositional relations by assuming the AND, NULL, and possibly ATTRIBUTE relations together with feature restrictions on concepts. Such a systematization would benefit both training of coders and the automatic generation and analysis of text.

3. Our coding of a transformation operation is also supported by the propositional structures of the two segments. First, the multiple types of information of segment 7 (*everything in the newspapers, musings, propaganda explosions*) becomes in segment 2 the UNIVERSAL *all*. Second, the CONDITION relation of the multiple types of infor-

mation with the outlook information of think-aloud segment 6 becomes the THEME relation of proposition 2.1 in written segment 2. Of course, both these similarities imply knowledge transformation operations that require defining criteria for their recognition.

4. Halliday's terminology for these constituents actually is *theme/rheme* rather than *topic/comment*; the latter pair is reserved for the special case of theme/rheme structures where the theme is made up of "old" information previously presented in the text. However, *topic/comment* is the more widely used terminology.

5. The tracking of part of the content of written segment 2 from goal status through knowledge transformation operations in the think aloud has been presented in Figure 3 and its accompanying text.

6. The journalist also used an identity frame for the initial sentence of the article. This sentence is a classical lead sentence for a newspaper article in that it tells *who, what, when, where,* and *why,* with the *why* being realized as a noun phrase in sole topic position (*The overriding question in world affairs today...*).

7. This characteristic of process research is only a manifestation of the more general characteristic of scientific inquiry—there is no direct access to evidence for theoretical constructs (see especially Lakatos, 1970, Section 2 on *Fallibilism versus Falsificationism,* pp. 93-132).

REFERENCES

Beaugrande, R. de. (1980). *Text, discourse, and process: Toward a multidisciplinary science of texts.* Norwood, NJ: Ablex.

Bracewell, R. J., & Breuleux, A. (1989). Le diagnostic cognitif dans la rédaction [Cognitive diagnosis in writing]. In G. Denhière & S. Baudet (Eds.), *Questions de Logopédie: Le Diagnostic du Fonctionnement cognitif dans la Compréhension de textes.* Braine-le-Comte, Belgium: Union Professionelle des logopèdes francophones.

Bracewell, R. J., & Breuleux, A. (1990, April). *Problem solving models of strategy implementation in expert and pre-expert writing* (Technical Report 90.2, Laboratory of Applied Cognitive Science, McGill University). Paper presented at the annual meeting of the American Educational Research Association, Boston.

Breuleux, A. (1990). *L'élaboration et l'exécution de plans dans une tëche de rédaction* [The construction and execution of plans in a writing task]. Unpublished doctoral thesis, University of Montreal.

Breuleux, A. (1991). The analysis of writers' think-aloud protocols: Developing a principled coding scheme for ill-structured tasks. In G. Denhière & J. P. Rossi (Eds.), *Texts and text processing* (pp. 333-362). Amsterdam: North-Holland.

Chafe, W. L. (1970). *Meaning and the structure of language.* Chicago: University of Chicago Press.

Cooper, M., & Holtzman, M. (1983). Talking about protocols. *College Composition and Communication, 34,* 284-296.

Crammond, J. (in preparation). *The development of argumentative writing skill.* Doctoral dissertation, McGill University.

Dobrin, D. N. (1986). Protocols once more. *College English, 48*(7), 713-725.

Ericsson, K. A., & Simon, H. A. (1984). *Protocol analysis: Verbal reports as data*. Cambridge: MIT Press.

Fillmore, C. (1968). The case for case. In E. Bach & R. Harms (Eds.), *Universals in linguistic theory* (pp. 1-88). New York: Holt, Rinehart & Winston.

Frederiksen, C. H. (1975). Representing logical and semantic structure of knowledge acquired from discourse. *Cognitive Psychology, 7,* 371-458.

Frederiksen, C. H. (1986). Cognitive models of discourse analysis. In C. R. Cooper & S. Greenbaum (Eds.), *Written communication annual: Vol. 1. Linguistic approaches to the study of written discourse* (pp. 227-267). Beverly Hills, CA: Sage.

Gleitman, L. R., & Gleitman, H. (1992). A picture is worth a thousand words, but that's the problem: The role of syntax in vocabulary acquisition. *Current Directions in Psychological Sciences, 1*(1), 31-35.

Grimes, J. (1975). *The thread of discourse*. The Hague: Mouton.

Halliday, M.A.K. (1985). *An introduction to functional grammar*. London: Edward Arnold.

Lakatos, I. (1970). Falsification and the methodology of scientific research programmes. In I. Lakatos & A. Musgrave (Eds.), *Criticism and the growth of knowledge* (pp. 91-196). London: Cambridge University Press.

Leech, G. N. (1970). *Towards a semantic description of English*. Bloomington: Indiana University Press.

Newell, A. (1980). Reasoning, problem solving, and decision processes: The problem space as a fundamental category. In R. Nickerson (Ed.), *Attention and performance* (Vol. 8, pp. 693-718). Hillsdale, NJ: Lawrence Erlbaum.

Nisbett, R. E., & Wilson, T. D. (1977). Telling more than we can know: Verbal reports on mental processes. *Psychological Review, 84,* 321-359.

Pinker, S. (1989). *Learnability and cognition: The acquisition of argument structure*. Cambridge: MIT Press.

Senecal, L. (in preparation). *A longitudinal study of the development of narrative writing skill*. Doctoral dissertation, McGill University.

Senecal, L., Crammond, J., & Bracewell, R. J. (1991). *Integrated frame analysis handbook* (Technical Report 91.1, Laboratory of Applied Cognitive Science, McGill University).

Simon, H. A. (1978). Information-processing theory of problem solving. In W. K. Estes (Ed.), *Handbook of learning and cognitive processes: Vol. 5. Human information processing* (pp. 271-295). Hillsdale, NJ: Lawrence Erlbaum.

Smagorinsky, P. (1989). The reliability and validity of protocol analysis. *Written Communication, 6*(4), 463-479.

Steinberg, E. R. (1986). Protocols, retrospective reports, and the stream of consciousness. *College English, 48*(7), 697-712.

Winograd, T. (1983). *Language as a cognitive process: Vol. 1. Syntax*. Reading, MA: Addison-Wesley.

Witte, S. P. (1987). Pre-text and composing. *College Composition and Communication, 38,* 397-425.

Witte, S. P. (1992). Context, text, intertext: Toward a constructivist semiotic of writing. *Written Communication, 9*(2), 155-207.

Yngve, V. H. (1960). A model and an hypothesis for language structure. *Proceedings of the American Philosophical Society, 104,* 444-466.

4

Reactivity in Concurrent Think-Aloud Protocols

Issues for Research

JAMES F. STRATMAN
LIZ HAMP-LYONS

The rise of process inquiry in reading, writing, and related problem-solving research has sparked much debate concerning data that purport to reveal problem-solvers' underlying cognitive processes. An increasingly used source for such data is a concurrent think-aloud (TA) protocol in which subjects report their thoughts continuously during various tasks. Cognitive research has benefited from experimental investigations into the method's validity (Ericsson & Simon, 1984). A common finding in many of the methodological studies reported is that concurrent TA protocols frequently slow down subjects' progress, relative to subjects' progress under normal task conditions. But direct investigations of the method's validity, however, are still quite rare, and perhaps the most important question shadowing the method is its *reactivity*: Do subjects' verbalizations of thoughts during a task actually alter the cognitive processes required to carry out the task—in ways that either enhance or obstruct the cognitive processes subjects would use when not under the TA condition? As we will discuss, for reading and writing researchers the importance of answering this question has grown in proportion to its neglect in controlled research. In many ways, the growing reliance upon concurrent think-aloud protocols is like the growing reliance of the nation upon nuclear-generated power in the 1960s: In both cases, the use of the "technology" has raced rather far ahead of the users' understanding of the technology's nature and impacts.

THE REACTIVITY PROBLEM
AND ITS SIGNIFICANCE

Our interest in this issue springs from three different but ultimately related problems. First, recent empirical work investigating reactive effects of protocols reveals troubling inconsistencies in Ericsson and Simon's (1984) theory of concurrent protocol generation, the most comprehensive cognitive theory of protocol generation at present. In particular, these inconsistencies may go to the heart of Ericsson and Simon's basic prediction that substantial cognitive interference will occur only if a task requires subjects to extensively recode information in short-term memory into an oral form, and thereby unnaturally prolong their attention to that information in order to verbalize about it (pp. 61-89). For instance, if blindfolded, but otherwise unconstrained subjects are asked to think aloud while untying various knots, we might well expect interference, because considerable extra effort will be required for subjects to generate descriptive terms for these thoughts and sensations. Thus, according to Ericsson and Simon, if recoding to an oral form is an intrinsic requirement of a task, not only will subjects' verbalizations be disrupted, but also their cognitive processes (p. 249). However, some recent research suggests that interference may occur even during tasks with which subjects might be presumed to be familiar, and in which no extensive recoding to an orally compatible form is thought to be required (Russo, Johnson, & Stephens, 1989). Along with other implications we discuss below, we are concerned that task-dependent as well as other variables may influence the amount of cognitive interference that results from giving a concurrent TA.

A second reason for our interest springs from the widespread use of concurrent TA protocols in studies comparing expert with novice task performance. This particular use raises many questions. Ericsson and Simon theorize that "we should expect the [concurrent] verbalizations of highly skilled individuals to be less complete than those of less skilled ones" (p. 91; see also pp. 115, 124). In their view, the basic reason for this relative incompleteness is that, in a given problem domain, more experienced, more expert subjects will have so deeply learned (automated) certain procedures that they need not allocate conscious attention to them during performance. And if they do not allocate attention to them, the processes will not be as readily available for oral recoding.

This question concerning the relative *completeness* of experts' and novices' concurrent protocols, however, must be kept distinct from the question concerning whether experts and novices experience different degrees and kinds of *interference* when providing protocols. That is, though many researchers have assumed that experts' reports will be less complete than those of novices, researchers have also assumed that concurrent reports will (more or less) disturb experts' and novices' cognitive processes to the same degree and in the same ways. This second assumption is unexplored in direct empirical tests for reactivity. In other words: Does the fact that task experts provide fewer concurrent verbalizations mean that they are experiencing greater or less interference from the TA requirement?

Intuitively perhaps, the requirement to verbalize thoughts while performing a task would seem likely to interfere more with the unpracticed novice's cognition than with the expert's. This supposition, like the supposition that the degree of recoding determines the amount of interference, stems from the general theory that short-term memory has a limited capacity, and therefore subjects can manage only so many mental procedures simultaneously. An example may help clarify the issue. Relative to an expert, a novice chess player might find a concurrent TA protocol a more disruptive condition. The novice's attention, already stressed by the demand to examine a complex array of pieces on the board and to make a move within 3 minutes, would seem further burdened by the demand to think aloud. Both quality of play and quality of verbalization could be expected to suffer. Yet, quite possibly, verbalizing thoughts during play would help the novice player while disrupting the expert. Novices, through the extra acoustic encoding that verbalization provides, might retain stronger impressions of the effect of their previous board moves, and thus gradually accelerate their learning of strategy (Anzai & Simon, 1979; Prietula & Feltovich, 1988). Experts, on the other hand, might not benefit in this way, but suffer through the distraction of vocalizing procedures long ago learned.

In our review of the literature, in fact, we find little controlled experimentation that clarifies these possible reactive effects of TA protocols on experts' and novices' cognition. The lack of such work may be one reason for the tacit assumption that the degree of cognitive interference experienced by experts and novices when providing protocols will be similar. However, for reasons we articulate more fully below, the possible relation between degree of task expertise and the reactive effects of concurrent TA protocols is one that merits more rigorous attention by users of the concurrent TA method than it has so far received.

The third reason for our interest in the issue of protocol reactivity is that, in the extant rigorous studies of protocol reactivity, the tasks scrutinized have been more "well-defined" than "ill-defined" (Simon, 1973). That is, the tasks usually involve solving mathematical problems, visual-spatial pattern problems, or decision-making problems presented in a discrete format, with well-specified goals (e.g., Fidler, 1983; Russo et al., 1989; Schweiger, 1983; Smead, Wilcox, & Wilkes, 1981). In one view, the use of such tasks is necessary and appropriate, because it allows for definitive scoring and comparison of subjects working in protocol and control (non-protocol) conditions. But some researchers (e.g., Witte, 1987) have supposed that experimental tests for protocol reactivity during "ill-defined" tasks are inherently infeasible, because it would be hard to find dependent variables related to such tasks suitable for controlled experimentation. Later, we will examine this second assumption with particular care.

We are concerned that the preponderant use of well-defined tasks to investigate the presence and nature of reactive effects may obscure our understanding of these effects during tasks which, like reading, writing, and text-analysis, involve one or both of the following features: (a) when subjects must specify partly or completely their own goals; (b) when subjects may generate many equally satisfactory "solutions." Reading legal cases in preparation for in-class "Socratic" recitation in law school (Lundeberg, 1987), determining a corporate acquisition strategy based upon natural language accounts together with quantitative data (Melone, 1987), and planning and writing appellate court briefs (Stratman, 1990), are just a few of the many "ill-defined" tasks that researchers have investigated using concurrent TA protocols. In few such studies, however, do we know much about the potential reactivity involved, nor have the researchers conducted formal tests for reactivity effects. Expanding inquiry into the possible reactive effects of concurrent protocols on the processes underlying these less discrete, more ill-defined tasks seems to us a critical step for educational and literacy researchers. As Smagorinsky (1989) notes, due to a lack of such inquiry we can at present only speculate how much the findings concerning reactivity in well-defined, problem-solving research (e.g., Russo et al., 1989) bear upon writing, reading, and text-revision tasks (p. 466).

REACTIVITY EFFECTS IN MODELS OF READING, WRITING, AND TEXT ANALYSIS TASKS

Apart from our interest in effects of protocol reactivity during "ill-defined" tasks generally, our special interest has been educational research that explores "ill-defined" skills in reading comprehension, written composition, revision, and editing. Concurrent think-aloud protocols are an increasingly used source for attempting to understand real-time cognition in a wide variety of reading and composition-dependent educational tasks (e.g., Applebee & Langer, 1987; Flower, Hayes, Carey, Schriver, & Stratman, 1986; Hayes, Flower, Schriver, Stratman, & Carey, 1987; Olson, Duffy, & Mack, 1985; Rymer, 1988; Smagorinsky, 1989, 1991; Witte, 1987). Significantly, though the degree of reactivity contaminating reading, writing, and revising protocols has been fiercely debated in the educational literature (e.g., Cooper & Holzman, 1983, 1985; Dobrin, 1986), very few formal empirical checks for reactivity effects have been reported in any of the studies using the method.

Olson, Duffy, and Mack (1985), for instance, carried out multiple regressions to see if the pause times of silent readers after single sentence presentations of text corresponded with the length of verbalizations produced by TA readers reading the same text, also a sentence at a time (pp. 272-273). They found that "Places where subjects in the TA task generate more talking . . . are the same places where independent subjects slow down while reading silently," concluding that "This supports the claim that the TA data are related in an important way to what readers are doing during more ordinary types of reading" (p. 273). At best, this is weak evidence for the claim that TA does not influence readers' normal processes, because there is no way to assess what mental activities the silent readers in their study were engaging in. In general, though, this kind of careful empirical attempt to assess the effects of TA on cognitive processes is extremely rare in reading, writing, and text-analysis studies. Critics and champions have apparently believed it infeasible to emulate the direct experimental designs used in studies of well-defined tasks to assess possible reactivity effects (Smagorinsky, 1989, p. 474).

Many criticisms leveled by educational researchers at protocols, especially for their incompleteness, may be moot if generating a protocol can be shown to change the very processes it is intended—if only in fragments—to reveal. A few educational studies mention the "extreme indicator" of a reactivity problem, by disclosing the number of subjects who find that the protocol disturbs them too much for them to continue working on a task (e.g., Berkenkotter, 1983; Rymer, 1988). In other studies, the use of protocols is usually premised upon theoretical grounds provided by Ericsson and Simon's (1984) review.

We particularly note no educational studies addressing directly the question of differential effects of the think-aloud constraint upon novices and experts. Yet the possibility of differential interference is a very serious one for educational researchers whose goal in using concurrent protocols has been to retrieve from expert task performances those aspects that might be modeled for classroom or programmed instruction. For example, in a study of cognitive processes in revision skill, Hayes et al. (1987) directed both experts and novices to think aloud during a complex revision task. Possible differences in the ways experts and novices might react to the protocol condition were discussed initially, but not explicitly analyzed in relation to the output measures reported (pp. 183-185). These researchers acknowledge "that what may appear to be a difference between experts and novices in underlying writing or revising processes may sometimes partly be an artifact produced by the interaction between the degree of expertise a subject possesses and the constraint of giving a protocol" (p. 184). In the study's results, for instance, it is unclear if the novice subjects' "means-ends" behaviors (coded from the protocols) were more negatively impacted by the TA condition than were the experts' (pp. 229-232). Indeed, though the overall picture of revision skill differences between experts and novices is quite dramatic in this study, it remains uncertain how far the differences are due to an interaction with TA. In a similar way, expert-novice studies of domain-based reading and analytic skill possibly confound true expert versus novice differences with an interaction between the degree of expertise factor and the protocol constraint. In Lundeberg's (1987) study of experts' and novices' legal case-reading processes, for example, there is also little discussion of differential reactivity between experts and novices. Certainly it would be encouraging news for the models presented in these otherwise valuable and pioneering educational studies if any strong interactions of this kind could be ruled out. On the basis of existing research, however, they cannot. Alternatively, if such interactions can be empirically shown, they might be carefully incorporated with researchers' interpretations regarding the structure of task processes, so that we have a more accurate picture of expert-novice differences.

Before we discuss results from a recent pilot study investigating the feasibility of testing TA subjects for reactivity, we need to look a bit more closely at current theories concerning how and why TA protocols may interfere with subjects' cognitive processes. To organize this discussion, we first review the theory as developed in the studies of well-defined problem-solving, then review tacit theories concerning the nature of reactive effects during ill-defined problem-solving, focusing especially on writing, reading, and text-revision tasks.

THEORIES OF
CONCURRENT PROTOCOL REACTIVITY

Current theory and the best methodological studies suggest five factors closely associated with the use of concurrent protocols that may cause reactivity: (1) experimental task directions to subjects that elicit an inappropriate level of verbalization (see Ericsson & Simon, 1984, pp. 78-83); (2) limited short-term memory capacity for talking and attending at the same time; (3) hearing one's own voice, (4) learning that occurs because thinking out loud increases subjects' critical attention to their activities; and (5) direct or indirect experimenter influence through verbal or nonverbal cues (Ericsson & Simon, 1984; Payne, Braunstein, & Carroll, 1978; Russo et al., 1989).

Though both the theory and the research predict the task conditions under which these factors will interfere generally (positively as well as negatively) with *any* subject's cognition, there are disturbing inconsistencies between current theory and recent empirical results. For example, the most recent rigorous experimental study of reactivity, by Russo et al. (1989), compared a group not required to produce a concurrent protocol with an experimental group required to produce one, and examined effects of requiring concurrent TA protocols over four dissimilar problem-solving tasks: mental addition, anagrams, gambles, and Raven's matrices. For two tasks, no significant differences between groups were evident. But for the addition and gambles tasks, the percent of correct answers in groups required to give protocols differed significantly from non-protocol groups. Protocols appeared to increase correct answers on the gambles task, while decreasing correct answers on the addition task (p. 762).

The important outcome of the addition and gambling tasks was that they appeared to directly contradict the predicted results, for these *types* of tasks, indicated by Ericsson & Simon (1984). As Russo et al. (1989) carefully noted:

> The generally benign view of TA protocols, supported until now by the virtual absence in the literature of empirical reports of significant and consequential reactivity, must be questioned . . . it would appear to be more difficult than previously thought to specify a priori whether or not a task will be altered by the generation of a concurrent protocol . . . our theoretical understanding of protocol generation is not yet adequate to provide sufficient assurance about the absence of reactivity to justify foregoing an empirical check. (p. 764)

Indeed, we would emphasize the implication here that trying to extend the results of reactivity tests examining well-defined tasks to ill-defined tasks (such as writing, reading, and text-revision) is highly problematic. Though some educational researchers might argue that testing for reactivity in studies of expert-novice performance on ill-defined tasks is unnecessary because the studies are exploratory and use a small number of subjects, we would argue nonetheless that such testing is crucial. The reason the testing is crucial, as Russo et al. (1989) suggest, is that "the causes of reactivity are not general but due jointly to the demands of the task and to verbalization" (pp. 762-763).

Extending this line of thinking, we wonder if researchers have directed sufficient critical attention at these joint demands in TA studies of real-time cognitive processes during reading, writing, and text-revision processes. Specifically, researchers interested in composing processes have assumed that when subjects engage in a text-revision or text-analysis task, their "reportable" short-term memory contents are in an orally compatible form, fairly easy to verbalize, and therefore that reactivity effects will be slight (e.g., Flower & Hayes, 1981, 1984). This assumption, however, has never been put to the test. As Ericsson and Simon carefully note, even with think-aloud instructions that clearly ask only for verbalization of "information" in short-term memory, subjects may present descriptions of complex mental operations instead, operations for which descriptive terms are not readily available—as if subjects were asking themselves, "What am I doing now?" (p. 244). As Ericsson and Simon comment:

> We would not be safe in extrapolating to this kind of verbalization the conclusions [about non-interference] that we have reached about think-aloud protocols that report mainly STM (short term memory) contents. . . . Verbalization of activities may possibly influence the problem solving process, although we are not aware of specific evidence that it does. (p. 244)

Presumably, then, the more we observe subjects trying to report "activities," the more their "normal" underlying cognitive processes may be altered.

Perhaps a check on transcripts for subjects' attempts to report activities, as a routine procedure, should standardly be reported in studies that try to describe cognitive processes during ill-defined tasks, even in "exploratory" studies with small numbers of subjects. In few think-aloud studies of reading, writing, and text-revision do researchers try to distinguish (in their transcript data) between subjects' apparent attempts to report "activities" and their attempts to report other information requiring less "translation" to an oral code. It is thus unclear how extensively subjects must recode short-term memory contents to an orally compatible form during these tasks. In the one portion of their treatise, where they comment explicitly upon the use of concurrent TA protocols to investigate the cognitive processes associated with reading and writing tasks, Ericsson and Simon only assert the theoretical "reportability" of short-term memory contents during these tasks. They do *not* comment upon whether, and in what ways, thinking out loud might or might not react upon the underlying cognitive processes (p. 243), except to suggest (as noted above) that attempts to report "activities" may lead to greater reactive distortion.

The lack of explanations in reported research concerning the extent to which subjects try to report "activities" during protocols leads us to question specifically whether experts and novices would differ in the extent to which they try to report such activities. Notably, the Russo et al. (1989) study did not include expertise as a variable; they endeavored from the start to assure that the degree of expertise across subjects was equal. Thus, their study does not speak directly to the possibility of systematically different reactivity *between* experts and novices when both are asked to provide think-aloud protocols.

EDUCATIONAL RESEARCHERS' VIEW
OF TA REACTIVITY EFFECTS

Among educational researchers using the TA method to compare experts' and novices' reading, writing, and text-revision behavior, a tacit view is that while TA protocols are likely to change both experts' and novices' processes, they are unlikely to do so in any *systematically different ways*.

Following Ericsson and Simon (1984), Smagorinsky (1989) argues, for instance, that while thinking out loud during other perceptual-motor processes can seriously interfere with expert or novice subjects' performance, it is unlikely to do so during writing and text-revision tasks, because the perceptual-motor processes associated with transcription (using pen or pencil) are highly automated for adult subjects (p. 467). Otherwise, he suggests, subjects' response to the TA condition while writing, planning, and analyzing natural language texts is (probably) unpredictably variable. Thus, in some subjects, despite TA practice, one might see a great deal of interference, while in other subjects no apparent contamination is involved. Smagorinsky (1989) further doubts that there is any way to predict when subjects will be disturbed or in what ways; he speculates that if a study uses a large random population (which, notably, is rarely or never the case in TA protocol based studies), these individually variable responses would probably "even out." Similarly, Faigley and Witte (1981), Witte and Cherry (1986), and Witte (1987), while assuming that TA does alter subjects' processes to a greater or lesser degree, seem to share this view of TA reactivity during writing and revision tasks as a randomized and unpredictable effect. Witte (1987) believes that to discern reliably effects of TA on underlying processes constitutes "a methodological problem of enormous proportions" (p. 399).

Like Russo, Johnson, and Stephens (1989), we have doubts about these tacit views. We wonder if the TA requirement during combined reading, writing, and revision tasks might *systematically* interfere with subjects' cognition—beyond the assumption of randomized, individually variable propensity to violate strict TA instructions and report "activities." For instance, it seems plausible that during a complex text-revision task like that used by Hayes et al. (1987), generating a protocol may enhance detection of surface errors (e.g., missing or misspelled words), by creating auditory feedback during reading out loud. It seems equally plausible to hypothesize that protocol generation may suppress both detection and revision of more complex problems of information organization if verbalization significantly reduces short-term memory capacity needed for projecting and testing partial solutions for such problems, in trying to form what Witte (1987) has called "pre-text."

Perhaps because of the small number of controlled studies of reactivity effects, much theoretical work in cognition and literacy has proceeded on the assumption that subjects' propensity to report "activities" is randomly dependent on individual differences, and that these differences would "wash out" in a large controlled study. But are reactivity effects dependent on "expertise" as well as upon the intrinsic requirements of the task? This is the line of inquiry that has not so far been rigorously pursued in educational studies of experts and novices, but one that we continue to explore in our work. We think that the methodological problem of investigating these effects is not so "enormous" as has been supposed, and that it is possible to investigate these effects in a systematic way.

METHODOLOGICAL APPROACHES
TO ASSESSING REACTIVITY EFFECTS

To be sure, one reason that assessing TA protocols for their possible interference with subjects' cognitive processes is seen as a difficult problem is that no one knows what would be an accurate model for completing most kinds of ill-defined writing, reading, and text-analysis tasks. A criterion process description—one providing a veridical picture of subjects' "normal" or "natural" thought behaviors—is certainly not available from subjects pursuing these tasks silently (i.e., in a non-protocol condition). As is often remarked (see Flower & Hayes, 1980; 1981a; 1981b; Spivey, 1990), writers and readers create their own goals, and may produce (usually) many different texts (as writers) or interpretations (as readers), which would serve equally well as "solutions" to their original exigency.

However, as Russo et al. (1989) argue, a useful test for reactivity can begin with output measures used in carefully controlled experimentation (also see Taylor & Fiske, 1981). In doing so, one must accept that there are definite limits on the validity of output measures alone as indicators of interference (or non-interference). Just because TA and non-TA groups achieve equal scores on test measures, for example, does not guarantee that their cognitive processes were the same, or that TA subjects' "natural" processes were not disturbed. It is possible that the underlying cognitive process required for a given task is altered by a TA protocol, even when the overall accuracy between protocol and non-protocol groups is not significantly different. Nonetheless, major differences between TA protocol and non-TA subjects' measures would seem to implicate significant underlying process differences. In carefully controlled experiments, these differences may reasonably be inferred to be associated with the TA and non-TA conditions.

Indeed, previous empirical research investigating text-revision processes provides intriguing output measures that may be used, if not as "smoking guns," at least as feasible starting points for assessing reactivity (Bartlett, 1981; Bereiter & Scardamalia, 1982; Faigley & Witte, 1981, 1984; Hayes et al., 1987; Scardamalia & Bereiter, 1983). All three of the following output measures might be used to explore experimentally interference with experts' and novices' cognition during task performance: (1) subjects' ability to *detect* text errors and problems and their ability to *produce* acceptable alternative revisions, that is, "corrections" that effectively remove the problems or errors while preserving the original meaning of the text; (2) their ability to *avoid introducing new* errors or problems into the revised text, even when they have eliminated those present in the original; (3) their ability to preserve the meaning of the original *or* the extent to which they introduce new content in texts they are revising.

While these variables might seem only to have relevance to the question of effects upon cognition in a text-revision task, we are interested in exploring if they could also be related to potentially reactive effects of TA in a variety of reading, writing, and verbal information analysis tasks. For example, assuming TA subjects in a controlled text-revision task introduced far less new content than they do in a non-TA condition, we might be seeing evidence that TA restricts semantic memory search in some way. Conversely, if TA subjects introduce much more new content, we might theorize the opposite, that is, that TA enhances such search. Thus, though a priori we cannot say how useful these variables might be for informing the broader theory of the reactive effects of TA, we do think previous research has shown these variables to be sufficiently robust to merit discussion in theories explaining TA interference with tasks requiring analysis, interpretation, and/or restructuring of written texts.

OUR EXPLORATORY STUDY

To explore the feasibility of using these measures in a rigorous test for reactivity, we recently undertook a pilot study, partially funded by the University of Colorado at Denver (Stratman & Hamp-Lyons, 1992). We discuss this pilot in some detail here because its results, together with the research already cited, point to a way to begin resolving the perplexing questions about protocol reactivity in reading, writing, and text-analysis studies. Essentially, we compared the same subjects revising faulty text under TA and non-TA conditions to see if the three output measures (listed previously) might be differentially affected. Our question was whether the supposition that a reactivity effect would be random and unpredictable (and therefore "wash itself out") could be supported, or whether we would find a nonrandom difference between TA and non-TA conditions.

As Russo, Johnson, and Stephens (1989) note, researchers investigating protocol reactivity using "product" or output measures face trade-offs in deciding whether to use a between-subjects design or a within-subjects design. In our pilot we used the latter to reduce a possible confound due to differences between subject groups. Specifically, we used a $2 \times 2 \times 2$ counterbalanced design (see Table 4.1). To minimize effects of carryover,

TABLE 4.1: Within Subjects, Counterbalanced Design in Pilot

Time 1 (12 Subjects)		Time 2 (Same 12 Subjects)	
TA (6)	Non-TA (6)	TA (6)	Non-TA (6)
Glue (3)	Print (3)	Glue (3)	Print (3)
Glue (3)	Print (3)	Glue (3)	Print (3)

subjects performed the same revision task (disguised) at two points in time, the second task occurring about 8 weeks after the first. To effect the disguise, the second task used a passage *isomorphic* with the passage used in the first; that is, the syntax of each sentence remained almost identical, words of the same number of syllables and of the same degree of familiarity were used, and so on. Further, we planted the same type and number of problems and errors in each, and at the same location (Hayes et al., 1987; Hayes, Waterman, & Robinson, 1977). Each isomorph used the same "compare-contrast" macrostructure; that is, two objects were compared on three dimensions or attributes. The topic of the two passages differed: One compared two types of household glues for bonding strength, moisture resistance, and drying time; the other compared two types of computer printers for their operating principles, print quality, and speed. We also carefully designed task directions for both TA and non-TA conditions to be superficially different but isomorphic in their precise requirements. Obviously, the important goal with this camouflage design is that at Time 2 subjects must not suspect that the passage is isomorphic with that encountered at Time 1 and thereby introduce a serious learning confound. Nor must subjects discover the purpose and demand characteristics of the experiment until after the Time 2 task is completed (Greenwald, 1976).

To reduce learning effects due to condition-order, this order was also counterbalanced: Half of Time 1 subjects were required to provide a protocol as they worked; the other half were not. At Time 2, their condition assignment was reversed. Similarly, to prevent a confound due to passage order, passage order was also counterbalanced within each task condition order. Finally, we attempted to eliminate any effects due to sensitization, by conducting tasks at Time 1 and Time 2 with different researchers and in different buildings. Time 1 TA and non-TA conditions were administered to students enrolled in different graduate and undergraduate courses, to prevent intergroup communication, and the tasks themselves were presented as part of subjects' regular classwork. All subjects received TA training prior to the experimental TA session, and in both TA and non-TA conditions subjects were given as much time as needed.

Pilot Study Results:
Error Detection/Removal
Under TA and Non-TA Conditions

Though we did not have enough subjects per cell and sufficient repeated measures to draw statistical generalizations in this pilot, we did find the results intriguing in a number of ways. First, as Table 4.2 shows, we found that TA slightly depressed subjects' ability, on average, to detect and remedy information organization errors. These errors included three kinds: sentences wrenched from their original position and placed where they disrupted cohesion and topical focus; paragraph boundaries that did not correspond to topic shifts or breaks in lexical equivalence chains (Bond & Hayes, 1984); and a misstatement of the number of attributes for which types of glue (or printers) were being compared. On the assumption that TA would constrain short-term memory needed for storing partial results of proposition integration or reordering, we had thought we might see a larger depression in TA correction scores here. On the other hand, there is certainly no evidence here that TA does *not* interfere with or alter subjects' abilities to deal with these problems. As a result, we feel it is extremely important to replicate this part of the experiment with many more problems of this type as well as with more subjects.

Second, as Table 4.2 shows, the TA condition appeared to slightly enhance the detection of faulty pronoun references, which seems consistent with the theory that acoustic feedback during reading out loud enhances rehearsal and thus the detection of such errors. Third, the TA condition appeared to make little difference in subjects' ability to detect phrase-level redundancies and word-level errors. The lack of robust effects on any of the word-level measures suggests to us they may not be worth investigating further. If subjects' cognitive processes associated with these low-level problems are altered by the TA condition, the alteration is not so great as to lead to strong enhancement or reduction of these detection and correction measures.

TABLE 4.2: Comparison of Error Detection/Removal Rates Under TA and Non-TA Conditions

Average number of detections of organizational and information ordering errors (displaced sentences, faulty paragraph boundaries, misstatement of number of attributes covered in comparison).

| Perfect Score = 8 | TA = 6.67 | Non-TA = 7.33 |

Average number of detections of faulty pronoun references.

| Perfect Score = 3 | TA = 3 | Non-TA = 2.75 |

Average number of detections of redundancies.

| Perfect Score = 3 | TA = 2.4 | Non-TA = 2.4 |

Average number of detections of "word-level" errors (morphological, tense, and spelling errors).

| Perfect Score = 6 | TA = 5.75 | Non-TA = 5.58 |

Average number of *new* "word-level" errors *introduced* (morphological, tense, and spelling).

| (N/A) | TA = 2.41 | Non-TA = 1.16 |

However, as Table 4.2 shows (bottom), we did note that the TA condition appeared to lead to the *introduction* of roughly twice as many *new* word-level errors. This finding is of potential theoretical concern, because it suggests a possible infringement by TA on text-generation and text-inscription processes. This particular finding, in turn, led us to extend our analysis to the amount of meaning-changes subjects may have made to the texts. We turn to these data next.

**Pilot Results:
Content Changes Under
TA and Non-TA Conditions**

We compared eight subjects' revisions drafted under TA and non-TA conditions for the extent to which they altered the passage content. Signifi-

cantly, instructions in both conditions explicitly directed subjects to preserve the meaning of the original text as much as possible while correcting
its defects. We speculated that the TA condition might induce subjects to be
more inattentive to the meaning of the original than they would be in the
non-TA condition, thus resulting in more meaning changes in the TA produced revisions. To carry out this analysis, we applied categories for scoring text changes developed by Faigley and Witte (1981, 1984) in their study
of expert-novice differences in revision behavior. However, rather than tab-
ulate both "meaning-preserving" and "text-base" changes in our subjects'
drafts as these researchers did, we concentrated on the latter (text-base)
changes, and on two levels: microstructural and macrostructural. As we will
discuss below, like Faigley and Witte (1981, 1984), we found the macro-
structure categories somewhat unsatisfactory for analyzing the kind and
extent of these content changes, and we plan to modify these procedures in
later work. The results of this particular analysis are nonetheless intriguing
and seem to us well worth exploring more rigorously.

Meaning-Changes on
the Microstructural Level

On the microstructural level, we tabulated the number of sentences in the
original (unrevised) text whose meaning was altered by each of three types
of change: additions, deletions, and substitutions. Additions could be words
or phrases placed in an original sentence that were not there before and that
could not be inferred from the original passage's text-base. Subjects might
also add entire sentences to the original. Conversely, deletions could be
words or phrases removed from an original sentence with the effect of
altering its meaning. Subjects might also delete entire sentences from the
original text. Substitutions are words or phrases that subjects might clearly
use to replace existing words or phrases, but again altering the original
sentences' meaning. To avoid double-counting, we did *not* include in this
analysis those additions, deletions, or substitutions that subjects made as
"corrections" to our planted errors.

To consistently score these three categories, we used a relatively conser-
vative technique. Basically, for each subject, we scored the number of sentences in the original texts that were affected by each type of change. For
example, a subject might delete the italicized material from the third sentence in one of the text isomorphs as follows: "*Other times* they have two
unlike surfaces, *say, wood and vinyl,* and they don't know what to do."

TABLE 4.3: Number of Original Sentences Whose Meaning Was Altered by Additions, Deletions, and Substitutions

	Additions		Deletions		Substitutions
	W-P	S	W-P	S	W-P
TA	19	8	40	21	32
Non-TA	40	3	55	20	41

NOTES: W-P = words or phrases; S = number of sentences added or deleted.

Rather than scoring two deletions here (or even six, since six words are deleted), we scored this as one deletion, because it affected the meaning of *one* original sentence (#3). We followed the same procedure when scoring sentences for the presence of additions and substitutions. Though in this pilot we did not formally assess scoring reliability using independent scorers, the two principal researchers and a graduate research assistant did informally inspect each other's analyses for blatant errors. We expect that in the larger study currently planned, we will statistically assess reliability using independent scorers.

Surprisingly, as shown in Table 4.3, more than twice as many original sentences in the non-TA condition were altered by word or phrase additions than in the TA condition. TA thus appeared, contrary to our hunch, to inhibit these kinds of changes. At the same time, however, TA seems to stimulate the production of entirely new sentences (S). Overall, when under the TA condition, subjects added more than twice as many new sentences than when not. Indeed, whereas four subjects in the TA condition added at least one new sentence each, only one subject accounted for the three new sentences in the non-TA condition. If these effects could be replicated with a statistically significant subject sample, they might be evidence for a possibly systematic effect of TA during writing and revision tasks.

As Table 4.3 also shows, the number of original sentences deleted is nearly equal between conditions. However, TA appears to inhibit "local" phrase or word deletion; whereas 40 original sentences were altered by this behavior in the TA condition, 55 were altered in the non-TA condition. The data similarly suggest that TA may have an inhibiting effect on local (phrase or word) substitution. The number of entirely new sentences "substituted" for original ones is not shown specifically in Table 4.3 because we used the "addition" and "deletion" categories for this purpose.

TABLE 4.4: Effect of TA and Non-TA Conditions on Subjects' Permutations, Distributions, and Consolidations

	Permutations	Distributions		Consolidations
	W-P	W-P	SD	S
TA	2	2	2	7
Non-TA	5	12	1	13

NOTES: W-P = number of original sentences altered; SD = number of whole original sentences distributed; S = number of discrete instances of multisentence consolidation.

Complex Meaning-Changes on the Microstructural Level

More complex means for altering the meaning of the original on the microstructural level are permutations, distributions, and consolidations. Permutations are reorderings of words, phrases, or sentences which, while changing the meaning of the text, did not affect the underlying frame of the comparison as given in the original. Distributions occurred when words or phrases were shifted from one sentence into another. Some distributions are quite complex, as when an original sentence is taken completely apart and its components reinserted in other sentences. Consolidations occur when phrases (in different original sentences) or different sentences are combined into one sentence. Complex consolidations might condense four or five original sentences into one. As this definition of consolidation might suggest, this change cannot be scored in the same way as the others. Moreover, with both distributions and consolidations, as Faigley and Witte (1981, 1984) note, it becomes more difficult to discern whether the change brought about thereby is microstructural or macrostructural in nature. The procedure we adopted for both permutations and distributions was to count, as before, the number of original sentences whose meaning was affected by them. However, for consolidations, the procedure we adopted, admittedly unsatisfactory, was to count the total number of discrete, multi-sentence instances in each subject's revised text.

As the data in Table 4.4 may suggest, TA seems to have had a very slight inhibiting effect on these more complex changes; and the number of sentences altered by these means is far smaller than those altered by addition, deletion, and substitution. The number of subjects making these kinds of changes in each condition is nearly equal. For instance, the two sentences

TABLE 4.5: Effect of TA and Non-TA Conditions on Subjects' Macrostructure

	Divided	Alternate	Mixed/Miscue
TA	5	2	1
Non-TA	5	1	2

affected by distribution in the TA condition are accounted for by two subjects; the 12 sentences affected by distribution in the non-TA condition are also accounted for by two (different) subjects, and one of these subjects accounted for 11 of the 12. Similarly, the 7 instances of multi-sentence consolidation occurring in the TA condition are accounted for by five subjects; the 13 instances occurring in the non-TA condition are accounted for by six subjects. As with all of our pilot data, a larger sample would provide a stronger indication that TA impacts or does not impact complex meaning changes at the microstructural level.

Changes to the Macrostructure

As a final exploration of possible reactivity, we measured subjects' revised texts for changes to the organizational pattern in the original. The original text, before we disorganized it, presented the comparison in a "block" or divided pattern; e.g., in the "printer" text, all of the features of dot matrix printers were discussed before the corresponding features of the laser printer were described. Once disorganized, this block pattern was probably less discernible to subjects, but the resulting isomorphs still conformed more to this pattern than to what is conventionally known as the "alternating" pattern. In an alternating pattern, the printer text would be organized around the three features of printers being compared (operating principle, print quality, speed) so that laser and dot matrix printers would be redistributed as subordinate topics under each feature.

We wondered if TA might make it difficult for subjects to reorganize explicitly using either of these patterns, leading them to produce a revision in which these patterns were mixed or confused. As can be seen in Table 4.5, five of the eight subjects in both TA and non-TA conditions preserved the original "block" pattern.

Though it might be tempting to conclude from this data that TA does not interfere with subjects' text-organization processes, we would again stress the need for more subjects. Further, we would opt for a disorganized text that is initially less biased in the direction of either the divided or the alternating pattern. This modification, by making the underlying macro-structure of the text less salient (i.e., more mixed or confounded), could provide a better test of the effects of TA on these particular processes.

RATIONALE FOR
EXPERIMENTAL STUDIES OF TA REACTIVITY
DURING READING, WRITING, AND TEXT-ANALYSIS TASKS

Now, one could argue that the potential theoretical significance of this kind of experimental study is negligible. It could be seen as suggesting, at most, that the TA condition merely reduces the *amount* of certain kinds of verbal processing, without fundamentally altering the *nature* of the processes themselves. While that view cannot yet be contradicted, we doubt its plausibility and take a somewhat different view, for two reasons.

First, it would be difficult to explain how fundamental processes could *not* be affected by TA if, for instance, the contrasting findings above for whole sentence additions and word/phrase level additions could be shown to be statistically significant (see Table 4.3). Second, and more crucially for expert-novice theories, we do not know how the degree of subjects' exper-tise might adjust these findings. Recent models of revision skill differences or reading skill differences between experts and novices might need serious reconsideration, since a difference in the amount of specific kinds of verbal processing is exactly what these models try to describe or predict (Hayes et al., 1987; Lundeberg, 1987; Scardamalia & Bereiter, 1987). At the very least, these results suggest the potential importance of including an expert-novice variable in any reactivity study.

Further, we think all of the data above—and perhaps especially the data suggesting TA may systematically influence the correction of organiza-tional-level errors, and the amount and kind of microstructural meaning-changes (see Tables 4.2 and 4.3, above)—argue for expanded, modified versions of the study. Our pilot findings, though not in any way conclusive, lead us to suspect that effects of TA on "ill-defined" writing and revision tasks may *not be as random or as dependent on individual differences* between subjects as some commentators have supposed. Regrettably, our pilot did not control for degree of expertise as a variable (five were under-graduates, seven were graduate students), and we continue to suspect that TA might differentially affect experts' and novices' output measures. If that is shown to be the case in a larger experiment with this or a similar design, it would be important for future expert-novice studies on these kinds of tasks to explicitly account for these differential effects, and to *not* assume that TA affects expert and novice cognitive processes in the same ways. Alternatively, if these output measures show no differential impacts of TA between experts and novices, then, on these kinds of tasks, there might be more grounds for assuming that TA is nonreactive. We might have more confidence that task models generated from expert/novice studies (e.g., like that of Hayes et al., 1987) are not contaminated by interactions of TA with subjects' degree of expertise.

To summarize, we began this chapter by noting the continuing concern over the validity of using concurrent think-aloud protocols as a data source in constructing models of real-time cognition, and for distinguishing between expert and novice cognitive strategies. As Russo et al. (1989) astutely noted, the comprehensive theory developed by Ericsson and Simon (1984), to predict when concurrent TA protocols will interfere with subjects' processes, is actually based upon relatively few direct studies of reactivity. Building upon their work, we have noted two crucial gaps in the methodological studies that do exist: One is the lack of studies that examine reactivity effects during "ill-defined" tasks (such as reading, writing, and verbal information analysis); and the other is the lack of controlled investigation of possible differences in reactivity between experts and novices.

The chief benefit to be obtained by filling these gaps is that as the concurrent TA protocol method becomes more widespread among educational researchers interested in developing theories of literacy skills, we may begin to be able to separate "true" expert-novice differences from effects of the TA method per se. As noted above, a great deal of theoretical work in cognitive development and literacy has proceeded on the assumption that concurrent TA protocols are either benign, or else that their reactive effects are dependent on individual differences and would "wash out" in a large controlled study. To move beyond reliance on this assumption, we think that studies of the type we presented here, which can begin to assess rigorously the question of reactivity between experts and novices during reading, writing, and text-analysis tasks, would be quite valuable to cognitive researchers in literacy. Beyond this benefit, however, studies of this type may bring more definition to theories (such as Ericsson and Simon's) that predict the task-demand factors that cause reactivity, specifically the thesis that the oral compatibility of short-term memory contents is the key to whether a TA protocol will or will not seriously interfere with subjects' underlying cognition.

REFERENCES

Anzai, Y., & Simon, H. (1979). The theory of learning by doing. *Psychological Review, 86*(2), 124-140.

Applebee, A., & Langer, J. (1987). *How writing shapes thinking: A study of teaching and learning.* Urbana, IL: National Council of Teachers of English.

Bartlett, E. (1981). *Learning to write: Some cognitive and linguistic components.* Washington, DC: Center for Applied Linguistics.

Bereiter, C., & Scardamalia, M. (1982). From conversation to composition: The role of instruction in a developmental process. In R. Glaser (Ed.), *Advances in instructional psychology* (Vol. 2, pp. 1-64). Hillsdale, NJ: Lawrence Erlbaum.

Berkenkotter, C. (1983). Decisions and revisions: The planning strategies of a publishing writer. *College Composition and Communication, 34*(2), 156-169.

Bond, S., & Hayes, J. R. (1984). Cues people use to paragraph text. *Research in the Teaching of English, 18*(2), 147-168.

Cooper, M., & Holzman, M. (1983). Talking about protocols. *College Composition and Communication, 34,* 284-293.

Cooper, M., & Holzman, M. (1985). Counterstatement reply. *College Composition and Communication, 36,* 97-100.

Dobrin, D. (1986). Protocols once more. *College English, 8*(7), 713-726.

Ericsson, K., & Simon, H. (1984). *Protocol analysis: Verbal reports as data.* Cambridge: MIT Press.

Faigley, L., & Witte, S. (1981). Analyzing revision. *College Composition and Communication, 32*(4), 400-414.

Faigley, L., & Witte, S. (1984). Measuring the effects of revisions on text structure. In R. Beach & L. Bridwell, (Eds.), *New directions in composition research* (pp. 95-108). New York: Guilford Press.

Fidler, E. (1983). The reliability and validity of concurrent, retrospective and interpretive reports: An experimental study. In P. Humphreys, O. Svenson, & A. Vari (Eds.), *Analyzing and aiding decision processes* (pp. 429-440). Amsterdam: North-Holland.

Flower, L., & Hayes, J. (1980). The cognition of discovery: Defining a rhetorical problem. *College Composition and Communication, 31,* 21-32.

Flower, L., & Hayes, J. (1981a). A cognitive process theory of writing. *College Composition and Communication, 32,* 365-387.

Flower, L., & Hayes, J. (1981b). Plans that guide the composing process. In C. Frederiksen & J. Dominic (Eds.), *Writing: Process, development, and communication.* Hillsdale, NJ: Lawrence Erlbaum.

Flower, L., & Hayes, J. (1984). The representation of meaning in writing. *Written Communication, 1*(1), 120-160.

Flower, L., Hayes, J., Carey, L., Schriver, K., & Stratman, J. (1986). Detection, diagnosis and the strategies of revision. *College Composition and Communication, 37*(1), 16-55.

Greenwald, A. (1976). Within-subjects designs: To use or not to use? *Psychological Bulletin, 83,* 314-320.

Hayes, J. R., Flower, L., Schriver, K., Stratman, J., & Carey, L. (1987). Cognitive processes in revision. In S. Rosenberg (Ed.), *Advances in applied linguistics: Vol. II. Reading, writing and language processing* (pp. 176-240). Cambridge, UK: Cambridge University Press.

Hayes, J. R., Waterman, D., & Robinson, C. (1977). *Identifying relevant aspects of a problem text* (National Science Foundation Grant GS-38533, NIH Grant MH 07722). Pittsburgh: Carnegie-Mellon University, Department of Social and Decision Sciences.

Lundeberg, M. (1987). Metacognitive aspects of reading comprehension: Understanding legal case analysis. *Reading Research Quarterly, 22*(4), 408-432.

Melone, N. (1987). *Expertise in corporate acquisition: An investigation of the influence of specialized knowledge on strategic decision-making.* Unpublished doctoral dissertation, University of Minnesota.

Olson, G., Duffy, S., & Mack, R. (1985). Thinking out loud as a method of studying real time comprehension processes. In D. Kieras & M. Just (Eds.), *New methods in the study of comprehension processes* (pp. 253-286). Hillsdale, NJ: Lawrence Erlbaum.

Payne, J., Braunstein, M., & Carroll, J. (1978). Exploring predecisional behavior: An alternative approach to decision research. *Organizational Behavior and Human Performance, 22,* 17-44.

Prietula, M., & Feltovich, P. (1988). *Expertise as task adaptation.* Paper presented at the Eighth Annual International Conference on Information Systems. Graduate School of Industrial Administration, Carnegie-Mellon University, Pittsburgh.

Russo, J., Johnson, E., & Stephens, D. (1989). The validity of verbal protocols. *Memory & Cognition, 17*(6), 759-769.

Rymer, J. (1988). Scientific composing processes: How eminent scientists write journal articles. In D. Jolliffe (Ed.), *Advances in writing research (Vol. 2).* Norwood, NJ: Ablex.

Scardamalia, M., & Bereiter, C. (1983). The development of evaluative, diagnostic and remedial capabilities in children's composing. In M. Martlew (Ed.), *The psychology of written language: A developmental approach* (pp. 67-95). New York: John Wiley.

Scardamalia, M., & Bereiter, C. (1987). Knowledge telling and knowledge transforming in written composition. In S. Rosenberg (Ed.), *Advances in applied linguistics: Vol. II. Reading, writing and language processing* (pp. 142-175). Cambridge, UK: Cambridge University Press.

Schweiger, D. (1983). Is the simultaneous verbal protocol a viable method for studying managerial problem-solving and decision-making? *Academy of Management Journal, 26,* 185-192.

Simon, H. (1973). The structure of ill-structured problems. *Artificial Intelligence, 4,* 181-202.

Smagorinsky, P. (1989). The reliability and validity of protocol analysis. *Written Communication, 6,* 463-479.

Smagorinsky, P. (1991). The writer's knowledge and the writing process: A protocol analysis. *Research in the Teaching of English, 25,* 339-415.

Smead, R., Wilcox, J., & Wilkes, R. (1981). How valid are product descriptions and protocols in choice experiments? *Journal of Consumer Research, 8,* 37-42.

Spivey, N. (1990). Transforming texts: Constructive processes in reading and writing. *Written Communication, 7,* 256-287.

Stratman, J. (1990). The emergence of legal composition as a field of inquiry: Evaluating the prospects. *Review of Educational Research, 60,* 153-235.

Stratman, J., & Hamp-Lyons, L. (1992, April). *Reactivity in concurrent think aloud editing protocols.* Roundtable paper presentation, annual meeting of the American Educational Research Association, San Franciso.

Taylor, S., & Fiske, S. (1981). Getting inside the head: Methodologies for process analysis and in attribution and social cognition. In J. Harvey, W. Ickes, & R. Kidd (Eds.), *New directions in attribution research* (Vol. 3, pp. 457-522). Hillsdale, NJ: Lawrence Erlbaum.

Witte, S. (1987). Pre-text and composing. *College Composition and Communication, 38,* 397-425.

Witte, S., & Cherry, R. (1986). Writing processes and written products in composition research. In C. Cooper & S. Greenbaum (Eds.), *Studying writing: Linguistic approaches* (pp. 112-153). Beverly Hills, CA: Sage.

Part II
Retrospective Accounts of Writing Process

5

"Once Upon a Time"
The Use of
Retrospective Accounts in
Building Theory in Composition

STUART GREENE
LORRAINE HIGGINS

I don't want to narrow this down to one particular situation. I sort of want to allow everyone to compare themselves to this. So you know I don't want to nail down one time and one place. But it's helpful to give little images here and there. That's basically what I'm trying to do with phrases like "nervously fingers the bridge of his glasses" and "smiles blindly with dry lips into the glare of the stage lights" . . . while it's not really specific, it does begin to give you a picture of what's going on, what he's feeling.

This excerpt from a student's retrospective account reflects some of the thinking that motivated the choices he made in composing an essay for an advanced writing class. His story is compelling because we learn about the reasoning behind his decisions to use certain words and phrases as he attempts to balance his own goals as a writer with the expectations he feels his readers in a writing workshop bring to his text. At the same time, such an account is an artifact of memory, one that represents this writer's sense of why he made the choices and decisions he did at a point somewhat removed from the moment he actually wrote his text. This is the nature of retrospective data—what we define as a writer's oral or written report of the processes involved in constructing a text at an earlier time.

AUTHORS' NOTE: The authors would like to thank Michael W. Smith and David Wallace for their generous and helpful comments on an earlier draft of this chapter.

Retrospective accounts can take a number of forms. Researchers can conduct face-to-face interviews with writers to prompt them for information about the techniques they had used or the factors they had considered as they wrote. These interviews can be open-ended or structured (e.g., Herrington, 1985; Higgins, 1992), focusing on specific portions of an actual text or specific aspects of the writing, such as attention to audience (e.g., Odell, Goswami, & Herrington, 1983). Some researchers have used "stimulated recall" interviews in conjunction with videotaped or audiotaped recordings of writers at work, first taping the writer in action, then locating interesting segments, such as places where the writer appeared to be stalled, took an unexpected turn, or seemed puzzled. The researcher can then ask the writer to respond to these tapes or to reconstruct what was happening at that moment. (See DiPardo, this volume, for a review of stimulated recall methodologies.) Other researchers have collected writers' written or taped reflections on their own texts or writing processes. For example, the excerpt that opens this chapter came from a study (Greene, 1992) in which students were instructed to tape themselves, in whatever setting they chose, as they reflected upon the decisions they made in composing their essays. Retrospection can also take the form of a writing diary or log. After each episode of thinking about, reading, or composing for a writing task, writers create an entry, recording the date and details of their activity, keeping a written account of what was done (e.g., Nelson, 1990; Walvoord & McCarthy, 1990). This method allows researchers to collect data over a long period of time, as the task unfolds. While this list of data collection methods is not exhaustive, it illustrates the variety of forms that retrospection can take, from written reflections to oral responses to a structured interview. The form, focus, and the amount of structure in retrospective methods can vary according to the researcher's theoretical orientation and area of interest.

Since retrospective accounts are constructions based on a writer's selective evaluations and inferences of what occurred during a previous episode of composing, the validity of retrospective accounts has been called into question. Nisbett and Wilson (1977) have argued that, at best, these verbal reports reflect writers' plausible explanations of how they have gone about completing a given task. Do writers have access to the workings of their own minds? And if so, to what extent are the stories writers tell valid or complete? While some criticisms of retrospective data may be warranted, we argue in this chapter that retrospective accounts can nonetheless play an important role in building theory in composition. In what follows, we outline some of the conditions under which researchers might choose to use this method. Using examples from our own research, we then discuss and respond to some of the criticisms and concerns that surround the collection and analysis of such data.

WHY USE RETROSPECTIVE ACCOUNTS?

Studies in composition have shifted during the past 20 years, from analyzing written texts to understanding how texts are constructed. Renewed interest in rhetorical invention (Young 1976) has brought with it an important research method: protocol analysis (see Smagorinsky, this volume). Protocols have been quite useful in helping researchers understand more about the "what" of writing by documenting some of the strategies and processes of invention that underlie written texts. More recently, however, researchers have begun to pose a different set of questions, not so much about what writers do, but *why*. These *why* questions arise from our increasing concern with rhetorical situations and our growing sensitivity to the diverse assumptions and goals that influence writers as they move in and across these different contexts.

One of the most striking examples of this shift is in the study of novice writers. A decade ago, researchers (e.g., Flower & Hayes, 1981) were using protocols to describe whether and how novice performance differed from that of experts. Today researchers are building on this work by asking why such differences exist, why writers recognize and attend to some strategies but not others, and whether the idiosyncratic behaviors we observe in different groups of writers possess a "logic" of their own (e.g., Hull, Rose, Fraser, & Castellano, 1991).

Researchers who ask such questions argue that differences in performance and strategies are not always best described in terms of deficits and failures. They point out that other factors—for example, writers' past experiences with writing (Hull & Rose, 1989), the evaluative climate of the classroom (Nelson, 1990), or their assumptions about the task (Flower, Stein, Ackerman, Kantz, McCormick, & Peck, 1990)—can influence their writing decisions and performance. The purpose of this growing body of research is to clarify and understand some of these situational and cognitive influences. Retrospective reports, used alone or in conjunction with other methods, have enabled researchers to build a richer understanding of the relationship among texts, situational factors, and writers' constructive processes.

By themselves, concurrent protocol analysis and traditional text analysis may not reveal important information that retrospective accounts can provide. Although concurrent protocols can be useful in documenting what writers do, when they are the sole source of data they can be less helpful in explaining why. When writers encounter difficult problems in their writing, they sometimes stop to verbalize alternatives and explain the reasoning behind their decisions (e.g., Flower, 1990), but typically, protocols are not designed to capture this type of self-conscious reflection. In fact, protocol instructions often ask writers not to explain their thinking but simply to verbalize it as it happens, with the hope of getting an accurate and uninter-rupted account of the writing process (Ericsson & Simon, 1980; Swarts, Flower, & Hayes, 1984). As Steinberg (1986) points out, the very act of explaining one's thinking might actually distort or modify that thinking, undermining the purpose of taking a protocol. Because retrospective ac-counts allow researchers to get a glimpse into writers' strategies and deci-sions after the fact, they have the advantage of allowing writers to explain and reflect on their decisions without interfering directly with their atten-tion to the task, freeing a writer from the "cognitive load" (Afflerbach & Johnston, 1984) that the concurrent verbalization of a think-aloud would require.

Although others have used text analysis to identify patterns in students' writing (e.g., Bartholomae, 1985; Crowhurst, 1991), these methods may be limited in their ability to tell us why these patterns occur. Researchers must be particularly cautious in drawing conclusions about students' abilities from their texts alone. Aston (1987), for example, discussed a college stu-dent's descriptive essay of her neighborhood, one that typified patterns we often see in younger writers, such as sparse elaboration and an absence of vivid detail. Although we might be tempted to conclude that this writer lacked keen observational skills or elaboration strategies, Aston revealed, through the use of a retrospective interview, that this student was quite able to describe her neighborhood in painful, accurate detail. In fact, she had drafted an earlier version that depicted used-up needles littering the hall-ways of her apartment building, and the nonstop sirens and screaming that went on at all hours of the night. Heeding the advice of her mother, how-ever, she tempered these harsh and frightening details, fearing that they might paint her as a student from a low-class neighborhood, a perception that might have affected her grade or treatment in class. This example illustrates how retrospective data can reveal hidden competencies that do not always turn up in a text. When prompted to reflect on their decisions and processes, writers often reveal to us what their texts do not.

Other researchers have also been successful in using retrospective data to understand the choices and decisions writers make in reading (Afflerbach &

Johnston, 1984; Garner, 1982; Greene, 1992), writing (e.g., Faigley, Cherry, Jolliffe, & Skinner, 1985; Higgins, 1992), and interpreting tasks (Greene, 1993a). This growing body of research has provided a rich source of information about the contextual and affective factors that influence the processes of both comprehending and composing. In their study of retrospective accounts of language learning, Sternglass and Pugh (1986) asked graduate students to keep learning logs to record the "language experiences and processes as they develop[ed]" their ideas about the issue of introspection in writing summaries, analyses, and syntheses (322). These logs revealed the role that writers' prior knowledge plays in their interpretation of a given task, and the ways that students sought cues from the instructional context in order to understand how to perform a task of writing a summary or synthesis. Nelson (1990) also asked students to keep logs in order to track the processes involved in conducting library research. Her findings underscore contextual factors that can shape students' evolving interpretations of a given task, and the strategies they use in writing research papers. Students' approaches to writing in a number of different fields depend, in large part, on the quality and frequency of teachers' feedback on students' drafts, their criteria for evaluating writing, and their stated goals for assigning writing.

How Reliable Are Retrospective Accounts?

As valuable as retrospective accounts can be in providing some insight into the cognitive and social factors motivating writers' choices and decisions, they are not, as we suggested earlier, without criticisms and drawbacks. In what follows, we examine three frequently discussed concerns related to the issue of reliability, and we introduce a fourth concern, one that has not received much attention in the literature.

The Limitations of Short-Term Memory

The first concern focuses on the limited capacity of short-term memory, the extent to which people have access to the "workings of their own minds" (Nisbett & Wilson, 1977, p. 232). Given this concern, we would qualify the claim of Ericsson and Simon (1984), who point out that:

> [R]etrospective accounts can reveal in remarkable detail what information [subjects] are attending to while performing their tasks, and by revealing this

information, can provide an orderly picture of the exact ways in which tasks
are being performed, the strategies employed, the inferences drawn from information, the accessing of memory by recognition. (p. 220)

We would argue that all research methods, especially those that require
writers to reconstruct experience from memory, are limited in their ability
to describe the "exact ways" any task is performed. However, while we
recognize that data based upon retrospection are incomplete, we would be
reluctant to say that they are not valuable. As Perkins (1981) observed, there
is "always some sort of gap. . . . But when one sees this gap as simply the
normal lapse between direct experience and the individual's conscious awareness of it, it is easy to see that this is the closest we can ever come to instan-
taneous recording of experience" (p. 7). Retrospective accounts can at least
offer a plausible explanation, providing more detail than we might obtain
by simple speculation or by other methods alone. As Ericsson and Simon
(1980) themselves note, incompleteness may make some information unavailable, "but it does not invalidate the information that is present" (p. 242).

The Constructive Nature of Working Memory

The second concern, one that we define quite broadly, revolves around
the constructive nature of working memory. Remembering is an act of
reconstruction (Bartlett, 1932) that entails simplification, compression, and
generalization in order to give some coherence to experience. When people
are asked to report on their own processes, their report may not bear a close
relation to the actual cognitive processes used (Ericsson & Simon, 1980;
Garner, 1982). The principles of gestalt psychology remind us that writers
may use a single experience and generalize from this instance to typify their
approach to writing. When they do not clearly remember certain aspects of
their experience, writers may fill in with more general information based on
their knowledge of what writers usually do or should do, or they may gloss
over or omit idiosyncratic aspects of their performance that do not fit this
prototype. Given that writers selectively attend to certain kinds of information and make connective inferences, it may not be surprising that they may
omit information or even distort their experiences. These concerns may
become even more of an issue when retrospection takes the form of writing,
an activity that entails a great deal of selective evaluation, inference, and
generalization. (For reviews of these issues, see Ericsson & Simon, 1980,
1984; Sternglass, 1988.)

The Purposes and Questions that Surround
the Use of Retrospective Accounts

A third concern relates to writers' interpretations of the questions and purposes surrounding the use of retrospective data and the nature of the questions themselves. One typical problem is that writers may misunderstand key terms in the questions we ask. For instance, in asking writers to report on their "plans," some may assume that we want to know about the outlines they produced before writing; others may assume that we want to know more about the larger purposes and intentions for their work. In what sense are we using this term, and how can we be sure that our writers are interpreting it as we do? Writers may also misconstrue the purpose of a retrospective interview, feeling that they must give a "right" answer or demonstrate their competence, rather than giving an accurate portrait of what occurred as they composed.

Tomlinson (1984) has questioned the validity of both professional writers' and students' (cf. Emig, 1971) "testimonies" of how they have written, arguing that they are giving a performance rather than reporting what they have done. In fact, writers may tend to perform more in instances when they want to please or impress the researcher. In short, the relationship between researcher and subject is by no means neutral. This relationship always involves some degree of role playing, one that is defined by the authority of the researcher and can influence "the type and accuracy of the information" we collect (Tomlinson, 1984, p. 436; see also Smagorinsky's discussion of the researcher-subject interaction in this volume).

Some prompts may actually encourage distortion and incompleteness. Prompts that contain leading questions, for example, suggest an answer in the way that they are worded. The question, Did you use X as a subgoal? invites a "yes" response in that it subtly implies that X is or should be a possible subgoal, because the researcher had thought to ask about it. Nisbett and Wilson's (1977) review of research on memory and personality also brings into focus the problems with prompts that require people to speculate about hypothetical situations or to draw inferences based on information that they were not asked to attend to in the task. In their own studies, Nisbett and Wilson (1977) asked their subjects how they would behave if the conditions in a given experiment were changed or altered in some way— how would they respond to a story if some passages had not been presented? A question such as this one invites speculation and inference. As others (Cooper & Holzman, 1983; cf. Rose, 1984) have argued, prompts need to be "ecologically valid," relating only to the specifics of the context surrounding a given writing task.

The Reporting of Retrospective Data

Fourth, and finally, we raise a serious concern that has not been widely discussed in the literature, but which we discuss at length in the final section of this chapter. Readers often have difficulty evaluating the use of retrospective accounts in composition research, because many studies fail to explain why this methodology makes sense in light of the research questions addressed. Moreover, researchers often do not explain the logical path between the retrospective data they cite and the conclusions they draw.

Though these concerns call into question both the validity and the reliability of retrospective accounts in describing processes of composing, these data can still offer a potentially rich source of information. After all, as Nisbett and Wilson (1977) pointed out:

> The individual knows a host of personal historical facts; he knows the focus of his attention at any given point in time; he knows what his current sensations are and has what almost all psychologists and philosophers assert to be "knowledge" at least quantitatively superior to that of observers concerning his emotions, evaluations, and plans. (p. 255)

Thus, rather than focus on what might inevitably be lost in collecting retrospective accounts, it makes sense to refocus our attention on what can be gained through retrospection. We may not capture the writing event in all its complexity (Rose, 1984), but the "stories" writers tell may prove to be invaluable, particularly when, as Ericsson and Simon (1980) point out, "they are elicited with care and interpreted with a full understanding of the circumstances under which they [are] obtained" (p. 147).

The Rhetorical Nature of Research on Writing

Perhaps the key question to ask at this point is not whether retrospective reports are reliable or valid, but rather, how can researchers collect and analyze this kind of data in a responsible way? How can researchers reduce the possibility of misinterpretation, helping writers recreate and describe those aspects of their performance that we want to understand in more detail? Moreover, how can we interpret and report this information so that other researchers can assess the reliability and accuracy of this data and our interpretations of it? Research is, after all, a form of argument based on interpretation; our claims can only be judged plausible if we carefully reconstruct our reasoning from the data to the claims we make.

Suggestions for Collecting Retrospective Data

In light of the four concerns we have discussed, we offer a number of suggestions that can make retrospection an important tool for understanding the logic that motivates what writers do.

Collect Data Immediately After Performance When Possible

First and foremost, the design of our methods needs to reflect our knowledge of working memory. Given the limitations of working memory, it is important to obtain a report immediately after a writer completes a task, minimizing the interval of time between process and report (e.g., Ericsson & Simon, 1980, 1984; Nisbitt & Wilson, 1977; White, 1980). As previous research has suggested (e.g., Garner, 1984), "recency" plays as important role in the completeness of a retrospective account. (For a different perspective, see DiPardo, this volume.)

Focus on Critical Incidents and Contextual Cues

Since remembering is a constructive act, and writers have a tendency to generalize information, we need to provide prompts or cues that can help writers better access detailed information from their short- and long-term memory. The use of concrete examples, contextual cues, and "critical incidents" (Flanagan, 1954) is helpful for this purpose.

When researchers ask writers to reflect on concrete examples of writing, rather than writing in general, they are more likely to obtain more detailed information. For example, if we want to understand whether and how writers use personal examples to write a critique of source texts, we might simply ask them this general question: "Have you ever used your own personal examples in writing a critique?" But this question might prompt a general "no" response, for many writers might assume that personal information is not objective or relevant to such a task. Asking the general question alone forces students to interpret for themselves what it means to use personal experience and to draw only a general statement about that. Their response might be far more focused, accurate, and detailed if they were asked to discuss their strategies for producing one or a few particular (and preferably recent) critiques in which they had used source texts. Talking from a specific text or set of source materials might help writers recreate the thinking that motivated the critiques they produced; these written materials can provide cues that help them access specific ways in which their own experiences had come into play as they read and evaluated these texts and as they chose examples and quotes for inclusion in their essays.

If we hope to elicit information from long-term memory—the way a college student had approached writing in high school, for instance—it would be even more critical to focus on specific examples and to provide contextual cues to help him or her reconstruct the situation and the specific strategies used, without cueing particular responses. Writers may have a hard time explaining their strategies when they do not have a specific experience or example in mind. We can provide contextual cues that remind the writer of the context. For example, Higgins (1992) used the following prompt in a study she conducted on argument:

> You said that your teachers often encouraged you to use your own ideas. Can you remember a specific instance in which a teacher did that? What did she say? What kind of assignment was she referring to? In that assignment, did you feel you were able to use your own ideas?

These kinds of cues direct writers toward specific incidents and help them remember the details of the rhetorical situation.

In the same study, Higgins used retrospective interviews to investigate the strategies and experiences students brought to the classroom, asking them to describe previous experiences with argument in and out of school. The interviews included two sets of parallel questions that prompted students to recall specific incidents in which they had used argument, in school and in their personal lives or on the job, to recreate the situation in which they had argued, and to retrace the steps they had taken as they constructed their arguments in these situations. These questions were interspersed throughout each interview:

> Now we're going to discuss some examples of how you have used writing to argue in different situations. Give me a typical example of when you have

used writing to argue outside the classroom. What was the SITUATION; what did your AUDIENCE expect; what did YOU expect? What STEPS did you take to think through and plan your writing? How did you SUPPORT your argument? Why? What kinds of STANDARDS did your audience use to evaluate this argument. What features made it a good argument in their view; which features made it weak?

Give me a typical example in which you used writing as a way to argue in school. What was the SITUATION; what did your TEACHER expect you to do? What did YOU want to accomplish? Explain the STEPS you took to think it through and write it. How did you SUPPORT your argument? Why? What kinds of STANDARDS did your teacher use to evaluate this argument; that is, which features made it a good argument in her/his view; which made it weak?

As the interviewer asked each question, she probed the student to elaborate (e.g., Is there anything else you want to add? Can you explain that a bit more?). These detailed prompts helped the students reconstruct their experiences in more detail than a general prompt might have, for example, "Discuss the strategies you have used for writing arguments."

"Critical incidents" (Flanagan, 1954) refer to specific but also dramatic events, which are typically remembered with more vividness and detail than routine events. If we wanted to understand a writer's negative attitude toward school writing, we might simply choose a previous assignment for her to discuss. But we would probably get much more information if we asked the writer to center her discussion on a critical incident, an assignment involving a particularly negative experience, one that had a forceful impact on her.

Clarify the Purpose
of Retrospective Accounts

In obtaining retrospective data, researchers also need to ensure that writers do not misinterpret the purpose of giving a retrospective account. Researchers can be very direct in explaining their purpose. Higgins (1992) asked students to discuss the goals and strategies they had used on a recently completed draft of an argument written for a college course. Naturally, students had some questions about who the interviewer was and why she had chosen to speak to them. Before conducting private interviews with the students, the researcher explained her purposes, assuring students that they were not being tested and that the information they gave would not affect their standing in the course:

The reason I am doing this interview is to get a student's perspective. I want to find out what you actually think and do when you write, not what your teacher thinks or expects you to do. Tell me exactly what you did. Your teacher will not see this information, and it won't be used to grade you. There are no right and wrong answers here.

Design Clear Prompts

The nature of a prompt or question is another area of concern in controlling for possible distortions in collecting retrospective reports. First, we need to ensure that the terms we use in our prompts and questions are clear. If a researcher is interested in obtaining information about a writer's argument strategies, she may need to clarify what she means by the term *argument*. For many, arguments are commonly perceived as quarrels or strong verbal disagreements. But argument, in a more specialized sense, can refer to a series of claims and evidence, whether written or oral. We may need to offer writers a series of contrasting meanings to clarify the definition we have in mind.

We also want to ensure that we base our questions on activities that have already occurred, because hypothetical questions can force writers into speculations that have little bearing on their experiences. Imagine the difference between asking a writer to describe the type of evidence she used in a particular writing assignment and asking her to predict the kind of evidence she might have used in an instructional task that she did not actually complete.

Leading questions can often put answers into writers' mouths. To avoid this, we can begin with open-ended questions or general prompts. For example, instead of asking, "Did you set any of the following goals (X, Y, Z) when you began your paper?" we can ask, "What goals, if any, did you have when you began to write?" If we hope to get more specific information about these goals, we may do well to arrange these questions from general to specific. This is easiest to do in face-to-face interviews with students. We can pick up on interesting "threads" that emerge in students' explanations and we can ask students to elaborate on these as they emerge:

RESEARCHER: What goals, if any, did you have when you began to write this argument paper?

WRITER: It was important to use my own ideas.

RESEARCHER: So how did you use your own ideas? Show me . . .

Use Converging Methods

Retrospective accounts, regardless of the nature of the prompts and questions we use, can only reveal part of the process of composing. In fact, the questions we ask a writer are an artifact of the theories that frame our research, so that our understanding of writing will be shaped by a framework that brings some dimensions of writing into focus, but not others. In order to capture the richness and complexity of what is involved in composing, we can use converging methods. Moreover, when we collect retrospective accounts, in addition to protocol data and texts, it is possible to check the consistency and completeness of these accounts. This is critical since, as Ericsson and Simon (1980) observed:

> [I]nconsistent retrospective reports can be produced as a result of probes that are too general to elicit information actually sought, and as a result of subjects' use of inferential processes to fill out and to generalize incomplete or missing memories. (p. 247)

As we saw earlier, Aston's (1987) combined analysis of a writer's text and verbal explanation helped to shed light on why the writer chose not to include detail in her essay. Investigating the ways in which students used their own ideas and experiences in constructing arguments, Higgins (1992) also used both retrospective interviews and text analysis. Students' drafts of an argument showed that they rarely included personal experiences and ideas outside the assigned sources to support their claims in text; however, they frequently tacked on a personal opinion paragraph at the end of their papers. Upon interviewing students, she discovered that the texts alone revealed only a limited number of ways in which students had used their own ideas, and she learned more about students' attempts to integrate their own opinions. Students explained that they had relied heavily on their own ideas as they read about new concepts in the source texts, invoking personal experiences to understand and relate to source concepts so they might paraphrase them better in their texts. Some students relied exclusively on personal beliefs and experiences when evaluating source ideas for inclusion in their papers, only choosing to cite evidence that they themselves had experienced or agreed with on a personal level. Although personal experience seemed to inform their arguments, they explained that they had excluded it from their texts because they were afraid of digressing from the assigned materials and ruining the organization that the source texts provided them.

The interviews showed that students negotiated the urge to use their own ideas by using them to choose concepts but then excluding them from their texts, or by separating their own ideas in an unrelated summary paragraph, which they had learned was acceptable in their reading course.

Suggestions for Analyzing and Reporting Retrospective Data

When researchers fail to explain their choice of retrospective methods and their procedures for analyzing retrospective data, then the conclusions they offer become almost impossible to evaluate. The use of this method is weakened considerably, even if the researcher has taken great pains to ensure against some of the problems mentioned earlier in this chapter. Thus studies that employ retrospective accounts should always explain the rationale for the method used, in light of the questions that a researcher has posed. Moreover, researchers need to map out the logical path from the data to their claims, so that others can make a judgment about the plausibility of those claims. How much data was collected? What procedures were used? In what ways did the researcher examine and account for writers' verbal responses? In what sense was this analysis reliable? Was a coding method used?

Although these issues of reliability and rigor seem quite basic to any research, they are sometimes ignored in reporting retrospective data. Perhaps, because retrospective data have often served the purpose of illustrating or bolstering conclusions reached through the use of other methods, researchers have not given a great deal of time or space to explaining retrospective data as *evidence*—data that are systematically collected and analyzed to support a claim. Instead, it has become common to simply lift a few quotations from writers' retrospective accounts and to use these as illustrations as evidence to support one's claims. But, even if a researcher is only using one or two quotations to elaborate on these claims in the discussion or conclusion section of a research report, these supportive comments should, in fact, be treated as data. It is not sufficient to say "Later, in an interview with this student, she confirmed this by saying . . . " The reader is left wondering, who conducted this interview and when? Was this interview planned as part of the study, or was it an afterthought? Why wasn't it mentioned in the methods section? How representative was this writer's account, given the rest of her explanation? Was the entire response analyzed in this way?

If researchers expect retrospective data to be taken seriously, then they must be responsible in reporting this data (Higgins & Greene, 1992). In the remainder of this chapter, we discuss in some detail the rationale and procedures behind a study (Greene 1992, 1993b) that focused, in large part, on retrospective data. Our description of this study will illustrate how researchers can:

- shape retrospective methods around their particular research questions or theoretical framework;
- derive methods of analyzing or coding from their questions and theories;
- assess the reliability of their interpretations;
- allow the reader to see how the conclusions have been derived from the data.

Exploring a Sense of Authorship in Reading: A Case in Point

Perhaps the best way to illustrate these points is to start where we began—with our student's comments about the choices he made in writing an essay for class:

> I don't want to narrow this down to one particular situation. I sort of want to allow everyone to compare themselves to this. So you know I don't want to nail down one time and one place. But it's helpful to give little images here and there. That's basically what I'm trying to do with phrases like "nervously fingers the bridge of his glasses" and "smiles blindly with dry lips into the glare of the stage lights" . . . while it's not really specific, it does begin to give you a picture of what's going on, what he's feeling.

His account of *why* he took the approach he did was part of a study designed to explore the extent to which students consider the following rhetorical elements in reading their own texts as writers: (a) providing a *context* for a reader by establishing the purpose of one's essay; (b) using *text structure* to further one's goals; and (c) fashioning *language* in order to situate one's writing within a given community of readers and determining the appropriateness of the choices one makes about language in a rhetorical situation.

This inquiry was motivated by constructivist theories of reading and writing, which suggest that as experienced writers read others' texts and create their own, they not only focus on content but on certain rhetorical features in a text. They also begin to make choices about language and text structure in keeping with their understanding of the context that surrounds their writing (cf. Ackerman, 1991; Haas & Flower, 1988). Bazerman's (1985) research in the sociology of science, for instance, points to the constructive nature of reading and writing, with an individual's personal map of the field consisting of consensual knowledge about the field, its methods and current practices, the problems on which the field is working, and the ways problems are worked out. Meaning, he suggests, seems to come from being able to integrate new information into what one already knows. Moreover, readers selectively evaluate what they read within the larger rhetorical concerns they have as authors.

A critical question is whether this characterization of reading is solely a feature of experienced readers. Given an open-ended assignment to write a persuasive essay that does not specify a certain format, to what degree will students attend to decisions about context, structure, and language? The answer to this question is important for teachers because it can increase our understanding of students' awareness of the rhetorical choices they make in a given situation, and the extent to which they are aware of the options that are available to them. In turn, we can be in a better position to help students further their own goals as writers, assume greater authority as readers, and establish a position from which they might speak in composing their own essays.

In light of the question motivating this study, one that focused on students' awareness of different rhetorical features of writing and the reasoning behind the choices they made in composing, it seemed sensible to use retrospective accounts. Why did students take the approach they did in writing their essays? Text analysis could reveal the way a writer established a context for writing, imposed structure, or used language; however, this kind of analysis could not tell us whether these choices were made consciously in light of larger rhetorical concerns, such as purpose and audience. Think-aloud protocols could show students' strategies for composing, but the reasoning behind a writer's choices are often tacit. After all, students' concerns for what they are actually writing at the moment are often more overriding than the reasons motivating their choices. As an alternative, retrospection, when the task is unstructured, can be useful in identifying the rhetorical concerns that are most salient to students.

Collecting Retrospective Accounts

To collect the data for this research, the investigator gave six students enrolled in an advanced writing course a relatively open-ended task that invited them to write about an issue that had come up in this course or in any other class they were taking. Immediately after writing a draft of their papers, students provided retrospective accounts, or what may be construed as retrospective protocols. They were given the following instructions: After writing a draft of your paper, turn on the tape recorder and think aloud for about 15 minutes or so and analyze what you did. Try to account for the choices and decisions you made as a writer. Students taped themselves privately in whatever setting they chose. This helped to reduce the researcher effect we discussed earlier in this chapter, eliminating as much as possible the sense that the researcher was testing students about how they approached the task of writing. To account for the phenomenon of recency, students were instructed to provide these accounts immediately after they finished their drafts. Since the task of thinking aloud was new to these six students, they practiced this procedure, so that they would feel more comfortable talking into a tape recorder. This entailed having students think aloud into a tape recorder as they reconstructed the choices they made in solving a math problem. They did not practice thinking aloud with a reading or writing task in order to avoid the possibility that students would be influenced by what they could perceive as a model.

Analyzing the Data

The data students provided were transcribed and read by the researcher in light of the research question: What did writers attend to in reading their own texts? In particular, to what extent did they focus on rhetorical features of their writing, such as context, structure, and language? First, the transcripts were parsed into T-units, which consisted of independent clauses and any subordinate clauses that may have been embedded. The brief transcript below, taken from the student's account of why he began his essay with an image of someone "nervously finger[ing] the bridge of his glasses" exemplifies what a parsed transcript of a retrospective account looks like. The actual raw data from which this excerpt was taken appear in the Appendix.

1 (I think you know while it's not really specific it does really give you a picture of what's going on. What he is feeling.) (You know what the

   scene looks like.) (You know basically what I'm trying to do is,
   you know, use phrases to sort of get across images here so that the
5 reader can picture in his mind what's going on.) (When I write I have
   a very specific picture in my head) (and what I'm trying to do with an
   essay is try and give it to the reader.) (I don't really like to think that
   other readers have totally different ideas of what I'm trying to say.) (I
   have a basic idea of what I'm trying to say and I'm trying to get it
10 across.)

   The second step consisted of coding each of the T-units, using categories
that related to the research question and the theoretical concerns that framed
this inquiry. Again, the key question motivating this study focused on the
extent to which students attended to different rhetorical concerns in reading
their own work. These concerns included context, structure, and language,
and provided the basis for coding the transcripts of students' retrospective
accounts. Thus these three rhetorical concerns served as a set of categories
that were established a priori, though it was also important to look carefully
at the data in order to account for what students attended to.
   Reading the transcripts entailed examining each of the T-units and identifying whether a student was focusing on context, structure, or language. In
a number of instances, students' attention to different rhetorical concerns
was quite sustained, extending beyond one or two T-units, and could be
labeled as an episode. The excerpt below illustrates one such episode that
was coded as context, even though the student was concerned with the
content of her essay as well. Here Lauren reflected upon how she went
about establishing the context for her essay, providing a rationale for the
argument she tried to advance about the nature of writer's block. She not
only considered the content she included, but why she took the approach
she did in writing the introduction to her paper:

context

1 (What I tried to prove was that there are five cognitive dimensions that
context
   lead to writer's block.) (And they lead to writer's block because they
content
   first lead to anxiety.) (And anxiety leads to writer's block.) (And in
context
   the beginning of my paper what I did was I just introduced what I was
context
5 going to talk about) . . . (I didn't explain them, I just listed what they

<pre>
                              context
were.) (I just wanted to introduce what I wanted to do.) (Then I
          content   context
went on in my paper) (and I was still introducing certain other things.)
                              content
(I used the writing model developed by Flower and Hayes) (and I did
                              context
this just so the reader would have an idea of what I was talking about.)
                              context
10 (So I didn't really start my argument on the first page.) (I just spoke
                    context
about what I was going to be arguing about.)
</pre>

Coding a transcript in this way is inevitably an interpretive process, one that reflects a researcher's theory about how people construct meaning. As a consequence, the decision to code data in a particular way is never clear-cut. In the excerpt above, for example, the entire episode was labeled as context, even though the student focused on content. This was because Lauren's attention to the subject matter of her essay was guided by her attempts to make sense of why she included the Flower and Hayes model in establishing the context of her paper.

Analyses of the transcripts also showed that when students attended to structure, they often described the organizational pattern of the essay; at times, students considered the rhetorical structure, certain kinds of evidence, or specific images. Students began with a text-based strategy that focused their attention on what they said, but moved away from the text, demonstrating an awareness of why they chose a given path in writing their essays. The example below is an excerpt from one student's transcript that has been parsed and then coded as structure because this seems to be Brian's most salient concern. Still, this particular example demonstrates how structure, content, and rhetorical context can be inextricably linked to one another. In fact, the last T-unit could be coded as both structure and content.

<pre>
                         structure
(My essay's not structured to where I develop different points) (or
                    context
to where I have to be very persuasive) . . . (I don't think you'll find
                    context
anybody who's a drinking and driving advocate) . . .) (It's more along the
                    structure/content
lines of a narrative, a story about what happens to a group of people.)
</pre>

As suggested above, some students also focused on choices about language, why certain words or phrases might be appropriate or not:

              content   content   content
     (He's just sitting there.) (He's frozen completely) (but his mind is going)
                        content
     (and he's thinking about this thing.) (And I have him say, "He thought
                              language
     surprisingly clearly to himself." "Surprisingly clearly," describing his

     thought because I wanted to make it very clear that what Brad was

     thinking is basically what I think.)

Though analyses of students' retrospective accounts focused on the extent to which they attended to context, structure, and language, they also reconstructed the choices and decisions they made about content, such as what to include or not to include in the essay, in light of their goals. Thus, in order to make the analyses as comprehensive as possible, a fourth category included all comments related to content. These comments reflected students' awareness of what they wanted to say and why certain details and ideas may or may not have been appropriate.

> (Brian) I didn't go into detail about the car that was wrapped around a tree. I didn't go into things like that or the shock of the drivers or anything like that. I just went into, I said, you know, this is what happens and two people were killed and that's it. That's all I need to say and the rest can be left up to your imagination and because things like that aren't pleasant to imagine. They shouldn't be for the essay. I think I can spare people the gore, I can make my point completely without it . . .

By accounting for all of the data in this way, not just the ways students attended to context, structure, and language, it was possible to analyze the proportion of comments devoted to one kind of strategy in relation to students' overall strategies.

Once this kind of analysis is made, it is important to establish the reliability of the coding. For this study, a second coder read 20% of all of the data collected. This meant developing a scheme for classifying the data that would be teachable (Swarts, Flower, & Hayes, 1984). After the researcher parsed the transcripts and discussed the categories with a second reader, this reader practiced identifying the strategies that she saw students using in reading their own writing on some data. Based on a pairwise comparison,

TABLE 5.1: Frequency of Students' Strategies for Reading Their Own Texts as Measured in T-units

	Context	Structure	Language	Content
Brian	10	9	2	39
Lauren	6	4	4	23
Andy	11	10	3	34
Alisa	2	2	1	30
Marc	3	6	0	22
Colleen	10	5	1	23
Total	42	36	11	181
Total Percentage	15%	13%	4%	67%

agreement between the researcher and this rater was 80%. This means that a match was made on 80% of the units that were coded. As noted earlier, there was some double-coding, for example when T-units were coded as both structure and content. In such instances, agreement was established if both raters identified at least one of the categories—structure or content.

Table 5.1 includes data from each student's retrospective accounts, revealing both the frequency with which they used different strategies and the proportions. This kind of analysis helped to put into perspective the extent to which students focused on the rhetorical features that were of interest in this study. Clearly, they considered content more (67%) than context (15%), structure (13%), or language (4%), though they attended to issues of context and structure with some degree of frequency. Interestingly, the proportion of T-units focusing on language was quite small.

Reporting the Results

In making any sort of claims about students' reading strategies, it was necessary to include enough data in a report so that readers could make their own assessments about the value of research based on retrospection. Reporting the findings of this study entailed some of the following: providing a systematic account of the questions that the study was designed to answer; the theory that motivated these questions; a discussion of how the data had been collected and analyzed, including the instructions given to the students for taping themselves, examples of the transcripts, and samples of the coding; and an explanation of the extent to which the coding of data was reliable. It was not sufficient to say that students attended to certain rhetorical features in reading their own texts; instead, it was necessary to define these features, explain their source of interest, and illustrate students' concerns in a task for which there was a sense of purpose.

Much of the persuasive power of retrospective accounts rests on showing that the analysis has been systematic, that the data have been parsed, and that frequency counts had been made. The persuasiveness of these accounts also rests on providing a moment-to-moment description of students' thinking as they reconstruct some of the choices they have made in reading their own texts. Although limited in its ability to capture all of the richness of students' thought processes, retrospection is a compelling source of data because these accounts enable us to hear individual students' voices. What may not be altogether clear, however, are the decisions that a researcher makes in choosing to select some examples and excluding others. In particular, what motivates the sorts of decisions we make about what to include? Given the pages and pages of transcripts that were transcribed, how do we determine what data is relevant?

In large part, the answers to these questions about what data to include in a report depend on the theory framing the study, the questions we have posed, and the argument we wish to make. For this research, a key question was whether students attend to the kinds of rhetorical concerns that expert readers address. Thus sorting through the data entailed choosing examples that showed students focusing on context, structure, and language. Since the analyses also revealed that students attended to content, it was useful to give an example that illustrated what was at issue for them as they considered the substance of their writing. Selecting data also entailed choosing examples that readers could identify as an illustration of a given rhetorical feature. This was particularly the case with the account we included at the beginning of this section and at the outset of our chapter, where a student reflected on the language of his essay. At times, it was useful to include data that provide a context for understanding what was of interest. In the following example, also mentioned above, a description of the scene the writer has composed conveyed a sense of why language was important:

> He's just sitting there. He's frozen completely but his mind is going and he's thinking about this thing. And I have him say, "He thought surprisingly clearly to himself." "Surprisingly clearly," describing his thought because I wanted to make it very clear that what Brad was thinking is basically what I think.

The key "finding" in this study was that students attended to different rhetorical features of their texts, at times reflecting an important meta-awareness about why they chose the strategies they did in advancing their arguments. Their concerns in reading their own writing reflected strategies that are often associated with more experienced writers. Thus, this kind of exploratory research provided a sense that the strategies these students used could be taught to others. Teachers can encourage students to develop a sense of the options they have as writers, and can help them articulate their reasons for making the choices they do in different rhetorical situations (Greene, 1993). In making these claims, it was necessary to provide readers with enough data to make their own assessments about the value of research based on retrospection.

CONCLUSION

We have offered four suggestions that can make the use of retrospective accounts valid, reliable sources of data. These include: (a) minimizing the time between process and report; (b) designing prompts that enable writers to gain access to both short- and long-term memory; (c) clarifying the purpose of retrospective accounts; and (d) reporting one's findings in ways that enable readers to see a clear path from data to claims. In providing these suggestions, we argue that the processes of gathering and analyzing data are quite complex and arduous, even when collecting retrospective accounts may be driven by a well-defined theory of what a researcher is looking for and what is important. Still, retrospective accounts can provide both researchers and teachers with a tool that can enable us to tap a rich source of data about how people approach the tasks of reading and writing. And we can use such a tool in a number of ways to uncover the hidden logic that comes to the surface through the stories that writers tell us about why they made the choices they did in composing.

APPENDIX

Okay, my essay. Um okay let's see, it starts out with the first sentence. What I basically try to do was draw the reader in. I think, I hope that is effective because I mean it's really as a beginning sentence it's meaningless to someone who just comes up and reads it. It's not like a topic sentence like some of my teachers write in school and start every paragraph with. It's more like a read more kind of sentence you know. Eventually . . . (inaudible) but it doesn't really make sense unless you keep reading which is hopefully what everybody will do. Uh so the next couple of lines it sort of gets into more detail. However, uh, I really don't explain exactly what's going on here which is on purpose. Uh, I basically sort of give a lot of images and a lot of scene but not a lot of specifics like where it is, what exactly is going on and what sort of concert this is. You know things like that. Um, I do that for a reason because I'm trying to be sort of ambiguous and sort of universal. I don't want to narrow this down to one particular situation. I sort of want to allow everyone to to uh compare themselves to this. So you know I don't want to nail this down to one time and one place. But it's helpful to give little images here and there. That's basically what I'm trying to do with phrases like nervously fingers the bridge of his glasses and smiles blindly with dry lips into the glare of the stage lights. I think you know while it's not really specific it does really give you a picture of what's going on, what he's feeling. You know what the scene looks like. You know basically what I'm trying to do is you know use phrases to sort of get across images here so that the reader can picture in his mind what's going on. When I write I have a very specific idea in my head, a very specific picture and what I'm trying to do with an essay is just try to give it to the reader. I'm not really, uh, I don't really like to think that readers have like totally different ideas of what I'm trying to say. I have a basic idea of what I'm trying to say and I'm trying to get it across.

REFERENCES

Ackerman, J. M. (1991). Reading, writing, and knowing: The role of disciplinary knowledge in comprehension and composing. *Research in the Teaching of English, 25,* 133-178.

Afflerbach, P., & Johnston, P. (1984). On the use of verbal reports in reading research. *Journal of Reading Behavior, 16,* 307-321.

Aston, J. (1987). *A participant observer case study conducted in a traditional developmental writing class in an urban community college of high risk, non-traditional women students who demonstrate apprehension about error production.* Unpublished doctoral dissertation, University of Pittsburgh.

Bartholomae, D. (1985). Inventing the university. In M. Rose (Ed.), *When a writer can't write* (pp. 134-165). New York: Guilford Press.

Bartlett, F. (1932). *Remembering.* Cambridge, UK: Cambridge University Press.

Bazerman, C. (1985). Physicists reading physics: Schema-laden purposes and purpose-laden schema. *Written Communication, 2,* 3-23.

Cooper, M., & Holzman, M. (1983). Talking about protocols. *College Composition and Communication, 4,* 288-293.

Crowhurst, M. (1991). Interrelationships between reading and writing persuasive discourse. *Research in the Teaching of English, 25,* 314-338.

Emig, J. (1971). *The composing processes of twelfth graders* (Research Report No. 13). Urbana, IL: National Council of Teachers of English.

Ericsson, K. A., & Simon, H. (1980). Verbal reports as data. *Psychological Review, 87,* 215-251.

Ericsson, K. A., & Simon, H. (1984). *Protocol analysis: Verbal reports as data.* Cambridge: MIT Press.

Faigley, L., Cherry, R., Jolliffe, D., & Skinner, A. (1985). *Assessing writers' knowledge and processes of composing.* Norwood, NJ: Ablex.

Flanagan, J. C. (1954). The critical incident technique. *Psychological Bulletin, 51,* 327-358.

Flower, L. (1990). The role of task representation in reading-to-write. In L. Flower, V. Stein, J. Ackerman, P. Kantz, K. McCormick, & W. Peck, *Reading to write: Exploring a cognitive and social process* (pp. 35-75). New York: Oxford University Press.

Flower, L., & Hayes, J. R. (1981). A cognitive process theory of writing. *College Composition and Communication, 32,* 21-32.

Flower, L., Stein, V., Ackerman, J., Kantz, P., McCormick, K., & Peck, W. (1990). *Reading to write: Exploring a cognitive and social process.* New York: Oxford University Press.

Garner, R. (1982). Verbal-report data on reading strategies. *Journal of Reading Behavior, 14,* 159-167.

Greene, S. (1992). Mining texts in reading to write. *Journal of Advanced Composition, 12*(1), 151-170.

Greene, S. (1993a). The role of task in the development of academic thinking through reading and writing in a college history course. *Research in the Teaching of English, 27,* 46-75.

Greene, S. (1993b). Exploring the relationship between authorship and reading: A study of classroom research. In A. M. Penrose & B. Sitko (Eds.), *Hearing ourselves think: Process research in the classroom.* New York: Oxford University Press.

Haas, C., & Flower, L. (1988). Rhetorical reading strategies and the construction of meaning. *College Composition and Communication, 39,* 167-183.

Herrington, A. (1985). Writing in academic settings: A study of the contexts for writing in two college chemical engineering courses. *Research in the Teaching of English, 19,* 331-359.

Higgins, L. (1992). *Argument as construction: A framework and method.* Unpublished doctoral dissertation, Carnegie-Mellon University.

Higgins, L., & Greene, S. (1992). *The uses of retrospective accounts in writing research.* Paper presented at the annual meeting of the Conference on College Composition and Communication, Cincinnati.

Hull, G., & Rose, M. (1989). Rethinking remediation: Toward a social-cognitive understanding of problematic reading and writing. *Written Communication, 8,* 139-154.

Hull, G., Rose, M., Fraser, K. L., & Castellano, M. (1991). Remediation as a social construct: Perspectives from an analysis of classroom discourse. *College Composition and Communication, 42,* 299-329.

Nelson, J. (1990). This was an easy assignment: Examining how students interpret academic writing tasks. *Research in the Teaching of English, 24,* 362-396.

Nisbett, R. E., & Wilson, T. D. (1977). Telling more than we can know: Verbal reports on mental processes. *Psychological Review, 84,* 231-259.

Odell, L., Goswami, D., & Herrington, A. (1983). The discourse-based interview: A procedure for exploring the tacit knowledge of writers in nonacademic settings. In P. Mosenthal (Ed.), *Research on writing: Principles and methods* (pp. 221-236). New York: Longman.

Perkins, D. N. (1981). *The mind's best work.* Cambridge, MA: Harvard University Press.

Rose, M. (1984). *Writer's block: The cognitive dimension.* Carbondale: Southern Illinois University Press.

Steinberg, E. R. (1986). Protocols, retrospective reports, and the stream of consciousness. *College English, 48,* 697-712.

Sternglass, M. (1988). *The presence of thought: Introspective accounts of reading and writing.* Norwood, NJ: Ablex.

Sternglass, M. S., & Pugh, S. L. (1986). Retrospective accounts of language and learning processes. *Written Communication, 3,* 297-323.

Swarts, H., Flower, L., & Hayes, J. R. (1984). Designing protocol studies of the writing process: An introduction. In R. Beach & L. Bridwell (Eds.), *New directions in composition research* (pp. 53-71). New York: Guilford Press.

Tomlinson, B. (1984). Talking about the composing process: The limitations of retrospective accounts. *Written Communication, 1,* 429-445.

Young, R. (1976). Invention: A topographical survey. In G. Tate (Ed.), *Teaching composition: Ten bibliographic essays* (pp. 1-43). Fort Worth: Texas Christian University Press.

Walvoord, B. E., & McCarthy, L. P. (1990). *Thinking and writing in college.* Urbana, IL: National Council of Teachers of English.

White, P. (1980). Limitations on verbal reports of internal events: A refutation of Nisbett and Wilson and of Bem. *Psychological Review, 87,* 105-112.

6

Using Intervention Protocols to Study the Effects of Instructional Scaffolding on Writing and Learning

DEBORAH SWANSON-OWENS
GEORGE E. NEWELL

In a time of unprecedented interest in psychological phenomena, it is ironic that the discipline of psychology seems less capable than ever of providing a coherent account of the human mind. We know more about isolated mental processes and skills, but we seem incapable of generating an overall picture of mental functioning. We can often find regularities under controlled laboratory conditions, but as soon as we move to other, more natural settings these findings seem to disappear in the sea of "real life."

Wertsch (1991, p. 1)

These words, which introduce James Wertsch's recent discussion of his theory of mediated mental functioning, echo current discussions within the field of writing research and instruction. Studies of the composing process have been a powerful impetus in rethinking writing instruction—a paradigm shift, according to Hairston (1982), leading to the field's change from concerns with the written product to concerns with writing processes. Yet in spite of extensive analyses of verbal protocols of composing, and a plethora of instructional approaches based on process studies, the "sea of [classroom] life" has proven to be difficult to navigate. For process-oriented writing instruction, inasmuch as it has been adopted in writing classrooms, has failed to address fully the cognitive strategies students employ as they tackle writing tasks.

Clearly, much has been said about the importance of prewriting activities, activities that have the potential to help cultivate students' topic knowledge, and help them search for and organize information in long-term memory (e.g., Connors & Glen, 1992; Hillocks, 1975; 1979). This instructional paradigm shift has also encouraged teachers to construct more "meaningful" writing tasks and address rhetorical parameters such as audience and purpose for writing (e.g., Kirby & Liner, 1981; Lindemann, 1986). Beyond such directives, however, there is little information about the types of instructional scaffolds teachers can offer students to help them incorporate their knowledge of topic or audience or purpose into more expert-like composing strategies. The extensive research on the executive routines of novice and expert writers by Bereiter and Scardamalia and associated colleagues have led these researchers to believe that "the central problem of writing instruction [is] that of altering the way students operate on their knowledge when they write" (Bereiter & Scardamalia, 1987, p. 359). This concern has led us to use the "intervention protocol" in our studies of learning to write and writing to learn.

WHY ANOTHER METHOD FOR STUDYING THE COMPOSING PROCESS?

Though process-oriented approaches to teaching writing continue to dominate the scholarly and practitioner-oriented literature, the first wave of efforts to reform instruction, using a reconceptualization of what it means to write, has had mixed results. Perhaps the most compelling evidence for this problem is documented in *Learning to Write in Our Nation's Schools: Instruction and Achievement in 1988 at Grades 4, 8, and 12* (Applebee, Langer, Jenkins, Mullis, & Foertsch, 1990). The authors report that although the majority of students received instruction on structured approaches to the writing process, their performances were not statistically significant from those students who did not receive such instruction. There are other sources of concern too. Studies by Hillocks (1986) and Langer and Applebee (1987) examined the strengths and weaknesses of process-oriented approaches to writing and concluded that such approaches have been seriously underconceptualized; translating knowledge of what writers do into instructional approaches has proven to be more difficult than it seemed initially.

Rather than arguing against the contributions of process-oriented instruction, we believe, with Applebee (1986), that these studies suggest the need for a more sophisticated conceptualization both of writing processes and of how to incorporate these processes into instructional programs. Research can play an important role in developing a more sophisticated conceptualization of the use of process approaches in instruction. But to do so requires the application of methodologies driven by theoretical frameworks and procedures that are sensitive to writing processes in school contexts.

Beginning with Emig's (1971) work, the field has produced a flood of studies emphasizing the heuristic, problem-solving nature of writing about new ideas and experiences. Typically these studies have compared experts and novices completing tasks set by the researcher, tasks not necessarily tied to classroom instruction. Applebee (1986) has argued that as models for writing instruction, the studies are flawed in two ways: "they have misrepresented what experts do and have failed to consider how processes might best be taught" (p. 106). He then recommends two reconceptualizations:

1. Writing processes must be reconstrued as strategies for particular purposes— writers rely on different strategies depending on the nature of the task and on the knowledge and skills they bring to the writing. Writing a narrative might require the organization of readily available information into a complex structural plan; writing an analytic essay might require less concern for form and more effort at generating relevant information.

2. Learning must be reconceptualized as the process of gradual internalization of routines and procedures that the instructional environment provides—the role of the teacher is to provide the necessary support for students to understand the writing task and the appropriate strategies for successful completion of the task.

To Applebee's recommendations we add those of Bereiter and Scardamalia (1987):

3. Novice writers must be viewed as individuals who possess well-formed composing strategies that help them negotiate the kinds of expository writing tasks schools often ask them to complete. Even a relatively immature composing process (identified in their work as the knowledge-telling strategy) enables students to employ their content and rhetorical knowledge enough to help them produce texts which, to varying degrees, convey relevant content framed in genre-appropriate ways. Instructional scaffolds cannot afford to neglect students' current composing strategies in their efforts to encourage students to adopt more intellectually transformative processes of writing.

4. In conjunction with the prior recommendation, learning must be reconceptualized to embrace more than the acquisition of content or rhetorical knowledge.

Such knowledge is a necessary but not sufficient condition to transform the executive routines writers employ. Writers also need strategies "for deliberately formulating and pursuing personally meaningful goals in writing, for recognizing and overcoming problems, and for assessing and revising choices made at a variety of levels" (p. 360).

5. Instruction must provide the type of external support that helps writers readily negotiate the early stages of learning to carry out more complex writing routines. As part of this instruction, students need to understand the nature and purpose of this more complex writing process, for without such understanding, they are likely to internalize only the most superficial aspects of it (p. 363).

Put simply, just as writing teachers have been asked to embrace a broader range of concerns in their instructional repertoire, we believe writing researchers must employ research methods that will inform such instructional efforts. To a large extent, process and instructional research have operated on parallel and not intersecting empirical tracks, with process studies being largely detached from instructional issues, and instructional studies ignoring how individuals internalize instructional lessons and incorporate them into their composing strategies. What we now need are studies that employ methodologies that enable us to acquire a better understanding of the interrelationship between the role of the teacher and the role of the student as they interact in school contexts. Linda Flower, who promotes a sociocognitivist orientation to writing research, sums up this argument well:

We need, I believe, a far more integrated theoretical vision which can explain how context cues cognition, which in turn mediates and interprets the particular world that context provides. What we don't know is how cognition and context do in fact interact, in specific but significant situations. We have little precise understanding of how these "different processes" feed on one another. (1989, pp. 282-283)

THE INTERVENTION PROTOCOL
AS A USEFUL RESEARCH METHODOLOGY

With the above premises as our starting point, the methodology of intervention protocols enables us to (a) study how instruction shapes composing and learning processes; and (b) redefine the researcher's role as one of co-participant who supplies assistance to the participating student, creating situations in which learning can be observed as students work within the zone of proximal development (Vygotsky, 1978). In other words, this methodology allows us to study the effects of instruction by adopting the notion of composing as socially situated. While the insertion of external prompts during students' efforts to solve composing problems is not a new research method (numerous studies cited in Bereiter and Scardamalia [1987] employ such methods), we suggest that this research methodology be broadened to examine more directly the impact classroom lessons have on composing processes. Rather than derive prompts solely on the basis of an hypothesized element of a composing model (e.g., testing the psychological validity of discourse-grammar knowledge by giving students a set of discourse elements to arrange), we believe intervention protocols can be designed to use particular information provided by instructors to see how added scaffolding efforts might improve students' application of that information. As in other cognitive research, the functional nature of these scaffolds—that is, what students are asked to do with this information—should be guided by current problem-solving theories of writing. Rather than viewing the collection of think-aloud protocols as situations in which students "do it all" on their own, we believe that much can be learned about the intersection of instruction and process when researchers provide contexts that support writers to do more than they can do on their own.

How the Intervention Protocol Works

Although intervention protocols can be designed to work in a variety of ways, a basic component of this research instrument is that students are given external cues intended to aid, or gain access to, certain aspects of their composing processes. Following are three different configurations of this research methodology, each capable of providing pertinent information about the role of instructional content or scaffolding in problem-solving.

1. Think-Alouds With the Support of Ongoing Cues

Students in this composing condition are given a set of cue cards and encouraged to use them as prompts to aid them at a variety of decision points during writing. This particular approach to intervention protocols could be useful to researchers interested in studying ways of influencing composing strategies through the use of scaffolds designed expressly to alter or reinforce certain on-line behaviors.

Given the heavy cognitive demands of the writing task, and the fact that writers are likely to possess a familiar, though often immature, problem-solving routine to negotiate such demands, the researcher needs to minimize the disruptive effects of external aids. Design considerations might include: providing prompts that focus on only one type of composing decision (e.g., generating goals for the whole text or individual paragraphs, or comparing how well the content of a certain segment of text fulfills one's goals for that segment); discussing with the student not only the nature and functional value of confronting such decisions and trying to resolve them, but also how he or she currently tries to deal with the problem the prompts are designed to help; modeling how the cues or prompts can be used to solve a composing problem by demonstrating, for example, how the investigator might use them to set his or her goals for a specific writing task, generate plans to achieve those goals, evaluate a given text in light of some specified goals or plans, and so on; giving the student an opportunity, with direct guidance from the researcher, to use the cue cards to solve a relatively limited writing task before tackling a more complicated or extensive type of writing assignment. (For a detailed discussion of various on-line cues used to help students apply knowledge and examine their executive composing strategies, see Bereiter & Scardamalia, 1987.) As we noted earlier, the agenda underlying the prompts need not necessarily derive from theoretical accounts of the composing process; it may derive from particular aspects of classroom instruction that the researcher is simply trying to reinforce as the student tries to carry out the writing directives offered by his or her teacher.

2. Interrupted Think-Aloud Sessions: Retrospective and/or Planning Accounts of Processes

In this type of intervention protocol, students are asked to compose aloud with the kinds of directives well documented in other discussions of protocol research (see, for example, Steinberg, 1986, p. 701). In addition to composing aloud, students are told before they begin that they will be asked to stop periodically and respond to questions about the writing they've produced to that point, and/or about the writing they plan to do next.

Interventions with this design are particularly useful when the researcher is interested in studying the on-line effects of scaffolds that (a) foster comprehension monitoring strategies or planning behaviors, or (b) encourage students to consciously employ certain domains of knowledge (such as genre knowledge) to evaluate or plan text in the process of its evolution rather than before or after its completion. This protocol format can be equally valuable to researchers who are not interested in influencing the composing process per se, but hoping to gain access to goals, plans, strategies, and knowledge that are not stated during the composing process.

Because this protocol method deliberately interrupts the writing process, researchers must consider where and how often such interruptions should take place. Swanson-Owens (1987), for example, asked students to signal when they felt they had completed a paragraph. This design decision was based on the belief that the paragraph is a psychological construct (e.g., Eden & Mitchell, 1986) and that given the nature of this construct, paragraph boundaries were places where students would naturally reorient themselves and engage in more global planning and monitoring behaviors than normally occur while students are focusing on sentences within the paragraph (although high-level planning can certainly be triggered at any point during the composing process). Having students signal when they were ready to talk also helped reduce the risk of disrupting them in the process of trying to formulate a thought or translate it into words.

3. Planning and Retrospective Accounts
Collected During the Problem-Solving Process

Unlike the design of the prior intervention protocol, which yields both on-line composing data as well as planning and/or retrospective accounts, this intervention format generates self-report data only about planning and/or retrospective behaviors. When not responding to the prompts given by the researcher, students work silently on the task.

Intervention protocols of this type can be valuable to researchers who believe (a) that periodic discussions about the evolving text or immediate processes can encourage students to engage in more reflective thinking about their work (i.e., the prompts themselves yield a procedural effect); or (b) that such discussions provide rich data about the ways students, without procedural or substantive support from the researcher, construe and go about tackling the task before them. The latter is especially important to researchers interested in exploring the direct effects of classroom instruction on composing processes, and in studies that include students who are less inclined to use metalanguage *during* composing than when talking *about* composing. In truth, it would be difficult if not impossible to separate the influence of these two factors—intervention prompts and the background knowledge and strategies students bring to the session. Reported outcomes from such studies should bear this confounding effect in mind.

Advantages of the Intervention Protocol

Beyond the need for research that explores the intersection of instruction and process, which we discussed at the beginning of this chapter, we feel that the intervention protocol offers special opportunities to study the ways context cues cognition. Among them are the following:

1. Intended Effects of the Intervention

Smagorinsky (1989) cautions "on-line" protocol researchers to "be careful that conditions of the protocol and the task do not influence the thought patterns under study" (p. 468). While it is clear that significant distortions in composing processes may occur when students give "directed reports," reports on specific behaviors having to do with motives and intentions articulated during the process of composing, intervention protocols—especially those designed to enhance the effects of classroom instruction—*deliberately* aspire to influence the thought patterns under study. Designed to foster certain composing strategies, to address the problem of inert knowledge, or to encourage students to articulate their plans for and assessments of their texts, intervention protocols can provide useful information about the effects of particular types of instructional content or scaffolds.

To increase the empirical value of such data, researchers should carefully examine exactly what their prompts are asking students to do, reducing as much as possible potential ambiguities in, and thus multiple construals of, their prompts. For example, if asked, "What did you do in this paragraph?" students could construe the question as a request for a summary of its content, the planning strategy they used, or a list of the types of discourse elements they included—all of which are substantively different questions to address. Entrenched in the issues of their own research agenda, researchers also need to be careful not to "lead" or "confuse the witness." Asking a question like "How did you use your teacher's recommendations about essay organization when you were planning the essay?" presupposes that students have considered such recommendations, when in fact they may not have. Asking, "What kinds of text representations did you have in mind when you wrote this paragraph?" is likely to yield blank stares and little else.

Beyond such considerations, researchers should conscientiously analyze the data in terms of where such interruptions have occurred, be they self-induced by the writer (e.g., drawing upon a cue card in the process of composing) or prompted by the researcher (e.g., stopping the student after each paragraph is completed, halfway through the text, or intermittently according to a particular time schedule or location within a given paragraph). The context in which students respond to cues or prompts is as much a factor as the content of the prompts in interpreting students' overall reaction to a particular intervention.

2. Intermittent Versus After-the-Fact Accounts

A second design advantage of the intervention protocol is that students can be asked to give intermittent rather than after-the-fact retrospective accounts of their composing strategies. Problems with retrospective reports have been well documented (DiPardo, this volume; Ericsson & Simon, 1980; Greene & Higgins, this volume; Hayes & Flower, 1983; Steinberg, 1986; Smagorinsky, 1989). Questions about the validity of such data have to do with (a) the displacement and eventual disappearance of information from conscious memory through the interference of other information, and (b) the reconstructive distortions that can come about because people tend to forget goals and subgoals once they have accomplished them, a feature of retrospective accounts commonly referred to as the "Zeigarnik effect" (Smagorinsky, 1989). Asking students to give intermittent reports on relatively small chunks of text shortens the interval of time between performance and report, and provides useful information before goals and subgoals have been met. Having students report on motives and intentions between composing episodes is also less disruptive to the process than asking for directed reports during composing.

Potential Problems With Intervention Protocols

Although a number of these potential problems are obvious, we thought them worth noting so that researchers are careful to factor them into their decisions related to this research methodology.

1. Time and Labor Required for Data Collection

Anyone who has collected think-aloud protocols knows how time-consuming and labor-intensive the enterprise is. Adding additional demands to this process obviously extends the composing time and the energy expended by subjects. For these reasons the researcher thinking of using this protocol method must consider the time frame students have for composing, and the stamina they have for completing the task. Such considerations played a part, for example, in the design of the intervention protocols collected by Newell and Johnson (1993). With only a 50-minute class period within which to implement the intervention, they focused on only the most critical topics to examine, and after piloting this version of protocol study, decided not to collect think-aloud data but to concentrate only on the students' responses to prompts (version 3 of the intervention designs discussed above). By contrast, Swanson-Owens (1987), who worked with college freshmen composing out-of-class essays, asked students to compose aloud as well as give retrospective and planning accounts of their work, since students could meet with her and draft their essays during an extended period (2 weeks).

2. Confounding of Classroom Instruction and the Investigators' Intervention

To the extent that the intervention protocol is used to explore the effects of instruction on cognition, studies must be designed, as much as possible, to tease apart the influence of classroom instruction and that of the prompts or scaffolds provided by the researcher. Although we are not aware of any studies that have examined this issue, we assume that such prompts are likely to alter executive routines or monitoring behaviors. Even the most descriptive, as compared to analytic or explanatory, responses from subjects require them to abstract themselves from the process and consciously articulate it. We believe such externally induced responses can not help but have an impact on students' monitoring behavior, and potentially influence the writing decisions they make.

Thus, whether researchers are trying to examine the influence of classroom instruction on writing performance, or examine the effects of additional scaffolds on applications of classroom instruction, we believe that researchers should design their studies to control for the effects of the prompts or scaffolds themselves. For example, before testing the effects of two instructional conditions on students' composing processes, Newell and Johnson (1993) collected extensive background data on their subjects to determine the comparability of their prior writing instruction and their knowledge of writing about literature. Prior to testing the effects of her own instructional scaffold on students' application of discourse structure knowledge, Swanson-Owens (1987) collected baseline (nonintrusive) protocols and texts prior to collecting intervention protocols and the texts they yielded.

While baseline data are an obvious component of any treatment study, they are especially important in studies looking at the effects of instruction on process, since process itself is conditioned by many factors. For this reason the research has to be particularly sensitive to topic effects, the ways students can construe cues, and the undoubted influence of any intervention that forces them into reflection or response.

3. Procedural Versus Substantive Facilitation

Researchers using interventions that are deliberately constructed to foster certain composing behaviors need to account carefully for the type of scaffold used during the composing session. Scaffolds designed according to identified self-regulatory functions associated with expert performance—that is, scaffolds that offer students cues to help foster certain executive routines and applications of knowledge—reflect significantly different assumptions about learning from those that offer students the active collaboration of the researcher or teacher. Termed "procedural" and "substantive facilitation," respectively, by Bereiter and Scardamalia (1987), these scaffolds should not be confused with one another, since in the former case, the researcher or teacher tries to reduce the information-processing burden of students rather than offering substantive input to the student. Such a scaffolding system is useful for examining both how to help students make better use of the knowledge they already have, and how to influence the problem-solving strategies they possess. (For a detailed discussion of this type of scaffold, see Bereiter and Scardamalia, 1987, especially Chapter 10.)

Substantive facilitation, by contrast, tries to reduce the executive burden of composing by having the teacher or researcher, or more knowledgeable other, assume part of this burden by becoming an active collaborator (cf. Applebee & Langer, 1983). As Bereiter and Scardamalia point out, this form of instructional scaffolding is typical in much school practice inasmuch as teachers set goals, provide and critique content, or suggest ways of organizing information for a piece of writing. Researchers using intervention protocols to facilitate composing processes need to be aware, both in their design and in their interpretation of the research, of the differences between these two scaffolding systems since they provide information about very different kinds of instructional support.

4. Establishing the Theoretical Framework

Intervention protocols build an added dimension of theoretical complexity into an already complex body of data. Unlike standard think-alouds, intervention protocols—especially those designed to provide an added scaffold to classroom instruction—require that the researcher be well informed about the theoretical bases for the intervention itself. Such bases provide the researcher with an analytic vantage point for making sense of the data and assessing what the intervention has accomplished.

5. Data Analysis

Because the validity of protocol data for assessing cognitive processes has been discussed extensively elsewhere (Cooper & Holzman, 1983; Dobrin, 1986; Hayes & Flower, 1983; Smagorinsky, 1989; Steinberg, 1986), we will limit our comments here to three general issues, one of which pertains to any kind of protocol analysis, the other two of which are related to intervention protocols in particular.

As Hayes and Flower so aptly put it: "Analyzing a protocol is like following the tracks of a porpoise, which occasionally reveals itself by breaking the surface of the sea" (1980, p. 9). While following those tracks presents numerous problems for the researcher, we believe that they offer strong enough traces of thought processes, in particular those associated with the writer's focal attention, to justify such data as being rich and informative. Because of their promise, we feel it is crucial for researchers not to underestimate the complexity of these data if their analysis and interpretation are to be of any real value for writing researchers. In his critique of protocols, Dobrin (1986) makes a strong case for the difficulty of interpreting the types of constraints operating for any given statement or behavior. He cites an example of a writer rereading his or her text " 'to see how it sounds' and then chang[ing the word] 'ameliorate' to 'improve' [and saying] 'Charlie wouldn't like that' " (p. 721). As Dobrin points out:

"To see how it sounds" may indicate that the decision is made on esthetic grounds, or in order to meet audience constraints, or both. If you try to cash out what is meant by esthetic grounds, moreover, there may again be many competing explanations, all of which may be true. The rhythm of the sentence might be improved. "Ameliorate" might look ugly. "Ameliorate" might have been used already in the paragraph. "Ameliorate" might literally sound worse. Ditto with the audience considerations. "Charlie" might like it. An old teacher may have taught the person the Fogg index. The definition might even indicate that "improve" is more accurate. (p. 721)

Given the multiple interpretations possible for coding such statements, we feel researchers should heed Dobrin's injunction to supply an "exhaustive list of the constraints, some description of how and when they're exerted . . . and some description of how meeting those constraints meshes with other requirements" at a given composing juncture (p. 722).

An important consideration specifically related to analyzing intervention protocols is grounding the analyses in a theoretical framework and in the purposes of the study. For example, Newell and Johnson (1993) used their intervention protocol data to explore whether the patterns of writing performance in the two instructional conditions—teacher-centered and student-based—were a result of students' own meaning making or their attempts to respond to the writing task according to teacher expectations. Accordingly, a key issue in the study was the influence of the instructional conditions on students' construal of the writing task.

A content analysis of the protocols revealed four categories or areas of concern relative to task construal. Each of the four categories (conceptualizing task demands, overall planning of the essay, evaluating progress through the essay, and reflecting on the completed product) was used to describe only those portions of the protocols that addressed how students conceptualized the writing task according to instructional condition. In studies of composing, particular care must be taken to adapt and modify the development of categories according to the theoretical direction and the focus of the study, rather than assuming that coding schemes developed for use in other studies are valid and appropriate.

Beyond such considerations, intervention protocols provide an additional database—the verbal exchanges between student and researcher—that may require analysis. Analyzing the content of students' retrospective and/or planning accounts can help researchers (a) account for knowledge and strategies not necessarily verbalized in composing-aloud data, (b) assess the developmental competence of that articulated knowledge and strategic thinking, and (c) corroborate interpretations of think-aloud or silent composing behaviors. While valuable, such analyses embroil the researcher in the painstaking and time-consuming processes of developing, coding, and testing the reliability of pertinent coding systems.

USING INTERVENTION PROTOCOLS

Before closing this chapter, we will briefly illustrate how we designed intervention protocols to serve our respective research agendas.

Interested in how college writers make use of their discourse structure knowledge during the production of argumentative essays, Swanson-Owens (1987) used intervention protocols to study how a particular type of instructional scaffold might help them make better use of this knowledge in the process of writing. The design of the intervention itself was informed by earlier work, which not only indicated that such knowledge is largely tacit and thus not readily evident in protocol studies, but also posited that less-than-expert writers employ discourse structure knowledge to less effect because it is mediated by composing strategies that do little more than use this knowledge as cues for searching memory for content (Bereiter & Scardamalia, 1987; Scardamalia & Bereiter, 1986a, 1986b; Scardamalia & Paris, 1985). At the time of the study, the most comprehensive theoretical explanation of why such knowledge failed to serve as little more than memory cues was that relatively unskilled writers did not link such knowledge to the formulation of goals, to strategic decisions, and to "high-level representations of content that can be manipulated effectively during text planning" (Scardamalia & Bereiter, 1986b, p. 785). This explanation seemed highly plausible in light of the numerous studies that indicated that novice writers work with limited goals, planning behaviors, and representations of text (e.g., Bereiter, 1980; Flower & Hayes, 1980, 1981; Perl, 1979; Scardamalia, Bereiter, Woodruff, Burtis, & Turkish, 1980; Sommers, 1980).

While this theoretical and empirical work helped to define the instructional problem, the instructional scaffold itself was largely informed by the comprehension monitoring work of Palinscar and Brown (1984). Given the important role assigned to reflective processes in writing, it seemed important to design an intervention that would engage students in more reflective planning and monitoring activities. And, given the research question, it seemed important to explicitly link those reflective processes to the discourse structure elements emphasized by the teachers in this study. For these reasons, then, students were given a series of questions that asked them to consciously draw on their knowledge of discourse elements as they engaged in reflective thinking, a process that might help them link their discourse structure knowledge to higher-order representations of their texts (e.g., goals, plans, and gist representations).

To accomplish this, students working with the intervention were given a number of general prompts designed to help them set goals and construct plans before beginning any writing. (Pre-composing prompts are provided in Appendix A at the end of the chapter.) Once students started to write the essay, they stopped after each paragraph and were asked questions that were designed to do two things: (1) help them monitor their comprehension of the text produced so far, and (2) plan the next segment of text they were to write. Each of these instructional agendas was directly tied to a set of discourse elements used by the teacher to characterize the structure of an argumentative essay. Students were given a set of cue cards that listed and defined the structural elements emphasized by the teacher. Prompts were designed to cue their knowledge of these discourse elements as they engaged in the comprehension monitoring strategies of summarizing, clarifying, questioning, predicting, and evaluating. (A list of these prompts is also provided in Appendix A.)

Using students in two different sections of freshman composition, whose teachers had similar instructional goals and teaching styles, but characterized the rhetorical (structural) elements of argumentative essays quite differently, Swanson-Owens collected baseline protocol data from the two different sets of students before using an intervention format with half of the case-study students in each class. Baseline data consisted of think-aloud protocols on three essays from each of the case-study students. The intervention was carried out with half of the case-study students on essays four and five. Follow-up protocols, without the intervention, were collected for two more essays (one done 2 weeks later, the other after 5 weeks).

In a follow-up interview with all of the participants, students reported that composing aloud had actually helped them focus on their writing more than they might have otherwise. Students involved in the intervention reported that the process of analyzing their texts according to the specific discourse elements had helped them see gaps in their logic and flaws in the development of their thesis or central idea. (See Stratman & Hamp-Lyons, this volume, for an extended discussion of reactivity in protocol analysis.)

Newell and Johnson (1993) employed the intervention protocol for two purposes: (a) to examine the effects of instruction on students' approaches to an analytic writing task; and (b) to obtain a window on how less successful writers (general-track, 10th-grade high school students) respond to prompts focused on conceptualization of task demands, planning decisions, and evaluation of ideas developed during composing. To examine the effects of classroom discussion on how students write and learn about a short story, Newell and Johnson developed two instructional units, one employing a teacher-centered discussion, the other employing a small-group discussion.

The central hypothesis underlying the study was that these different instructional conditions would influence students' conceptualization of the task, and in particular, their understanding of the function of the writing assignment (to recall the teacher's interpretation of a story or to explore their own), their sense of audience, and their ownership of the text. Such conceptualizations would, in turn, influence students' planning decisions and evaluations of content in significant ways.

Newell and Johnson's decision to use intervention protocols was based, in large part, on the kind of data available in standard think-aloud protocols of younger writers. Earlier experiences with such protocols taught them that these writers are not as likely as older or more expert writers to articulate their goals, strategies, or rhetorical concerns. Since the purpose of this study was to explore the influence of different instructional conditions on students' task construal and the planning and evaluative behaviors associated with it, Newell and Johnson decided to use the intervention protocol because retrospective and planning accounts would give them more direct access to this information. (A list of the specific prompts used in the study is provided in Appendix B at the end of the chapter.)

Although asking students about their decisions as they compose raises the possibility that the intervention itself altered how students would normally write on their own, Newell and Johnson designed the study so they could demonstrate rather specific effects of each type of instruction. As noted earlier, they addressed the confounding effects of the intervention and instructional conditions by collecting background information, which, after analysis, indicated that students began the study with similar writing instruction from the prior year.

When students were debriefed about how the interruptions affected their thinking and writing, their reaction to the prompts seemed directly influenced by the type of instruction they had received in their classes. Students in the teacher-led condition complained that they did not need to pause and discuss their writing. "I knew what I was going to say and that just slowed me up. . . . I had a plan based on what we did in class, and there was just one way to do it." On the other hand, students in the reader-based condition commented that the prompts helped them see what they had written. "Well, writing this was like getting in a car and not knowing where you are going.

When you asked about that, I kinda saw what was going on. I guess I was thinking about my ideas a lot." Such responses are interesting because they illustrate the potential for an interaction to take place between an instructional condition and the intervention itself, an interaction that was not evident in the Swanson-Owens study.

CLOSING COMMENTS

For those of us concerned about the relationships between process studies and developmental and instructional issues, the limitations of making inferential leaps from what experts do to what instruction should do are acutely felt. Accordingly, we feel intervention protocols offer a methodology for studying writing and learning in situ. In one sense, this methodology may be conceived as "learning experiments" based on proplectic instruction, an instructional method that recognizes the role of inter-psychological processes in the development of intra-psychological processes (Vygotsky, 1978).

While we find this methodology promising for those interested in studying the interaction of context and cognition, there are numerous conditions that, if ignored, can compromise its potential value. Throughout this chapter, we have tried to identify a number of those conditions, citing as noteworthy the relationship between the type of research question asked and the type of intervention used, the time and stamina of subjects, the potentially confounding effects of classroom instruction and the intervention itself, the substantive differences between scaffolding designs, and the theoretical bases for, and linguistic precision of, the prompts or cues given students. Despite the challenges such conditions pose for researchers, we feel the intervention protocol to be an adaptable and potentially profitable instrument for studying writing processes in school contexts.

APPENDIX A

Intervention Protocol Prompts
Used in Swanson-Owens's (1987) Study

Pre-Composing Prompts:

1. Why do you think [teacher's name] has asked you to write this essay?
2. What are some of the issues that come to mind about this topic?
3. Who do you think of as your audience for this essay?

4. How much do you think they already know about issues like [content items students have raised]?

5. Do you think there are some issues [referring specifically to those students have raised so far] that your audience will have trouble accepting or agreeing with?

6. [If so], what are they and why might your audience have difficulty with them?

7. What are you trying to accomplish, what are your goals in writing this essay?

8. What do you think you'll have to do in order to achieve your goals?

9. What would you like to do first?

10. How do you plan to do that?

Composing Prompts
(Asked After Each Paragraph Written):

Note: These are the prompts used for only one of the two classes studied. The format was the same for both sets of students; the specific discourse elements referred to were different for each class of students. References to specific discourse elements are in **bold type**.

1. What is the **basic critical question** you're asking in this essay? (function: clarifying)

2. How does this paragraph address the **basic critical question** you're asking in the essay? (function: clarifying)

3. How does this paragraph relate the paragraph just prior to it? (function: clarifying)

4. Without looking back at your paper, I'd like you to tell me in one sentence the main point or idea you wanted to communicate in what you've just written. (function: summarizing)

5. Looking back at what you've just written, how many **arguments** are you using to make that point? (function: clarifying)

6. Summarize each of the arguments. (function: summarizing)

(Students are then given a cue card with the following list plus their definitions, derived from classroom lessons on argumentation:

—**argument on the other side of the question**
—**response to the argument on the other side of the question**
—**reason**
—**repetition**

—definition
—examples: evidence, exposition
—making an assumption explicit
—take-my-word-for-it statement
—question
—objection
—other: e.g., conclusion

7. How have you developed each of the arguments you offer in the paragraph? (Students go sentence by sentence through the paragraph, analyzing the function of each sentence in terms of the list presented on the cue card.)

8. How convincing is this [referring to a specific] argument? (Students have an additional cue card with the criteria specified by the teacher.)

9. Have you been **objective** in this paragraph? (function: evaluation)

10. What questions do you have about the ideas you've included in this paragraph? (function: questioning)

11. What (unanswered) questions might your reader have when reading this paragraph? (function: questioning)

12. What might you revise? (function: evaluation)

13. What do you want to accomplish in the next section of your essay? (function: goal-setting)

14. How do you plan to do this? (function: planning)

(Students then resume writing until they signal that they've finished the next paragraph.)

APPENDIX B

Intervention Protocol Prompts
Used in Newell and Johnson's (1993) Study

Instructions to Students

Before we begin, I want to go over a few things about what we are going to do. We are interested in finding out how students write about literature and how they use ideas from class discussion in their writing. So I'm going to ask you some questions before, during, and at the end of your writing of an essay about the story. You are free to take notes, outline, or whatever you usually do before you write. You can use the story or notes from class in whatever ways you want. In any case, try to write the way you usually do without trying anything special for me. For this assignment, you just need a rough draft, so you don't have to worry about spelling or mechanics.

Pre-Composing Phase

1. Explain in your own words what the assignment is. Why do you think your teacher asked you to write on this topic?
2. What are some of the ideas that come to mind about this assignment that you might want to include in your paper?
3. What do you want to say about [the topic]?
4. How are you going to accomplish those things?

Composing Phase

5. Okay, now tell me what you have tried to say so far.
6. What other things are you going to say in your paper? (Without any intervention, let the student finish the essay.)

Post-Composing

7. Were there any new ideas about the story that came to mind as you were writing? Tell me about those.
8. Now that you are finished, what do you think of your essay?

REFERENCES

Applebee, A. N. (1986). Problems in process approaches: Toward a reconceptualization of process instruction. In A. R. Petrosky & D. Bartholomae (Eds.), *The teaching of writing* (85th yearbook). Chicago: National Society for the Study of Education.

Applebee, A. N., & Langer, J. A. (1983). Instructional scaffolding: Reading and writing as natural language activities. *Language Arts, 60,* 168-175.

Applebee, A. N., Langer, J. A., Jenkins, L. B., Mullis, I.V.S., & Foertsch, M. A. (1990). *Learning to write in our nation's schools: Instruction and achievement in 1988 at grades 4, 8, and 12.* Princeton, NJ: Educational Testing Service.

Bereiter, C. (1980). Development in writing. In L. W. Gregg & E. R. Steinberg (Eds.), *Cognitive processes in writing.* Hillsdale, NJ: Lawrence Erlbaum.

Bereiter, C., & Scardamalia, M. (1987). *The psychology of written composition.* Hillsdale, NJ: Lawrence Erlbaum.

Connors, R., & Glenn, C. (1992). *St. Martin's guide to teaching writing.* (2nd ed.). New York: St. Martin's Press.

Cooper, M., & Holzman, M. (1983). Talking about protocols. *College Composition and Communication, 34,* 284-293.

Dobrin, D. N. (1986). Protocols once more. *College English, 48,* 713-725.

Eden, R., & Mitchell, R. (1986). Paragraphing for the reader. *College Composition and Communication, 37,* 416-430, 441.

Emig, J. (1971). *The composing processes of twelfth graders* (NCTE Research Report No. 13). Urbana, IL: National Council of Teachers of English.

Ericsson, K. A., & Simon, H. A. (1980). Verbal reports as data. *Psychological Review, 87,* 215-251.

Flower, L. (1989). Cognition, context, and theory building. *College Composition and Communication, 40,* 282-311.

Flower, L., & Hayes, J. R. (1980). The cognition of discovery: Defining a rhetorical problem. *College Composition and Communication, 31,* 21-32.

Flower, L., & Hayes, J. R. (1981). A cognitive process theory of writing. *College Composition and Communication, 32,* 365-387.

Hairston, M. (1982). The winds of change: Thomas Kuhn and the revolution in the teaching of writing. *College Composition and Communication, 33,* 76-88.

Hayes, J. R., & Flower, L. (1980). Identifying the organization of writing processes. In L. W. Gregg & E. R. Steinberg (Eds.), *Cognitive processes in writing.* Hillsdale, NJ: Lawrence Erlbaum.

Hayes, J. R., & Flower, L. (1983). Uncovering cognitive processes in writing: An introduction to protocol analysis. In P. Mosenthal, L. Tamor, & S. A. Walmsley (Eds.), *Research on writing: Principles and methods.* New York: Longman.

Hillocks, G. (1975). *Observing and writing.* Urbana, IL: National Council of Teachers of English.

Hillocks, G. (1979). The effects of observational activity on student writing. *Research in the Teaching of English, 13,* 23-35.

Hillocks, G. (1986). *Research on written composition.* Urbana, IL: National Council of Teachers of English.

Kirby, D., & Liner, T. (1981). *Inside/Out: Developmental strategies for teaching writing.* Upper Montclair, NJ: Boynton/Cook.

Langer, J. A., & Applebee, A. N. (1987). *How writing shapes thinking: A Study of teaching and learning* (NCTE Research Report No. 22). Urbana, IL: National Council of Teachers of English.

Lindemann, E. (1986). *A rhetoric for writing teachers.* New York: Oxford University Press.

Newell, G., & Johnson, J. (1993). How discussion shapes general track students' reasoning and writing about literature. In G. Newell & R. Durst (Eds.), *Exploring texts: The role of discussion and writing in the teaching and learning of literature.* Norwood, MA: Christopher Gordon.

Palinscar, A. S., & Brown, A. L. (1984). Reciprocal teaching of comprehension-fostering and monitoring activities. *Cognition and Instruction, 1,* 117-175.

Perl, S. (1979). The composing processes of unskilled college writers. *Research in the Teaching of English, 13,* 317-336.

Scardamalia, M., & Bereiter, C. (1986a). Research on written composition. In M. C. Wittrock (Ed.), *Handbook of research on teaching*. New York: Macmillan.

Scardamalia, M., & Bereiter, C. (1986b). Writing. In R. F. Dillon & R. J. Sternberg (Eds.), *Cognition and instruction*. New York: Academic Press.

Scardamalia, M., Bereiter, C., Woodruff, E., Burtis, J., & Turkish, L. (1980). *The effects of modeling and cuing on high-level planning*. Unpublished manuscript, the Ontario Institute for Studies in Education.

Scardamalia, M., & Paris, P. (1985). The function of explicit discourse knowledge in the development of text representations and composing strategies. *Cognition and Instruction, 2*, 1-39.

Smagorinsky, P. (1989). The reliability and validity of protocol analysis. *Written Communication, 6*, 463-479.

Sommers, N. (1980). Revision strategies of student writers and experienced adult writers. *College Composition and Communication, 31*, 378-388.

Steinberg, E. R. (1986). Protocols, retrospective reports, and the stream of consciousness. *College English, 48*, 697-712.

Swanson-Owens, D. (1987, August). *Accessing and applying discourse structure knowledge: Process and instruction at the college level*. Proposal for dissertation written as partial fulfillment for doctoral degree at Stanford University.

Vygotsky, L. S. (1978). *Mind in society: The development of higher psychological processes*. Cambridge, MA: Harvard University Press.

Wertsch, J. V. (1991). *Voices of the mind: A sociocultural approach to mediated action*. Cambridge, MA: Harvard University Press.

7

Stimulated Recall in Research on Writing

An Antidote to "I Don't Know, It Was Fine"

ANNE DiPARDO

> The basic idea underlying the method of stimulated recall is that a subject may be enabled to relive an original situation with great vividness and accuracy if he is presented with a large number of the cues or stimuli which occurred during the original situation.
>
> *Benjamin Bloom* (1954, p. 25)

> The utterance proves to be a very complex and multiplanar phenomenon if considered not in isolation and with respect to its author (the speaker) only, but as a link in the chain of speech communication and with respect to other, related utterances.
>
> *M. M. Bakhtin* (1986, pp. 92-93)

Emerging from the knottier challenges of my dissertation research, my interest in stimulated recall has less to do with recondite musings on matters methodological than with the power of practical urgencies. Mine was an ethnographic examination of a basic writing adjunct program (DiPardo, 1991, 1993)—a program which served a striking concentration of its university's tiny but growing population of non-Anglo students, and which

AUTHOR'S NOTE: Thanks to Sarah Warshauer Freedman for helpful comments on an earlier draft of this chapter. This research was supported by a grant from the NCTE Research Foundation.

represented something of a pivotal link in the campus's efforts to increase its retention of such students.[1] The program provided those enrolled in basic writing courses with 3 supplemental instructional hours in "collaborative" tutorial groups led by upper-division and graduate English majors, time set aside for responding to emerging ideas and successive drafts. As described by administrators, it seemed an almost model effort, a generously funded attempt to help students master the demands of academic writing by providing opportunities to explore alternate points of view, to argue ideas, and to gauge the effects of their written work in the presence of a comparatively nonthreatening audience (cf. Bruffee, 1984; Cazden, 1988; Hawkins, 1980). Popularized by theorists invoking a social constructivist perspective on linguistic growth (see, for instance, Bruffee, 1978, 1984), such groups are often seen as an appealing and relatively cost-effective means of providing the needed "invitations" into the academic "conversation"—benefits which are far from automatic in any case, but perhaps especially where students present a varied range of cultural and linguistic backgrounds.

My attempt to understand the dynamics of this program was similarly informed by a conceptual frame emphasizing the social nature of linguistic growth. Having surveyed the collaborative learning literature at some length (reviewed in DiPardo & Freedman, 1988), I was left with the itchy sense that much remained to be learned about how the familiar Vygotskian rationale (e.g., Applebee & Langer, 1983, 1986; Bruner, 1978; Vygotsky, 1978, 1986) might be enacted in specific teaching-learning encounters. I'd come, that is, to a sense that "collaborative learning" was a rubric perched with precarious authority over a broadening array of programs and strategies, often obscuring more than it clarified (cf. Erickson, 1989). As I collected pilot data for my project, I became particularly interested in these students' and tutors' reciprocal processes of change: how, as both moved through a period of shifting identities and competing loyalties, they were providing mutual opportunities for integration and growth, for new understandings about the nature of literacy and learning (see Wertsch's [1991] discussion of Vygotsky and Bakhtin). At the same time, I became aware of how these instructional interactions were related to a troubled process of institutional transformation at nested system levels (Cazden, 1988; Erickson, 1986; Erickson, Florio, & Buschman, 1980)—not only within the writing program and the English department, but also across the campus at large, as administrators and faculty struggled to translate the new "educational equity" mission into effective support programs and services. Over time, I came to regard the frictions between these equity students and their tutors as a microcosm of a troubled and somewhat unpredictable process of institutional change, to understand their unresolved conflicts as clues to the many complexities attending the campus's emerging diversity. Good intentions were everywhere apparent, such as in a recent policy announcement proclaiming a strong commitment to "providing quality education to students who are from groups historically underrepresented in higher education," and to "meeting and addressing the needs of these students." But meanwhile, such hopeful rhetoric was undercut at the levels of campus and program alike by a host of unresolved dilemmas, particularly apparent in the conversations of these tutors and students as they together confronted the social and cultural issues attending linguistic entry into the academy. As I thought further about the design of my study, I realized that I could not consider these specific encounters without also considering the multiple levels of meaning in which they were entangled—layers of context that shaped the themes and issues that prevailed in these small-group interactions, and, to some extent, were shaped by them.

DESIGNING THE STUDY:
INITIAL CONSIDERATIONS

As I began to design the study, I thought about ways I might examine the relationship between the small-group sessions and these larger patterns of meaning (Erickson et al., 1980); that is, I wanted to look closely at particular small-group interactions, but I also wanted to consider their institutional and socialcultural matrices. My intention was to construct an ethnographic portrait of clarity and depth by weighing and comparing the perspectives of various informants (Denzin, 1970; Erickson, 1986; Goetz & LeCompte, 1984). As Lincoln and Guba (1985, p. 295) maintain, reality is composed of "a multiple set of mental constructions," as various individuals interpret a given set of phenomena from different vantage points, sometimes employing similar terminology informed by widely differing assumptions. I wanted to compare these constructions across the several levels I was investigating, considering policymakers' intentions, program administrators' translation, tutors' implementation, and students' responses. My primary aim was to approach these small-group interactions as key events, as interactions that might shed new light on the complexities of formulating adequate programmatic responses to linguistic and cultural diversity.

In order to chart the relationships among these small-group interactions and the layers of institutional context in which they were embedded, I interviewed a number of administrators at the levels of the campus and the writing program, and also selected two tutors and four equity students for case study. In addition to audiotaping all their small-group interactions over a full semester, I completed beginning- and end-of-term interviews with each, in which I explored their perceptions of the small-group interactions, their educational and vocational goals, and their perspectives on the campus's emerging diversity. For further background, I collected photocopies of all drafts of each focal student's writing assignments, as well as students' journals and tutors' logs; I also audiotaped all tutorial staff meetings, and attended the regular basic writing class on a weekly basis.

In the end, I hoped to construct a dynamic, multidimensional portrait of program and policy, a portrait whose internal validity would be supported by triangulation with varied data sources and by close study of a number of key informants over a period of several months (Doheny-Farina & Odell, 1985; Goetz & LeCompte, 1984; Lincoln & Guba, 1985; Merriam, 1988). In terms of external validity, I aimed no farther than what has been called "user" or "reader" generalizability (Merriam, 1988; Walker, 1980)—that is, to provide others an opportunity to "generalize personally to their own situations" (McCutcheon, 1981), to use these "images of the possible" (Shuman, 1986, p. 146) as an impetus to reflect upon their own contexts, to discover fresh directions of inquiry and discussion (see also Connelly, 1978; Connelly & Clandinin, 1990; Guba & Lincoln, 1989; Peshkin, 1985).

THE BEST-LAID PLANS:
A TROUBLED START

Early on, I found that the administrators, teachers, and tutors who participated in my study were generally expansive and generous in their replies to my questions, readily relaxing into extended responses. The students, on the other hand, presented a more formidable interviewing challenge. Although they often spoke eagerly about their backgrounds and general responses to life at this predominantly Anglo campus, my questions about their composing and the role of the tutorial groups were typically met with downcast eyes and terse, mumbled replies. "I don't know," read line after line of my early transcripts, "the class is fine, the group's fine, I guess." Despite careful planning, it began to seem that my depiction of the program would be long on teachers' and administrators' perspectives, but relatively bereft of students' own descriptions of their approaches to writing and responses to the tutorial groups.

While I had anticipated some reluctance on the part of the students, only after those initial interviews did I more fully grasp its nature and extent. These students were, after all, linguistic and cultural minorities struggling for academic as well as social footholds in this alien new environment. Many were embarrassed about being placed in a two-semester basic writing course, self-conscious about their grapplings with academic discourse, and less than eager to discuss these matters with an Anglo researcher who was, at least initially, a relative stranger. Further, even where they were willing to answer my questions, they often seemed stymied by a lack of experience in analyzing their own composing processes or instructional interactions; in many instances, even the least reluctant had little to say beyond the fact that they didn't feel they could write very well, and that although the tutors seemed to be trying their best, no miracles loomed imminent. Probing helped a bit, but I still came away from initial interviews with the sense that students' perceptions remained only half-articulated and, in many cases, half-conscious. Cultural and linguistic issues quite likely informed a good part of this reluctance: Several students, for instance, apologized for their lack of ease with spoken English (one in particular, a quiet, young Navajo woman, seemed to feel especially overwhelmed by my many requests for spoken information).

Happily, my final interviews with students would prove to be a much different matter—spilling over time limits, full of freewheeling and candid conversation. Time and the opportunity to get better acquainted were of course part of the story, but I also credit my decision to employ a form of stimulated recall in end-of-term interviews; that is, to play back audiotapes of particular sessions, asking students and tutors to interpret and comment. Though the strategy played a key role in eliciting more detailed reflections, it was far from a panacea. Indeed, as discussed in the following section, the usefulness of stimulated recall emerged as part and parcel of its incorporation into a larger pattern of inquiry, a process at once practical and conceptual, alternately commonsensical and vexing.

EMPLOYING STIMULATED RECALL: SOME METHODOLOGICAL CONCERNS

Prior Uses of Stimulated Recall in Research on Writing

Writing researchers' adaptations of stimulated recall have drawn from its earlier uses in other disciplines and in other areas of education. Researchers in psychology, (e.g., Fanshel & Moss, 1971; Kagan, Krathwohol, & Miller, 1963) and linguistics (e.g., Gumperz, 1976), for instance, have used stimulated recall to elicit participants' retrospective impressions of audiotaped social interactions or verbal performances. In a seminal study of students' thinking during classroom discussions, Benjamin Bloom (1954) played back audio recordings of just-completed sessions, asking students to reconstruct what they were thinking (see also Gaier, 1954). Studies of teaching effectiveness have used variations of Bloom's strategy as a means of accessing teachers' cognitive processes without interrupting instructional events (for discussions of this research, see Clark & Peterson, 1986; Shavelson, Webb, & Burstein, 1986; Shulman, 1986). Working from a markedly different paradigm, educational anthropologists have employed stimulated recall in ethnographic studies of classroom interactions, playing back videotapes deemed key or representative in order to elicit a more detailed sense of the informants' own perspectives (see, e.g., Erickson & Mohatt, 1988).

The use of stimulated recall in writing research has been largely confined to examinations of students' cognitive processes as they compose, the most frequently cited example being Mike Rose's studies of writer's block (1980, 1981, 1984). Building upon Bloom's work (1954), Rose videotaped university-level students as they wrote, one camera focusing upon the emerging text, the other upon the student; Rose then reviewed both tapes with the research subjects, stopping periodically to ask about their thought processes (a split screen allowed them to observe themselves composing on one side of the video display, their written productions on the other). Although Rose allows that the presence of a camera introduced an unnatural element, he contends that stimulated recall is less intrusive than think-aloud protocols, tending to produce more detailed and accurate portraits of writers' processes than do ordinary post hoc interviews. In Rose's more recent research with Glynda Hull (e.g., Hull & Rose, 1989, 1990a, 1990b; Hull, Rose, Fraser, & Castellano, 1991), a similar procedure was employed, this time in combination with a range of data sources (conventional interviews, writing samples, observations of classroom and conference interactions, and so on) that allowed further insight into student writers' products, processes, and developmental histories.

Stimulated recall is, then, less a unified approach than a flexible tool that has been adapted to widely varied agendas, and attended by a number of specific methodological choices. According to Clark and Peterson (1986), these include replaying only segments selected by the researcher as opposed to replaying whole tapes, posing specific questions as opposed to more open-ended invitations to comment, and retaining sole control of when to stop the tape as opposed to asking informants to share in this responsibility.

Integrating Stimulated Recall Into My Study

As I incorporated stimulated recall into my study, I needed to ensure that my particular methodological choices were appropriate to my theoretic foundation and lines of inquiry. In contrast to studies employing stimulated recall to probe students' solitary composing processes (e.g., Rose, 1980, 1981, 1984), my goal was to assess the webbing of social, affective, and linguistic issues in students' and tutors' talk about writing (Dyson & Freedman, 1991)—that is, how the small-group conversations related to students' struggles to adjust to life at this predominantly Anglo, middle-class campus, and how tutors' efforts to provide meaningful support related to larger patterns of institutional uncertainty. Of the studies I've mentioned, my goals and approaches most closely resembled those of Hull and Rose, whose focus extends beyond isolated literacy performances to the social and historical contexts that shape them (see Hull & Rose, 1989, 1990a, 1990b; Hull et al., 1991; the importance of addressing social context is also addressed by Rose, 1985). Just as my goals and purposes departed from studies of students' cognitive processes during composing, so too did my use of stimulated recall, which came to be integrated into my ethnographic approach and social-cognitive conceptual frame.[2]

The first step was selecting audiotaped episodes[3] for playing back to students and tutors in final interviews, a task that became enmeshed in a larger process of sifting repeatedly through the total data set in search of salient themes and issues, looking for counter-examples as a final check on the stability of the pattern (Bogdan & Biklen, 1982; Erickson, 1986; Spradley, 1980). Once I was satisfied that I had identified a set of themes and issues that effectively characterized the data as a whole, I combed through again to collect all talk related to each of these. I then reviewed the data I'd collected around each issue or theme, selecting interactions or talk that seemed representative or key, passages that seemed promising candidates for my final write-up. Finally, I pulled out small-group interactions from each of these stacks of sorted data, selecting episodes to play back in final interviews with students and tutors. In some instances these emerged as pivotal occurrences, moments where a long-simmering uneasiness became suddenly palpable, for example, or where a student was able to break through habitual hesitancy to assume a more assertive stance. In other cases, I selected an audiotaped interaction because it was highly typical of the way a particular tutor and student worked together; where possible in such instances, I also included an atypical session, this in the interest of moving tutors and students beyond easy generalities. Because I wished to limit each of the final interviews to 90 minutes and had substantial ground to cover (I additionally asked all the same questions I'd included in initial interviews), I selected three audiotaped segments per student, keeping total playback time in each interview to around 15 minutes.

When it came time to review the segments with students, I briefly reminded them of the context of each interaction (the nature of the assignment on which they were working, the point in the composing process at which a given encounter had occurred, and so on), and explained that they could stop the tape at any time if they had questions or comments. So that they might spontaneously review the sessions during our subsequent discussions, I also provided a written transcript of each episode. I then played back each tape, hitting the pause button only if the informants wished to interject a remark, and stopping after each segment to ask for their response. In order to avoid leading my informants, I framed these requests in very open-ended terms ("Comments?"; "What do you have to say about this?"; "What's your sense of what was going on here?"); for the most part, replies to such prompts were fluent and detailed, rendering unnecessary much additional probing. Each stimulated recall interview was audiotaped, fully transcribed, and analyzed in the same manner as my earlier data (i.e., I matched the themes and issues that were taken up in these interviews with those I'd identified earlier across the total data set).

While the interactions I played back to students had occurred weeks earlier, researchers focusing upon cognitive processes have cautioned that stimulated recall is an effective strategy only if the briefest possible time elapses between the actual event and its review, preferably a span counted in hours rather than days. (Bloom [1954, pp. 25-26], for instance, observed that subjects were 95% accurate in recalling events within 2 days of their occurrence, a figure that dropped within 2 weeks, in concert with "the usual memory curve decline," to 65%.) Again, given the rather different goals of my own study, a revised approach seemed warranted; that is, since I was more interested in inviting informants to construct a narrative of their semester-long relationships, retrospective impressions proved more valuable than immediate ones. In our informal conversations immediately following a number of the small-group sessions, I noted a tendency among students and tutors alike to simply review or summarize what had taken place; the richness of our end-of-term interviews, on the other hand, suggested that they could often see patterns and themes more clearly in hindsight than while immersed in the dynamics of the moment. While the longer lapse may indeed have diminished the "vividness and accuracy" with which informants recalled the specifics of particular encounters (Bloom, 1954, p. 25), it had the compensatory strength of providing an opportunity to locate these occurrences within a larger sequence of events.

Arguing the need for "multiple and converging" approaches to writing research, Rose (1985, p. 250) maintains that while methods must be compatible with a study's assumptions and goals, a given strategy's original uses are not always the best guide to its potential and flexibility. Methods, writes Rose, "are not necessarily limited to the constraints of their origins and can be adopted and even revamped to serve other problems built on models of human beings and definitions of knowledge different from those that gave birth to such methods" (p. 251). Though better known for its uses in more cognitively oriented research, stimulated recall proved a fortunate addition as I tailored it to my own examination of the social and cultural backdrop of college writing.

Getting Down to Cases: Sylvia

While stimulated recall certainly strengthened my interviews with tutors, it was particularly essential to my end-of-term interviews with the four equity students. By way of illustration, I focus here upon one: Sylvia, an 18-year-old Mexican-American whose family had emigrated to a prosperous West Coast farming community while she was still an infant.[4]

Struggles With Writing

Sylvia was a star mathematics student whose academic self-confidence had been badly jostled by her ongoing struggles with writing, the origins of which she traced to a pivotal moment in her early education. Spanish had been the only language spoken in Sylvia's home, and when she began kindergarten, she was placed in a bilingual program designed to accommodate her community's growing Hispanic population. Sylvia remembered her 2.5 years in the bilingual program as happy and productive, a time of moving without notable dissonance between the worlds of home and school. Then, in the middle of Sylvia's second-grade year, she was abruptly switched into an English immersion classroom, an experience she described as traumatic, disruptive, and scarring. As Sylvia began speaking only English in her new classroom, she lost the ability to communicate with friends and family in her native language. Periodic visits to relatives back in Mexico restored Sylvia's ability to speak Spanish, but even as a young adult, she remained reluctant to converse in her native language with anyone outside her immediate circle of family and close friends. While Sylvia's tutor and teacher assumed all semester that English was her first language, she continued to believe that she spoke both her first and second languages with a foreigner's accent: "It's like I have two cultures in me," she explained, "but I can't choose."

Sylvia was particularly ashamed of her Spanish-language writing, insisting that she was a far better writer in English. Even so, she was embarrassed by her reliance on the five-paragraph formula she'd first picked up in a high school writing workshop for Hispanic students (such formats allow you to "say only so much . . . and you can also leave out a lot," she observed). In an initial interview, Sylvia spoke of her desire to take more chances in her writing and to develop her ideas in fresh ways. But Sylvia's optimism was cautious, informed by a lingering sense that she was simply not a born writer: "It's just a block that I have within myself," she observed with a shrug.

Sylvia's Response to the Tutorials: Initial Impressions

Wishing to work on both her writing and on her reluctance to share it with others, Sylvia had initially welcomed the opportunity to meet regularly with a small tutorial group led by Morgan, an upper-division English major. By midterm, however, Sylvia had fallen into old patterns, attending sporadically and rarely bringing in rough drafts. Though she remained an occasionally spirited participant in group discussions, Sylvia maintained a careful distance when the focus turned to student writing, especially her own. "You're giving me that bored look," Morgan commented somewhat wearily during one of their later sessions. As had frequently become the case in such moments, Sylvia stared back impassively, refusing to yield.

"Tutors should have patience with the students," Sylvia told me in an early interview—unlike the many teachers she had known who "give up on the student, and say 'well, they're not going to do it, or they don't want to do it,' and say 'okay, next. Pick a number, say next.' " But if Sylvia was hoping for insightful understanding, she was also more than ready to assume primary responsibility for her own motivation and learning. In an end-of-term interview, she admitted that her progress toward the goals she had set for herself was not what she had been "looking forward to, or hoping." Quite characteristically, Sylvia was quick to assume full blame: "But that's only because of myself, because I brought it upon myself," she said. When I asked why her attendance at the tutorial hour had become rather spotty late in the term, she assumed a similar burden of responsibility:

I just lost interest in the tutoring. To me, my personal opinion, I wasn't taking advantage of it so I wasn't getting the help, and I was blaming everybody else, I was blaming other people, but I just said, "look at yourself, blame it on yourself." Because I wasn't taking advantage of it, when I should have.

Intrigued by the contrast between Sylvia's initial enthusiasm for the tutorials and this end-of-term malaise, I kept nudging her to say more. I tried rephrasing a question I'd already asked: Could the tutor have done anything differently, was there some way the sessions might have been made more beneficial to her? "I just lost interest," Sylvia said again, "and I didn't have my priorities set, because I would schedule something else at that time." She described her relationship with Morgan as "pretty good"; but in the next breath, she hinted at more negative perceptions, observing that Morgan lacked "that personal touch." When I asked for examples, Sylvia again answered by assuming "blame" for the tutorial dynamics: "When we started the semester, I was looking forward to tutoring," she explained, "but ever since I got the flu in the beginning of the semester, I've just been off in my own little world and doing it on my own."

But Sylvia was ill for only a few days, and the tutorials had taken place over a full semester. As I listened to the audiotapes of Sylvia's tutorial group, I sensed a more complicated story, one in which harmony and dissonance were held in a delicate tension, in which the conversation swung between moments of shared understanding and understated conflict. It was a tension I was waiting to hear about from Sylvia, who dropped hints about being less than fully satisfied with the tutorials, but greeted my every probe with renewed insistence that she was somehow to "blame."

Digging Deeper:
Employing Stimulated Recall

The stimulated recall segment of my final interview with Sylvia stood in marked contrast to these more traditional question-and-response episodes.

As I played back three moments from her tutorial sessions, Sylvia became both fascinated and reflective, repeatedly reconsidering and qualifying the generalities of her earlier replies, engaging in far more detailed analysis. As I switched off the tape player after each segment, I suddenly found I didn't need to say much to get Sylvia talking.

The first tape I played was from a rather upbeat session early in the semester in which Sylvia, her tutor, and a small group of classmates brainstormed "narrative" papers. Several had elected to write on their experiences as ethnic minorities at the campus, which had long mirrored the Anglo, middle-class demographics of its surrounding community. An African-American who had grown up in this community, Morgan talked at length about her own troubled response when fellow African-Americans regarded her as "not black enough." Although the session was not particularly focused upon students' writing—indeed, much of it was devoted to swapping stories, laughing, and offering mutual support—most seemed to be finding the hour engaging and meaningful. Sylvia was particularly vocal that morning, chatting with the group about the ways in which she, too, was sometimes misperceived: as a "rich girl," because she hadn't qualified for financial aid, or as a "coconut" who was often told "you don't act Mexican."

After listening to the tape, Sylvia allowed that she and Morgan held something important in common:

> We're in the same boat. . . . Because when her friends tell her, "you don't act black," to me, what is "acting black"? . . . And when they tell me "you're not Mexican," what is that? Just because I can't eat hot, spicy stuff, or I can't speak Spanish properly, or whatever?

Sylvia recalled that the session had helped her generate ideas she later explored in an essay. The episode seemed to underscore the more positive aspects of her relationship with her tutor: the session "helped out," Sylvia observed, "it really did."

The next tape I played was of a somewhat different tenor, as Morgan struggled to help Sylvia shape ideas for a "descriptive" writing assignment. When Sylvia announced her intention to write about her mother, a briskly business-like Morgan began pressing for details:

MORGAN: Your mother? Okay, are you like thinking of any characteristics you want to throw out, that you want to talk about? How would you approach writing about this person?

SYLVIA: (pause) Uh, I don't know (laughs).

MORGAN: You're a college student, you should know, that's why you're here. Any possible approaches?

SYLVIA: Just the way she has influenced me in my life.

MORGAN: What ways has she influenced you—positive, negative? Let's start from there.

Morgan continued to ask such questions for several moments longer, encouraging Sylvia to "make notes," to "start, you know, getting that together," and cautioning her not to make the essay "*too* personal." Sylvia revealed nothing here of the deeply emotional essay she would later write about her mother's battle with cancer, nor would she share this decidedly personal essay with her tutorial group on the day set aside for responding to drafts.

After listening to this tape, Sylvia reflected for a long while on her admiration for her mother, acknowledging that she hadn't felt "ready" to reveal these thoughts and feelings to her group. Sylvia was more pointedly critical in reacting to Morgan's comment that she "should know":

> I didn't like that comment! I mean, just because you're a college student, and because you're here, doesn't mean you know everything. She just threw me off on that one, like a curve ball there, you know. It didn't affect me, it's just that I know I'm a college student, and I know I don't know everything, but what I do know, I can say something about it, whatever. I don't know what she meant, to tell you the truth.

While Sylvia allowed that she sometimes benefited from Morgan's insistent questions, in this segment she detected evidence that her tutor had "lost interest": "I think she had high expectations of all of us in the beginning," Sylvia noted, "but then when she got to know us, I guess through our writing and through our discussions, I don't think she had high expectations [anymore]."

But even late in the semester, Sylvia's interactions with Morgan had been punctuated by moments of warm rapport, generally as the conversation returned to issues of ethnicity. The final tape I played was of a portion of one of their last sessions, in which the group brainstormed essays about "stereotyping." When Morgan asked who wanted to go first, Sylvia eagerly volunteered. "When I go back to Mexico," she explained to the group,

> I'm being stereotyped as a rich bitch. . . . Because, like, when I go into the smaller villages, they say oh, you're from the north, *el Norte,* which means

United States. . . . They just say, because you live in the United States you must be rich, and you don't work, or stuff like that. You know, you don't have a hard life . . . because my family that live in the villages do have a hard life.

Morgan responded by musing that she would have a comparably hard time if she were to visit Africa: "Well man, what the hell . . . If I go to Africa, I will be so torn. That's not who I am . . . people over there would just, you know, shun me."

Sylvia listened to this tape with a widening smile. In terms of a certain ethnic ambivalence, Sylvia observed, she and Morgan were "in the same boat." "I'm getting her input, and I'm getting her viewpoint," she acknowledged; "I mean, she has more experience than I do, and I can learn from her." Though visibly annoyed just moments earlier, Sylvia was once again focused on the more positive aspect of her relationship with Morgan. "Sometimes I really feel torn between the two cultures," she noted a few moments later, adding that "I'm glad Morgan can relate to this sometimes with me."

When I played these same three tapes for Morgan, she voiced strong identification with Sylvia's ethnic uncertainty, and equally strong impatience with Sylvia's tendency to pull back from discussing her actual writing: Sylvia had "really complex ideas in our discussions," Morgan observed, but "her writing is simple in a lot of ways. . . . It bothers her that she doesn't have it down the first time." But while Morgan had already spoken freely about these perceptions, Sylvia had offered little more than vague generalities in response to my many questions. Had Sylvia not reacted to the three tapes, her voice in my final account would have been limited to pronouncements that her relationship with Morgan had been "pretty good," and that she herself was to "blame" for moments when the connection faltered. I had gathered that Sylvia held mixed feelings about Morgan, but without Sylvia's own words—and without an opportunity to compare these to Morgan's responses to particular episodes—I would have been far more alone with the burden of interpretation. Especially in the stimulated-recall segment of my final interview with Sylvia, I gathered perceptions that would allow me to weave a more richly triangulated, multiplistic tale.

CONCLUSION

Those of us who study writing instruction are accustomed to a given phrase—"teaching the writing process," fostering "collaborative learning," and so on—meaning quite different things to different people. So too is the case with stimulated recall, a strategy that gathers power as it is shaped by a larger pattern of purposes and goals, and, in the case of my study, where it takes its place among an array of methods for learning about the densely tangled social, linguistic, and cognitive dimensions of students' composing processes. In the end, my study came to challenge hierarchical thinking about programs and policies, depicting research participants and institution caught in a mutual and inexorable process of change, and making a case for attending more carefully to the kinds of lessons equity students have to teach us about their needs and backgrounds. In other words, the power of my study came to rest in large part with students' voices—voices encouraged toward detailed and often revealing responses at least in part by my adaptation of a form of stimulated recall.

Though my research departed in rather marked ways from more cognitively oriented studies employing stimulated recall, I found my variation of the method helpful for the same general reason: because it encouraged all the tutors and students to address the specifics of their interactions, challenging them to move beyond bland generalities or polite reluctance. Since many of the segments I chose for playback were charged with both intellectual and emotional meanings, my respondents became immediately engaged, fascinated by the sound of their own half-forgotten words, locating these slices of time within a semester-long sweep of events that suddenly took on new interest and importance. Their reflections allowed me to make many telling comparisons between a given informant's beginning- and end-of-term perceptions, and, particularly, between a student's and a tutor's often markedly different perceptions of a single event.

There were, however, a number of issues to confront in my adaptation of the method. In selecting sessions that seemed pivotal or key, for instance, I made interpretive judgments, focusing informants' attention and discussion upon isolated episodes; I chose carefully, knowing that an ill-advised selection could result in an unenlightening portrait of events, but I always chose without absolute certainty that my selections would prove optimally worthwhile in eliciting reflections upon the themes and tensions that had emerged as salient across my months of data collection. My decision to limit the stimulated-recall component of each interview to 15 minutes further emphasized the need to select tape segments with considerable care.

Regarding the nature of educational phenomena as both multifaceted and shifting, qualitative researchers generally seek to capture various perspectives upon key events rather than quintessential "truths" about these events (Bogdan & Biklen, 1982; Erickson, 1986; Peshkin, 1985). Since, as Heath (1983, p. 9) points out, "the ethnographic present never remains as it is described," replicability has typically been seen as an inappropriate standard against which to measure the value of such studies (Connelly & Clandinin, 1990; Guba & Lincoln, 1989; Merriam, 1988; Van Maanen, 1988). In terms of *internal* reliability, however, a benefit remains in securing some sort of check on the consistency of the researcher's interpretive judgments, what Goetz and LeCompte (1984, p. 218) usefully term "inter-observer" reliability. Here, too, my study was plagued by potential pitfalls, since, as is so often the case in ethnographic work, I was a lone investigator; though I was assisted by helpful feedback and advice along the way, no one was as familiar with my unreduced transcripts as I was, and no one was truly in a position to say whether they agreed or disagreed with the logic I employed in selecting these tapes for playback. There was no easy way to resolve this problem within the context of my study; it becomes, rather, a rationale for collaborative research, wherein checks on interpretations and decisions can become both integral and ongoing.

From an ethical perspective, I also worried a bit about reminding research participants of interactions they'd perhaps rather forget, such as potentially embarrassing moments of open discord or awkward struggle. Though I'd repeatedly informed the tutors and students that they had every right to decline to answer any of my questions, I sometimes wondered if the use of stimulated recall made it harder for them to do so. Confronted with an audiotaped record of a troublesome interaction, they were sometimes possessed by a sudden urge to talk at length about thorny issues they had previously avoided. That, of course, is a prime reason for including stimulated recall in a study such as mine, but also cause for attention to the ethical danger of moving informants toward a momentary openness they may later regret.

While it would be an exaggeration to say that stimulated recall alone accounted for the emerging candor of my informants—I did have an opportunity, after all, to get to know them and gradually gain their trust—I found the method to be an exceptionally valuable addition to my overall research design. Integrated into a larger fabric of inquiry, it became a key tool in revealing some of the stubborn tensions that have a way of humming beneath surfaces—and, more substantially, of quietly complicating efforts to provide nurturing instructional environments to all.

NOTES

1. In subsequent references I'll use the term *equity student*—the designation by system-wide administrators who frequently pointed out that groups traditionally termed

minorities would soon comprise a majority of the state's population. Lacking a more accurately descriptive and politically neutral term, I use the term *Anglo* to designate non-Hispanic whites.

2. While my conceptual frame and research questions strongly suggested purely qualitative strategies, certainly a mixture of qualitative and quantitative methods is both possible and desirable under other circumstances (for a discussion of the relationship between qualitative and quantitative approaches, see Smith, 1983, and Hillocks, this volume).

3. Video would no doubt have further enhanced these stimulated-recall sessions, providing opportunity to review the language of posture, gesture, and facial expression as well as spoken words. Unfortunately, since the groups met at various locations as the whim of the moment dictated, videotaping was a logistical impossibility.

4. For detailed accounts of all four case-study students and their tutors, see DiPardo (1993).

REFERENCES

Applebee, A., & Langer, J. (1983). Instructional scaffolding: Reading and writing as natural language activities. *Language Arts, 60,* 168-175.

Applebee, A., & Langer, J. (1986). Reading and writing instruction: Toward a theory of teaching and learning. In E. Z. Rothkopf (Ed.), *Review of research in education* (Vol. 13). Washington, DC: AERA.

Bakhtin, M. M. (1986). *Speech genres and other late essays* (C. Emerson & M. Holquist, Eds.; V. W. McGee, Trans.). Austin: University of Texas Press.

Bloom, B. S. (1954). The thought process of students in discussion. In S. J. French (Ed.), *Accent on teaching: Experiments in general education.* New York: Harper.

Bogdan, R. C., & Biklen, S. K. (1982). *Qualitative research for education: An introduction to theory and methods.* Boston: Allyn & Bacon.

Bruffee, K. (1978). The Brooklyn plan: Attaining intellectual growth through peer-group tutoring. *Liberal Education, 64,* 447-468.

Bruffee, K. (1984). Peer tutoring and the "conversation of mankind." *College English, 46,* 635-652.

Bruner, J. (1978). The role of dialogue in language acquisition. In A. Sinclair (Ed.), *The child's conception of language.* New York: Springer-Verlag.

Cazden, C. (1988). *Classroom discourse: The language of teaching and learning.* Portsmouth, NH: Heinemann.

Clark, C. M., & Peterson, P. L. (1986). Teachers' thought processes. In M. Wittrock (Ed.), *Handbook of research on teaching* (3rd ed., pp. 255-296). New York: Macmillan.

Connelly, F. M. (1978). How shall we publish case studies of curriculum development? *Curriculum Inquiry, 8,* 78-82.

Connelly, F. M., & Clandinin, D. J. (1990). Stories of experience and narrative inquiry. *Educational Researcher, 19,* 2-14.

Denzin, N. K. (1970). *The research act: A theoretical introduction to sociological methods.* New York: McGraw-Hill.

DiPardo, A. (1991). *Acquiring "a kind of passport": The teaching and learning of academic discourse in basic writing tutorials.* Ann Arbor, MI: Dissertation Abstracts International.

DiPardo, A. (1993). *"A kind of passport": A basic writing adjunct program and the challenge of student diversity.* Urbana, IL: National Council of Teachers of English.

DiPardo, A., & Freedman, S. W. (1988). Peer response groups in the writing classroom: Theoretic foundations and new directions. *Review of Educational Research, 58,* 119-149.

Doheny-Farina, S., & Odell, L. (1985). Ethnographic research on writing: Assumptions and methodology. In L. Odell & D. Goswami (Eds.), *Writing in nonacademic settings.* New York: Guilford Press.

Dyson, A., & Freedman, S. W. (1991). On teaching writing: A review of the literature. In J. Jensen, J. Flood, D. Lapp, & J. R. Squire, (Eds.), *Handbook of research on teaching the English language arts.* New York: MacMillan. (First published as an occasional paper by the Center for the Study of Writing and Literacy at UC Berkeley and Carnegie-Mellon)

Erickson, F. (1986). Qualitative methods in research on teaching. In M. C. Wittrock (Ed.), *Handbook of research on teaching* (3rd ed.). New York: Macmillan.

Erickson, F. (1989). Learning and collaboration in teaching. *Language Arts, 66,* 430-441.

Erickson, F., Florio, S., & Buschman, J. (1980). *Fieldwork in educational research* (Occasional Paper No. 36). East Lansing: Michigan State University, Institute for Research on Teaching.

Erickson, F., & Mohatt, G. (1988). Cultural organization of participation structures in two classrooms of Indian students. In G. Spindler (Ed.), *Doing the ethnography of schooling.* Prospect Heights, IL: Waveland Press.

Fanshel, D., & Moss, F. (1971). *Playback: A marriage in jeopardy examined.* New York: Columbia University Press.

Gaier, E. L. (1954). A study of memory under conditions of stimulated recall. *Journal of General Psychology, 50,* 147-153.

Goetz, J. P., & LeCompte, M. D. (1984). *Ethnography and qualitative design in educational research.* Orlando, FL: Academic Press.

Guba, E. G., & Lincoln, Y. S. (1989). *Personal communication.* Newbury Park, CA: Sage.

Gumperz, J. (1976). *The sociolinguistic significance of conversational code-switching* (Working Paper No. 46). Berkeley, CA: Language Behavior Research Laboratory.

Hawkins, T. (1980). Intimacy and audience: The relationship between revision and the social dimension of peer tutoring. *College English, 42,* 64-68.

Heath, S. B. (1983). *Ways with words: Language, life, and work in communities and class-rooms.* Cambridge, UK: Cambridge University Press.

Hull, G., & Rose, M. (1989). Rethinking remediation: Toward a social-cognitive understanding of problematic reading and writing. *Written Communication, 6,* 139-154.

Hull, G., & Rose, M. (1990a). Toward a social-cognitive understanding of problematic reading and writing. In A. Lunsford, H. Moglen, & J. Slevin (Eds.), *The right to literacy.* New York: MLA.

Hull, G., & Rose, M. (1990b). This wooden shack: The logic of an unconventional reading. *College Composition and Communication, 41,* 287-298.

Hull, G., Rose, M., Fraser, K. L., & Castellano, M. (1991). Remediation as social construct: Perspectives from an analysis of classroom discourse. *College Composition and Communication, 42,* 299-329.

Kagan, N., Krathwohol, D. R., & Miller, R. (1963). Stimulated recall in therapy using video tape—A case study. *Journal of Counseling Psychology, 10,* 237-243.

Lincoln, Y. S., & Guba, E. G. (1985). *Naturalistic inquiry.* Beverly Hills, CA: Sage.

McCutcheon, G. (1981). On the interpretation of classroom observations. *Educational Researcher, 10,* 5-10.

Merriam, S. B. (1988). *Case study research in education: A qualitative approach.* San Francisco: Jossey-Bass.

Peshkin, A. (1985). Virtuous subjectivity: In the participant-observer's eyes. In D. Berg & K. Smith (Eds.), *Exploring clinical methods for social research.* Beverly Hills, CA: Sage.

Rose, M. (1980). Rigid rules, inflexible plans, and the stifling of language: A cognitivist analysis of writer's block. *College Composition and Communication, 31,* 389-401.

Rose, M. (1981). *The cognitive dimension of writer's block: An examination of university students.* Unpublished doctoral dissertation, University of California at Los Angeles.

Rose, M. (1984). *Writer's block: The cognitive dimension.* Carbondale: Southern Illinois University Press.

Rose, M. (1985). Complexity, rigor, evolving method, and the puzzle of writer's block: Thoughts on composing-process research. In M. Rose (Ed.), *When a writer can't write.* New York: Guilford Press.

Shavelson, R. J., Webb, N. M., & Burstein, L. (1986). Measurement of teaching. In M. Wittrock (Ed.), *Handbook of research on teaching* (3rd ed., pp. 50-91). New York: Macmillan.

Shulman, J. (1986). Paradigms and research programs in the study of teaching: A contemporary perspective. In M. Wittrock (Ed.), *Handbook of research on teaching* (3rd ed., pp. 3-36). New York: Macmillan.

Shuman, A. (1986). *Storytelling rights: The uses of oral and written texts by urban adolescents.* New York: Cambridge University Press.

Smith, J. K. (1983). Quantitative versus qualitative research: An attempt to clarify the issue. *Educational Researcher, 12*(3), 6-13.

Spradley, J. P. (1980). *Participant observation.* New York: Holt, Rinehart & Winston.

Van Maanen, J. (1988). *Tales of the field: On writing ethnography.* Chicago: University of Chicago Press.

Vygotsky, L. (1978). *Mind in society.* Cambridge, MA: Harvard University Press.

Vygotsky, L. (1986). *Thought and language.* Cambridge: MIT Press.

Walker, R. (1980). The conduct of educational case studies: Ethics, theory and procedures. In W. B. Dockerell & D. Hamilton (Eds.), *Rethinking educational research.* London: Hodder & Stoughton.

Wertsch, J. (1991). *Voices of the mind: A sociocultural approach to mediated action.* Cambridge, MA: Harvard University Press.

Part III
Analysis of
Collaborative Discourse

8

Interpreting and Counting
Objectivity in Discourse Analysis

GEORGE HILLOCKS, JR.

In 1915 cartoonist W. E. Hill published "My Wife and My Mother-in-Law" in *Puck*. When one looks at the picture, one sees either an old woman or a young girl. After we view the picture for a few moments, it seems to flip over spontaneously so that we see the other image, and then after a few more moments, it flips back. The line of the old woman's nose becomes the line forming the side of the young woman's cheek, chin, and jaw. The old woman's left eye becomes the young woman's left ear. The old woman's chin becomes the young woman's throat; her mouth becomes a necklace on the young woman's delicate throat. The scarf covering the old woman's head becomes part of the young woman's hat, perhaps feathers flowing from a fashionable bonnet. Psychologists explain this flipping from one image to the other as the effect of two competing learned schemata (Attneave, 1974). In the same year, psychologist Edgar Reuben introduced a picture of a "reversible goblet" to demonstrate figure-ground reversal (Attneave, 1974). As we gaze at the picture, for a moment we see two faces staring across a white space at each other. Suddenly instead of the faces our attention focuses on the white space, which is a goblet appearing on a black background. This image, too, flips back and forth from goblet to faces.

Jens Bjerre, a Danish writer and photographer who lived with the Kalahari Bushmen for a period of 6 months, writes of following two men as they proceed in hunting gemsbok. He notes, "They observe every clue which reveals the animal's movements—a bent straw, a hoofprint in the sand, a broken branch, seeds shaken from the branch onto the ground, and many

AUTHOR'S NOTE: The research reported here was supported by a grant from the Benton Center for Curriculum and Instruction, Department of Education, The University of Chicago. I am grateful to Robert Dreeben of The University of Chicago for his thoughtful comments on an earlier draft of the manuscript.

other signs which are invisible to me" (1960, p. 121). As one reads Bjerre's narrative of the hunt, one realizes that he is indeed very perceptive, noting, for example, how after the gemsbok has been killed, the hunters do not allow the shadows of their heads to fall across the body of the animal. But the signs by which the hunters track the animal he says are invisible to him.

As these three examples suggest, what we see is not dependent simply upon the capacity of our sensory receptors. In the case of the "reversible goblet," we interpret our perception one way and then another. When the black part of the drawing is the ground, we see the goblet, the figure. When the white part of the drawing is the ground, we see the faces. Gestalt psychology taught us that long ago (Kohler, 1947). In the case of the drawing "My Wife and My Mother-in-Law," we have a somewhat different situation. One schema helps us organize our perceptions to see a young girl, while another organizes our perceptions to see an old woman. Somewhere along the way we have acquired these schemata that govern our interpretation of incoming sensory data.

In the case of the Danish photographer, we have a different situation in which certain experiential and cultural knowledge has simply not been acquired. The Danish photographer does not know what to look for. Nor would we. For unless we have had prior experience as trackers, we are unlikely to see any pattern in the way the dust is scratched, the pebbles are disturbed, the grass is bent, or the twigs are snapped.

As these examples illustrate, what we think we see directly as data coming to us through our various sensory receptors is actually our interpretation of that data, the product of personal, social, and cultural experiences combined with perceptual capacity and, I believe, a disposition to observe. This inescapable condition affects our analysis of whatever we attend to, and has particularly important ramifications for how we proceed in investigating the meaning of language samples, such as those collected as think-aloud protocols and from classroom discussions for research on writing. Some people take this to be a sign that all observations and knowledge are therefore suspect because they are the products of necessarily different sets of experiences. Guba, for example, states that, "Realities are multiple, and they exist in people's minds" (1990, p. 26).

Proponents of this point of view typically reject what they call the positivist view of objectivity, the view that objectivity is possible by using methods that attempt to provide an unbiased examination of phenomena. These thinkers make a hard-and-fast split between what they call quantitative and qualitative, or positivist and constructivist methodologies. Guba, for example, designates positivist methodology as *experimental/manipulative* and explains its procedures: "questions and/or hypotheses are stated in advance in propositional form and subjected to empirical tests (falsification) under carefully controlled conditions" (p. 20). On the other hand, he designates a methodology of constructivism as *hermeneutic* [interpretive], *dialectic.* In these procedures, he claims, "individual constructions are elicited and refined hermeneutically, and compared and contrasted dialectically with the aim of generating one (or a few) constructions on which there is substantial consensus" (1990, p. 27).

These extreme positions, around which debate continues to appear in our journals (cf., *Educational Researcher,* 1992, *21*[5], 5-17), are not operationally feasible. Quantitative studies cannot ignore interpretation. Those that do frequently prove to be cul de sacs. At the same time, qualitative studies ignore the quantitative at their peril. I will argue that each camp has something to learn from the other and that without components of both, our research will be the weaker.

THE UBIQUITY OF
INTERPRETING AND COUNTING

Underlying Guba's descriptions of positivist and constructivist approaches to research is the implied claim that hermeneutics (interpretation) is the province of the constructivist. He phrases his description of positivist research such that interpretation appears to be excluded. Where is the need, after all, for interpretation in experimentation and manipulation? Guba would have us believe that experimentalists simply count the results of their manipulations. Before we agree that experimental research excludes interpretation, we need to determine what interpretation involves.

Interpretation

Hans-Georg Gadamer, perhaps the foremost exponent of hermeneutics, in explaining the nature of hermeneutics, provides the following example of interpretation:

> It is not so much our judgments as it is our prejudices that constitute our being. This is a provocative formulation, for I am using it to restore to its rightful

place a positive concept of prejudice that was driven out of our linguistic usage by the French and the English Enlightenment. It can be shown that the concept of prejudice did not originally have the meaning we have attached to it. Prejudices are not necessarily unjustified and erroneous, so that they inevitably distort the truth. In fact, the historicity of our existence entails that prejudices in the literal sense of the word, constitute the initial directedness of our whole ability to experience. Prejudices are biases of our openness to the world. They are simply conditions whereby we experience something—whereby what we encounter says something to us. (Gadamer, 1976, p. 9)

In this brief passage Gadamer interprets the idea of prejudice in an attempt to rid it of its negative meanings and to replace those with more positive ones. This transformation takes place through a process of interpretation that entails mediation by the use of successive terms. He informs us that today's meanings are not the same as the original meanings of *prejudice*. He explains that prejudices are "not necessarily unjustified" and that they do not "inevitably distort the truth." Having cleared that ground, he makes the first mediation with the phrase "constitute the initial directedness of our whole ability to experience." In other words, prejudices in this sense amount to what cognitive psychologists might call prior knowledge, the knowledge that we necessarily bring with us to any experience.

His second mediation comes in the phrase "our openness to the world." With this phrase, Gadamer so far removes prejudice from its usual sense of closed-mindedness that it takes on the opposite, almost diametrically opposed meanings. He again resolves this apparent contradiction by explaining that prejudices are "simply conditions whereby we experience something," a third mediation. After qualifying this position somewhat, Gadamer goes on to explain that in the hermeneutical experience "we are possessed by something and precisely by means of it we are opened up for the new, the different, the true" (p. 9). And here we have a fourth mediation in which the concept of prejudice becomes combined with the notion of hermeneutical experience as something not merely necessary, but without which we cannot be aware of the new, the different, or the true.

In this brief interpretation, Gadamer makes and justifies a series of shifts in semantic categories, from the negative associations with the term *prejudice,* to the necessity of prejudice as our "initial directedness" in any experience, to that which opens us up to the new, the different, and the true. As this passage illustrates, interpretation assigns, justifies, and shifts the boundaries of categories.

Interpretation in Quantitative Research

If we think of interpretation in this way, it becomes obvious that any research, no matter how positivist in orientation, involves interpretation. Even the simple act of categorizing objects requires at least two interpretive decisions. We must decide whether the similarities are strong enough and the dissimilarities weak enough that the two objects may be considered members of the same category. In addition, when we do this in a formal way we must provide some rationale for the existence of the categories, just as Gadamer does in his explanations of prejudice.

Such decision making is necessary even in the use of relatively low-inference categories, such as T-units and other categories used in describing written syntax. Decisions to categorize structures as T-units cannot be automatic, because their boundaries are often ambiguous and their constituents are frequently implied. In such cases coders must make interpretive decisions about whether particular units meet the criteria established. Often, those decisions push at the boundaries of established categories and result in a myriad of ground rules intended to cover special cases, but which in effect also provide an explanation of how the category set has been interpreted in light of the data at hand.

More important, the categories that we use in research require (but frequently do not receive) interpretation and justification, a rationale that explains their meanings and implications. Thus, when a researcher in economics takes family income to be an index of quality of life, the researcher ignores many other aspects of family life, subordinating all else to income. Presumably, that selection is not random. It must require an interpretive process that, at the very least, examines the implications of the index in some rigorous way and compares it to other possible indices in order to evaluate its power as an indicator. Unfortunately, researchers frequently appear to ignore that process.

Studies of schooling, for example, frequently assume some relatively abstract gauge, for example, per-pupil expenditure, to be an appropriate indicator of the character of education within a school. A host of studies, sometimes called "the black box" studies, used such indices to examine what went into the black box, but did not examine what went on inside the box. They concluded that schooling had no impact on differences in educational outcomes. Differences in educational achievement had to be attributed to differences in such factors as socioeconomic status. However, when researchers, such as Barr and Dreeben (1983), looked inside the black box to see what was happening in classrooms, they found highly differential effects depending upon the organization and operation of classrooms.

I recently read a newspaper story about the problem of garbage in the United States. It included a litany of "facts," among which was the statement that each resident of New York City produces on average 6 pounds of garbage per day. Assuming a population of 7 million, garbage production comes to 42 million pounds in a single day, or nearly 15.33 *billion* pounds per year. That is more than a ton of garbage a year for each man, woman, and child. How did the people who keep track of garbage arrive at the figure of 6 pounds per day? Certainly, it sounds like a factual matter—6 pounds a day, a direct and precise measurement. But it is not. It is an estimate based on a variety of information that may include the actual weights of garbage collected in some given time periods in particular districts of the city. It may be based in part on an estimate of the amount of garbage required to fill a certain dump site. The specific information used to devise the estimate of 6 pounds is the choice of those who do the estimating; and those choices, if not random, are the product of an interpretive process involving judgments and arguments about which sources of information are likely to produce the most stable estimates. When the final estimate is reported, it appears without any explanation of the interpretive processes underlying it.

Counting in Qualitative Research

Interpretations of categories, of sampling, of what counts as a member of a category, and what category membership means are inescapable. The more painstaking we are in revealing those processes, the more useful our research will be. But if interpretation underlies counting, counting also underlies interpretation. The relationship is symbiotic. Counting is hidden in every generalization, even in the work of qualitative researchers who appear to do without numbers.

The qualitative research of Clifford Geertz on *The Religion of Java* provides many examples. Early in the text Geertz sets out to describe religious ceremonies of one "subvariant within the general Javanese religious system" (1960, p. 5). As he begins to describe the marriage ceremony, he comments on his method:

> I shall describe the marriage ceremony in the fullest form in which it appears, but I shall include no practice not carried out on the occasion of at least one wedding I saw during the time I was in Modjokuto. It must be remembered not

only that ceremonies for middle daughters are usually somewhat less elaborate, but also that various people omit various parts of the ceremony pretty much at will. (p. 54)

A consciousness of numbers and counting is implied throughout that statement, even though specific numbers do not appear. The number observed is greater than one, each practice described must have been carried out in at least one wedding witnessed, and the range of practices within the wedding ceremony appears to vary widely, from a minimum of going to the mosque to pronounce the Moslem Confession of Faith to an elaborate series of practices over 2 days, with certain events in some weddings taking place after an additional interval of 5 days. Geertz sees no reason to present these numbers and ranges in a formal way.

The number of wedding ceremonies he actually witnessed is probably inconsequential unless we have reason to believe that the sample he did see either may have failed to indicate the range of complexity or may not have been representative. If he had witnessed only three ceremonies, for example, and two of the three were of the simplest kind while the third accounted for all of the other practices witnessed, we would have serious cause to doubt the usefulness of the account. Or, since the wedding is presented in its "fullest form," we may wonder whether that fullest form can possibly be representative. On the other hand, to present only some sort of average wedding would be to eliminate much that is of interest in the account. And if our interest is in the range of practices used, then the fuller account, of course, is not only justifiable but desirable.

A few chapters later Geertz wishes to make the point that Javanese know a great deal about specific illnesses along with their symptoms: "Analysis of symptoms is particularly appropriate to more specific illnesses with well-defined disease pictures and rests on a categorization of such pictures at once elaborate and, seemingly, quite accurate, which is widely diffused among the populace generally" (p. 92). At this point numbers are irresistible, and Geertz cites one boy who "listed 47 diseases . . . each with a special name and symptom pattern in the space of a half hour; and four other informants did almost as well" (p. 92). Geertz then goes on to list the diseases commonly named. We will be convinced by this argument if we have no reason to doubt either of two claims: (1) that the knowledge is elaborate, and (2) that it is diffuse among the general populace. The number of five informants and the list of diseases provides convincing support for the claim that the knowledge is elaborate. If one had cause, those same numbers might call into question the claim that such knowledge is diffuse among "the populace generally."

The point here is simply that counts and the necessity for counts lurk in the corners of all qualitative research. They are as ubiquitous in qualitative as are interpretations in quantitative research.

AVOIDING BIAS

Some writers charge that seventeenth-, eighteenth-, and nineteenth-century scientists and rhetoricians believed that, using scientific method, reality might be grasped objectively through the senses and reported directly through language, without mediation of any kind.[1] (See, e.g., Berlin, 1984, p. 7.) Critics such as Guba (1990) and Lincoln (1990) claim that *objectivity* of this sort is impossible. They say that because prior knowledge mediates whatever we see, we cannot come to know a reality existing outside ourselves, independent of our perceptual biases.[2] Most of us agree that coming to know reality in any absolute sense is impossible. A problem arises, however, when we reject all attempts at objectivity. We overlook the sense in which objectivity has to do with consistency and systematicity, and take no steps to ensure those, even though the problems of interpreting and classifying such data are sometimes enormous.[3]

In most cases, researchers are honest. They do not try to "cook" their data in order to make it support some hypothesis wherein they may see some personal profit. Most do not select cases with an eye to establishing some preconceived result. In experimental studies and case studies, responsible researchers do not select only the best writers for presentation or evaluation in order to promote some privately held value. They do not deliberately distort or select the words of their subjects in order that those words might support some predetermined end. Putting these ignoble sources of bias aside, there are still three sources of bias that must be reckoned with: (1) cultural knowledge, (2) fluctuations in personal knowledge during the processes of research, and (3) our sample. Each of these, in my mind, requires some attempt at objectivity, particularly in analyzing the discourse of groups or individuals.

Cultural Knowledge

We cannot operate without cultural and personal knowledge. They come with being human. They are what Gadamer refers to as our prejudices, without which we would be unable to recognize the new and different. At the same time they have potential for constricting our views. What we have in our cultural and personal knowledge is a Janus looking in two directions. One face allows us to perceive the new. The other restricts what we may perceive.

The bias resulting from cultural knowledge is probably more difficult to deal with because it is hidden from us. It imbues the stances we take and the assumptions we make. It is so deeply embedded in our psyches that it is hidden from us, as taboos are. When a strong taboo operates, those governed by it may not even be aware that the possibility for the forbidden action exists. Recently, two parents in a small Pennsylvania town were arrested for selling their children as prostitutes. When I heard the headline, I was shocked and waited for the news story, thinking I must have heard the headline incorrectly. I cannot recall having heard of such a crime before, although such crimes must have existed. Perhaps we repress such things, individually and socially. Such taboos may be recognized only in their violation. Cultural knowledge, of which taboos are a part, shapes our conceptions in the same way, without our conscious knowledge.

Perhaps a major goal of contemporary cultural criticism is to explicate the way our culture controls our assumptions and stances, our worldview, the way we conceive of ourselves and others. It does this by subjecting our categories, definitions, goals, methods, and such to continuous philosophical analysis. In cultural criticism, major clues to the unraveling of our assumptions, our cultural worldview, have come from those who are able to stand outside the mainstream culture and bring a different perspective to bear on it. Our goal should not be to eliminate the bias that comes with our cultural knowledge. For as Gadamer points out, that knowledge is the condition necessary to the hermeneutical experience that opens us to "the new, the different, the true" (p. 9). Any systematic inquiry, qualitative or quantitative, will be stronger and more perspicacious if it is founded upon an interpretive process that subjects goals, assumptions, methods, and so forth to continuing philosophical analysis.

Personal Knowledge

Personal knowledge is a somewhat different matter. By personal knowledge I mean that knowledge that differentiates individuals within a culture, knowledge acquired as a result of individual personal experience and study. We exercise conscious control over a large proportion of personal knowledge, particularly the knowledge we bring to bear in doing tasks. Even though we have greater control over this knowledge than over cultural knowledge or the personal knowledge that has helped to form our personalities, it still is a potent source of bias, especially in the analysis of protocols or discourse, for two reasons.

First, when we activate one schema or set of schemata, we tend to eliminate other possible schemata from consideration, even though the data may be susceptible to other, more productive analyses. Researchers working in discourse and protocol analysis have a tendency to believe that categories "emerge from the data." Although a given set of data will not be susceptible to any and all randomly selected categories, it is doubtful that some set of categories springs fully blown from the data set itself. The researcher necessarily brings sets of concepts that allow the formulation of categories that appear to be relevant to the data; then the researcher interprets the data in order to classify it in light of the categories so developed. The categories were never implicit in the protocols themselves. They are the result of an interpretive act on the part of the researcher.

Second, memory being what it is, consistent interpretive acts are difficult to come by, particularly in the analysis of language. Not only is each item for categorization different, but each appears in a different verbal environment that influences the perceived meaning of the item. Further, although we make use of categories and describe them as though they were discrete boxes bounded by clear wooden sides, the wooden walls are fictitious, set in place by the researcher in order to explain the conceptual system at work. Thus, the precise dimensions of the walls are redefined on each occasion, making use of all past experience with the categories.

Effects of Personal Knowledge on Analysis

To illustrate these points, let me turn to a portion of a classroom discussion that I have used as illustrative material elsewhere (Hillocks, in press). I use it again here because this was one of the first I examined and the first that helped me see not only the many possibilities for analysis, but also the way in which my own changing knowledge influenced what I saw in the data. The audio recordings of group discussions were collected as part of a pilot study of materials to be used in my ongoing research (Hillocks, in progress). One important purpose of that research was to examine the character of group discussions in hopes of providing some insight into how students learn in such discussions. Some of the discussions involved students in the examination of a set of scenarios in which characters responded to dangerous situations in various ways.

Each scenario was designed to reflect some particular criterion that Aristotle made use of in delimiting the idea of courage in the *Nichomachean*

Ethics. For example, the scenario that students discuss in the example that follows involves expert firefighters battling a fire on an oil derrick at sea. The relevant Aristotelian criterion has to do with the idea that expertise and high levels of experience decrease the danger of an act, thereby rendering it less than courageous. Students, of course, were not privy to Aristotle's criteria. In their discussion, they were to use their own ideas to determine whether the action should be considered courageous and to develop a criterion, a rule by which they might judge comparable actions. As a discussion of this scenario begins, one of the participants almost immediately compares it to another scenario (#2) in which a Secret Service agent throws himself in the line of fire to block a bullet intended for the president. The scenario about the fire fighters (#6) and the first 16 turns in the discussion appear in the box that follows.

Scenario #6: On Monday the fire had started on the oil derrick far out at sea. By Wednesday the men working on the derrick had been rescued, but the fire was out of control. "Red" Granger and his men were called in to fight the dangerous fire. "Red" and his men had fought many oil fires. They had the training and experience to put out the fire. Are "Red" and his men courageous when they fight the fire?

Group Discussion

1. SCOTT: God, all these contradict the other ones.
2. KEITH: Yeah.
3. SCOTT: Six contradicts the one with the agent, the Secret Service agent.
4. KEITH: I don't think they're courageous/ because they're experienced,/ but they're not actually putting themselves at risk./ They're just doing another job./ It's not actual...../
5. SCOTT: What did we have for number 2?
6. KEITH: Yes.
7. SCOTT: Yes. This one has to be yes./ It's a job.
8. KEITH: No,/ not necessarily.
9. AMY: No, it's different./ You're not putting yourself in front of a bullet./
10. KEITH: Yeah./ Chances are that some people are going to die in car wrecks every day./ Just because you get in a car doesn't mean you're courageous./
11. SCOTT: But really, it's their job to do something like that./ And you have to be courageous/ to take a job like that in the first place.
12. SUE: He has fought many oil fires it says.
13. AMY: Yeah, that guy was going in front of many bullets. [sarcastic]/
14. SUE: This emphasizes their training and their fighting many of them./ The other one was just like I saw them out of the corner of my eye./
15. AMY: So this one is not courageous./ They had experience,/ so they're not doing anything out of the ordinary./
16: KEITH: Yeah,/ even if the bullet doesn't kill him, he's pretty sure he's going to get hurt./ These, they might go in there and not get hurt at all./

When I began the analysis, I approached it from the concept of inquiry that I had in mind (Hillocks, 1986). I expected students to examine the data carefully; to quote from it; to make comparisons; to note contrasts; to bring prior knowledge to bear; to make generalizations; to draw inferences; and to develop hypotheses, conclusions, and of course, criteria. My assistants and I have been able to identify instances of all of these in the transcripts.

Scott, for example, in his very first turn points to a contrast he sees existing among all of the scenarios that he's dealt with to this point. In turn 3 he specifies the contrast, seeing in scenario #6 a contradiction to scenario #2. In fact, Scott's comments early in the discussion set up comparison/ contrast as a major operation that students will use through the first two-thirds or so of the whole discussion of this scenario. In turn 4, Keith uses the data of the scenario to draw the inference that "they're not actually putting themselves at risk. They're just doing another job." In turns 5 and 7 Scott reverts to comparison, deducing that since a Secret Service agent and the firefighter are both doing a job, both are courageous. In turn 9 Amy focuses on a difference she sees in the two scenarios. She says, "You're not putting yourself in front of a bullet." Her implication is that the danger to the Secret Service agent is much greater than the danger to the firefighters. Keith picks up on Amy's comment in turn 10 and brings his prior knowledge to bear, pointing out, "chances are that some people are going to die in car wrecks every day. Just because you get in a car doesn't mean you're courageous." Keith's remark along with Amy's earlier point suggest that the students are thinking of a continuum of risk. At one extreme is "putting yourself in front of a bullet." At the less dangerous extreme is driving a car. This becomes an important concept in devising the final criterion statement governing their judgment about the scenario.

In the following turn Scott continues to focus on the similarity he perceives because both involve a job. However, he shifts ground a bit and makes a new inference that one has to be courageous to take a dangerous job in the first place. In turns 12 and 14 Sue returns to the data of the stated scenario, pointing out the emphasis on the training and experience of the firefighters and contrasting that with the action of the agent in scenario #2. She implies that seeing something out of the corner of the eye does not allow for bringing experience and training to bear. In the remaining two turns Amy and Keith clarify the difference, focusing on the greater certainty of harm to the Secret Service agent. The discussion continues in this vein, with the students examining data, making comparisons ever more carefully and explicitly, bringing other knowledge to bear, developing hypotheses, and doing the kinds of things that appear to go on in inquiry.

This seemed to me to be a quite satisfactory approach to the analysis of the protocols of group discussions, and we have just recently completed our categorization of many pages of transcripts. However, long before the completion of that analysis, it happened that I was working with Toulmin's theory of argument (1958) and analyzing student writing in light of the structures that Toulmin includes in argument. It occurred to me, as I moved from one task to the other, that these students were engaged in very sophisticated argument. I wondered if it were the argumentative structure of the discussions that might be responsible for the impact of this kind of activity on student writing rather than simply the use of the strategies of inquiry. Or it might be that argument is integral to the ongoing process of inquiry. (I am beginning to see it as *necessary to inquiry*.) We began then to look at the discussions in terms of their use of grounds to support claims, warrants that connect grounds to claims, and qualifications and backing. To illustrate these, let us take Toulmin's example of a brief argument. "Harry is a British subject," is a *claim* that requires support. It is based on the datum or *ground* that "Harry was born in Bermuda." There is no necessary connection between the two statements. A *warrant* or rule is required to make this connection explicit: "A man born in Bermuda will generally be a British subject." The argument, of course, is still incomplete, as the warrant requires some sort of justification, what Toulmin calls *backing*. The backing for the warrant in this case will be the set of statutes and legal provisions that stipulate a person born in Bermuda is a British subject. In addition, the argument will require qualification, what Toulmin calls provision for possible *rebuttal*: "Unless both his parents were aliens/he has become a naturalized American/ . . . " (p. 105).[4]

Scott opens the argument by making a claim about what he sees as contradictions among the scenarios. He specifies that claim in turn 3. Keith makes a different claim, which will turn out to be in conflict with the one Scott reaches later. Keith says, "I don't think they're courageous." Immediately, he adds the grounds for that decision: "Because they're experienced." This is followed by an implied warrant: "They're not actually putting themselves at risk." Then he extends that idea: "They're just doing another job."

In turn 5, Scott asks what the group's response was to scenario #2. In turn 7 he reasons that if the answer for scenario #2 was yes, the Secret Service agent was courageous, then the answer for scenario #6 must be yes as well. He then adds an implied warrant: "It's a job." Scott's reasoning appears to be that because the action is undertaken as a job, it is courageous. In turns 8, 9, and 10, Keith and Amy both take issue with that warrant. Here they imply the continuum of dangerous acts, indicating that the danger of the job is the critical factor.

Over Scott's objection that one has to be courageous "to take a job like that in the first place," Amy and Sue cite grounds from the scenario and move toward establishing a different warrant, contrasting the degree of danger inherent in the two actions. In turn 15 Amy reiterates Keith's earlier claim: "So this one is not courageous." She follows that claim with the grounds, "they had the experience," and an implied warrant, "so they're not doing anything out of the ordinary." Keith begins to establish part of the backing in turn 16, the reasoning underlying what will be the criterion developed by the group: "Even if the bullet doesn't kill him, he's pretty sure he's going to get hurt. These, they might go in there and not get hurt at all." Keith's statement represents a clarification of the idea of the continuum of risk implied in Amy's turn 9.

What begins with conflicting claims (Scott versus Keith and Amy) moves through reasoning about the evidence and warrants underlying the claims to increasingly clearer distinctions. Scott's initial claim, though eventually rejected by the group, sets the stage for those distinctions. It prompts the others, particularly Sue and Amy, to turn back to the evidence and to draw inferences about them. Although the early inferences are not made explicit, they serve as crucial distinctions in the argument (cf. Amy's comment in turn 9, "You're not putting yourself in front of a bullet.")

Curiously, the more I thought about the function of the argumentative structure in the student discussions, the more I began to see that something else was needed. The simple categorization of claims, grounds, and warrants did not adequately explain how students learned from each other. At this point, I was serving as the chair of Carol Lee's (1991, 1993) dissertation committee. Carol's use of Vygotsky (1978 and 1986) in developing her instructional framework led me to consider the use of Vygotskian ideas in the analysis of group discussion, in particular the idea that language or signs enable children to move beyond the direct perception of data within a sensory field. It occurred to me that the scenarios used to prompt discussion might be thought of as comparable to sensory fields. My question was how students move to more complete and complex understandings of the issues involved. Vygotsky argues that visual fields are perceived as wholes, and that words enable children to "single out separate elements, thereby overcoming the natural structure of the sensory field and forming new (artificially introduced and dynamic) structural centers" (1978, p. 32). The words, indicating separate elements, stipulate a focus of attention and connect it with other elements through syntactic structures. Perhaps the same was true for the discussion of more abstract verbal fields such as the scenarios.

Indeed, as students make their contributions to the discussion, the words they use have the effect of establishing new structural centers of talk. For example, in his first turn, Scott establishes contrast as a structural center for the discussion that runs through the first 30 turns of the discussion. In turn 4, Keith establishes another structural center with his comment, "But they're not actually putting themselves at risk." Clearly, it is not the case that the firefighters have no risk. But Keith's phrase establishes level of risk as a topic for discussion, a topic later taken up by other students.

When Scott claims, in turn 7, that the firefighters' actions are comparable to the Secret Service agent's because both are doing a job, Amy quickly claims the contrary, "You're not putting yourself in front of a bullet." This comment by Amy mediates movement from Keith's early comment that the men are "not actually putting themselves at risk" to the much more explicit statement about degree of risk that Keith makes in turn 16. In turn 10, Keith provides another mediation in his use of the analogy about driving a car. In turn 13, Amy makes it clear that a Secret Service agent cannot gain experience in "going in front of many bullets." Indeed, almost every turn can be seen as a mediation from one idea to another.

By turn 16, Keith pulls together the two major structural centers in the discussion to this point: contrasting the difference in degree of risk involved in the two scenarios. In this statement he makes a much more explicit contrast in terms of degree of risk than has appeared in the discussion to this point.

My point is that the longer we work with a set of data, the more we are likely to see in it, simply by virtue of bringing the ideas of other writers and researchers to bear on it. As our personal knowledge changes, so does what we see in our data. I do not by any means wish to imply that the analysis of protocols is completely subjective. However, I think there can be no question that the categories we use in analyzing protocol data are the product of our knowledge interacting with the protocols. That is, the protocols must be amenable to the system of categories used. At the same time, the categories involved should have the power to show differences among protocols or the parts of protocols. Here is where counting (and quantification more generally) becomes important in the analysis, providing a measure of the diffusion and pattern of categories over the protocols analyzed and an index of their validity.

Consistency

Another aspect of personal knowledge requires consideration here, our ability to apply the category system consistently. As suggested earlier, the vagaries of memory, and the fact that each item to be categorized appears in a new linguistic environment that necessarily impinges upon its meaning, make consistency in the application of any analytic scheme difficult, whether that be a categorical system or a narrative analysis. The sort of difficulty involved can be illustrated with a quick examination of Keith's fourth turn. Let us simply use the Toulmin categories as an example. His initial statement ("I don't think they're courageous") is clearly a claim in Toulmin's terms. There is no ambiguity about it. However, the second unit ("because they're experienced") is not so clear. Should it be categorized as grounds or as a warrant? The word *because* suggests a warrant. In fact, in Aristotelian terms, *experience* may serve as a warrant because of the implication that experience serves to reduce risk and, hence, make an action less than courageous. However, Keith's third unit ("But they're not actually putting themselves at risk") seems a more explicit warrant than the second unit ("because they're experienced"). In addition, the term *experience* appears in the scenario itself. Because of that, it seems better regarded as grounds. In another environment, with appropriate modifiers, it might very well need to be classified as a warrant.

An even more difficult example appears in Amy's sarcastic comment in turn 13, "Yeah, that guy was going in front of many bullets." What are we to do with such a comment? Clearly, the intent is not literal but ironic. Amy means to emphasize the impossibility of the Secret Service agent's gaining experience in "going in front of many bullets." Should this be considered the claim of some unarticulated argument? Or should it be considered grounds for Amy's claim that the case of the Secret Service agent is different from that of the firefighters, in turn 9? When conflicts of this sort arise frequently, as they do in almost any protocol analysis, counts will determine the consistency with which the analysis can be made.

Sample

The *sample,* what we focus on, or the portion of it that we report, may be a third source of bias. Particularly in dealing with qualitative data, we may be tempted to select examples that make some desired point, while ignoring others that would deny it. In literary criticism, such a tactic may be appropriate because the reader may go the full text to evaluate whatever assertions are made. In the analysis of protocols, as well as other kinds of qualitative data, such a liberty places too great a strain on the reader's credibility. The reader in these cases will not have the full texts in hand.

I recently had occasion to read a paper that contained a generalization comparable to the following: Although Alan was a weak reader and although he did not have the terminology that a literary critic might use, he was able to classify stories. The support for this generalization was a single example, that Alan had classified a story as the best he had read. Leaving aside the problem with this peculiar use of the term *classify*, a single example hardly supports the generalization that "Alan was able to classify stories." Did he do this on more than one occasion? Did he use more than one category in classifying stories? These were issues that the paper failed to explore, leaving me, for one, unconvinced. Some counting and reporting of numbers would have been very useful.

Another example is the 16 turns of group discussion cited earlier. Those turns are only the first third of the discussion of that scenario. Are they representative? Decidedly not. By turn 27, Sue has begun to phrase the criterion and indicates she wants help from the others. By turn 34, the students have altogether abandoned their argumentative mode and have entered a highly collaborative one, in which they contribute to structuring a criterion:

34. SUE: Something they are trained and familiar with? [asking about criterion phrasing]
35. KEITH: Yeah.
36. SUE: What would you say, "A person is not courageous when they are trained and familiar with . . . "?
37. AMY: A situation.
38. SUE: Usually a fatal situation?
39. AMY: No, they're trained.
40. KEITH: So it's not going to be a fatal situation to them.
41. AMY: Yeah, they're going to know how to take steps to make it . . .
42. SUE: OK, what if you say, "A person is not courageous when they're trained and familiar with a situation"?
43. KEITH: Well, it's usual for them. I think that's the big thing.
44. AMY: It's something they're used to.
45. SUE: So should I write that?
46. KEITH: Yeah.

Clearly, if we concentrate on the first two-thirds of the discussion, we will have a distorted view of what the students actually do. That would be a great loss, for the level of collaboration is often remarkable, with one student beginning a sentence and one or even two finishing it. The concern, then, is not with a representative sample so much as it is with representing the sample. We need not only a description of those from whom the qualitative data are drawn, but also a characterization of the phenomena we identify in the data and some measure of its frequency, dispersion, and order. All of these serve as the grounds for our interpretations of the data.

There are two reasons, then, for counting in qualitative research. The first is to demonstrate the level of consistency in interpreting the data, in applying categories. No one conducts research on a single datum. We always deal with many pieces of data. Even a case study involves arrays of data, for example, several observations of a single child in a classroom. Any generalization about the child observed will presumably be based upon many pieces of information. As I have suggested earlier, even with low inference categories, there is always a margin of error. It is important to know what that margin of error is, how consistent the interpretations of the data are. The second reason for counting is to demonstrate the frequency, dispersion, and order of the phenomena in question.

At the same time, we need to remember that either quantitative analysis without interpretation or interpretation without quantitative analysis may be misleading. As the following excerpt from Boswell's *Life of Johnson* serves to remind us, both are indispensable.

JOHNSON: "Were I a country gentleman, I should not be very hospitable, I should not have crowds in my house."

BOSWELL: "Sir Alexander Dick tells me, that he remembers having a thousand people in a year to dine at his house; that is, reckoning each person as one, each time that he dined there."

JOHNSON: "That, Sir, is about three a day."

BOSWELL: "How your statement lessens the idea."

JOHNSON: "That, Sir, is the good of counting. It brings every thing to a certainty, which before floated in the mind indefinitely."

BOSWELL: "But *Omne ignotum pro magnifico est*: one is sorry to have this diminished."

JOHNSON: "Sir, you should not allow yourself to be delighted with errour."

BOSWELL: "Three a day seem but few."

JOHNSON: "Nay, Sir, he who entertains three a day, does very liberally." (April 18, 1783)

NOTES

1. There is considerable evidence that the great scientists were far more sophisticated, that they were keenly aware of the role of interpretation in their work. Lavoisier did not

observe oxygen directly. He interpreted many complex observations to conclude its existence. Kepler did not simply look at the sky and report elliptical planetary orbits. Indeed, using mathematics, he interpreted the observations of others to develop a theory of planetary motion. Newton did not observe gravity. He made observations of bodies in motion, invented a language (calculus) capable of describing continuous motion in quantitative terms, and formulated a theory of motion from which he extrapolated a theory of celestial motion, gravity.

2. Assertions of this sort are based on a definition of *come to know* and some idea of the level of certainty required to qualify something as *knowledge*. In everyday life we use our prior knowledge in conjunction with our perceptions, biased though they may be, to *come to know* sets of circumstances with enough certainty to act upon that knowledge. If this were not true, most of us would never venture from whatever safe haven we could find. We act upon what Dewey (1938) might have called "warranted assertions." Dewey liked that term because it connotes the idea that the process of knowledge seeking is ongoing and dynamic, not static or rigid. It implies the viability of degrees of certainty.

3. An important concept of objectivity involves the explication and interpretation of terms and the phenomena we associate with them. That is a topic for another essay.

4. In making an analysis of the student arguments, I modified the Toulmin system to some degree. Whenever we make a claim that entails a judgment, as in the case of judging courageous action, the judgment is based on a definition of the quality or trait being judged. That definition becomes the *backing* for the warrant in the argument. Statements of criterion, then, were coded as backing. Since students do not ordinarily use explicit rules in their discussion, we coded implied warrants as warrants. For example, if a student claims the firefighters were not courageous because they had a high degree of experience, they imply a warrant, as does Keith in turn 4: "They're not actually putting themselves at risk."

REFERENCES

Attneave, F. (1974). Multistability in perception. In R. Held (Ed.), *Image, object, and illusion: Readings from Scientific American.* San Francisco: W. H. Freeman.

Barr, R., & Dreeben, R. (1983). *How schools work.* Chicago: University of Chicago Press.

Berlin, J. A. (1984). *Writing instruction in nineteenth-century American colleges.* Carbondale: Southern Illinois University Press.

Bjerre, J. (1960). *Kalahari* (E. Bannister, Trans.). New York: Hill and Wang.

Boswell, J. (n.d.). *The life of Samuel Johnson.* New York: Random House.

Dewey, J. (1938). *Logic: The theory of inquiry.* New York: Henry Holt.

Educational Researcher. (1992), *21*(5), 5-17.

Gadamer, H. (1976). *Philosophical Hermeneutics* (D. E. Linge, Trans.). Berkeley: University of California Press.

Geertz, C. (1960). *The religion of Java.* Glencoe, IL: Free Press.

Guba, E. G. (1990). The alternative paradigm dialog. In E. G. Guba (Ed.), *The paradigm dialog.* Newbury Park, CA: Sage.

Hillocks, G. (1986). *Research on written composition: New directions for teaching.* Urbana, IL: National Conference on Research in English and ERIC Clearinghouse on Reading and Communication Skills.

Hillocks, G. (in press). Environments for active learning. In L. Odell (Ed.), *Composing theory.* Carbondale: Southern Illinois University Press.

Hillocks, G. (in progress). *Integrating qualitative and quantitative data: Studies of learning to write under three foci of instruction.*

Kohler, W. (1947). *Gestalt psychology: An introduction to new concepts in psychology.* New York: Liveright.

Lee, C. D. (1991). *Signifying as a scaffold for literary interpretation: The pedagogical implications of an African American discourse genre.* Unpublished doctoral dissertation, The University of Chicago.

Lee, C. D. (1993). *Signifying as a scaffold for literary interpretation: The pedagogical implications of an African American discourse genre* (Research Report No. 26). Urbana, IL: National Council of Teachers of English.

Lincoln, Y. S. (1990). The making of a constructivist: A remembrance of transformations past. In E. G. Guba (Ed.), *The paradigm dialog.* Newbury Park, CA: Sage.

Toulmin, S. E. (1958). *The uses of argument.* New York: Cambridge University Press.

Vygotsky, L. S. (1978). *Mind in society: The development of higher psychological processes* (M. Cole, V. John-Steiner, S. Scribner, & E. Souberman, Eds.). Cambridge, MA: Harvard University Press.

Vygotsky, L. S. (1986). *Thought and language* (A. Kozulin, Trans.). Cambridge, MA: MIT Press.

9

Discourse Analysis of Teacher–Student Writing Conferences
Finding the Message in the Medium

MELANIE SPERLING

One research road to travel when analyzing and interpreting the discourse of teacher-student writing conferences[1] embeds discourse analysis in long-term classroom observation. This chapter delineates one of the ways in which such research may proceed, and focuses on inherent problem spots, that is, unresolvable dilemmas and unavoidable pitfalls associated with following this research path. The point I wish to make is that the problems are theoretically important, for they are not only predicted by the routines of research, they also predict how researchers can understand what they see and interpret what they find. As a number of discourse analysts have pointed out (e.g., Tannen, 1989), discourse analysis is not a fixed procedure, but a varying and flexible methodology. Because many research paths for conducting discourse analysis of teacher-student writing conferences share the research problems that are the concern of this chapter, the problems themselves must be seen as critical signals, marking the points where theory and method are mutually constraining.

What follow are (a) a brief theory-grounded defense for analyzing writing conference talk in the first place, a section in which I raise what is perhaps the major problem in writing conference research, the frequent

AUTHOR'S NOTE: Funding for projects discussed in this chapter was provided to the author by a grant from the Research Foundation of the National Council of Teachers of English and by a Spencer Fellowship from the National Academy of Education. Thanks to the editor of this volume and to the editors of this series for their useful responses to earlier drafts.

difficulty in definitively relating the discourse of a student's writing conferences to the student's writing; and (b) a discussion of the problems inherent
in the research methodology, with examples taken from my own research
experience. This latter section considers the two major phases of research,
data collection and data analysis, phases that can in reality be intertwined
and are sometimes difficult to tease apart.

ANALYZING WRITING CONFERENCE TALK: DEFENSE AND THEORY

Often when we meet a problem we want to talk it over; the phrase "talk it
over" seems to imply something other than communicating ideas already
formed. It is as if the talking enabled us to rearrange the problem so that we
can look at it differently. (Barnes, 1976, p. 19)

The ways in which talk "rearranges" problems are of special interest to
researchers who concern themselves with the relationship of oral discourse
(talk) to learning to write. Such researchers often work from the premise
that the structure of linguistic interaction in classroom settings plays a
major role in the building of writing knowledge and meaning (see Barnes,
1976; Vygotsky, 1986). Within this linguistic framework the teacher-student
writing conference, when it takes place in conjunction with writing instruction, has been a key discourse event to study.

Researchers who analyze writing conference conversations for patterns
of discourse often seek to uncover links between oral and written language,
between social interaction and the thinking processes associated with writing, and between teacher-student collaboration and student learning. Yet,
ultimately, causal connections between writing conference discourse and
what students subsequently say or write are difficult to prove, and this
difficulty can become a major and overriding issue in the study of writing
conference discourse and its relationship to student writing. *Because the
teacher said X, and said it in this way, the student wrote sentence Y* is a
conclusion that may never be drawn from this work, given the complex and
often ineffable nature of human behavior. The writing conference is one of
any number of factors in the student's social and cognitive context, some
observable and measurable, others invisible, that converge behind the mo-
ment-by-moment decisions that drive a piece of student writing or particular writing processes. Yet even casual inspections of writing conference

conversation tell us that often in such conferences something important is going on with respect to the student as a writer (see, for example, Graves, 1983), and on the basis of such observations writing conferences have long held practical appeal for teachers as effective writing pedagogy (e.g., Harris, 1982; Murray, 1979; Rose, 1982).

What makes conference conversations appealing events to which to apply systematic discourse analysis is their essentially conversational structure coupled with their instructional purpose (see, e.g., Freedman & Katz, 1987; Freedman & Sperling, 1985)—a potent and mutable combination that depends for its ultimate content and character on variables such as the differences among the students and teachers who participate in the conferences, the different kinds of writing that may be their focus, the variety of pedagogical purposes they can serve, and the variety of teaching conditions under which they might occur.

As a discourse event with ties to ordinary daily intercourse as well as classroom life, the writing conference invites linguistic analyses adapted from more general studies of conversation (e.g., Clark, 1992; Sacks, Schegloff, & Jefferson, 1974) as well as analyses adapted from sociolinguistic studies of formal classroom interaction, such as the well-known studies of classroom lessons conducted by Mehan some years ago (1979; see also Campbell, 1986; Cazden, John, & Hymes, 1972; Green & Wallat, 1981; Wells, 1981). These two strands of research each emphasize the *social* and *constructive* elements of conversation. Conversation can be understood, in part, through participants' standing in particular relationship to one another, engaging in an unfolding process shaped and determined by (a) their own social and cognitive characteristics, (b) the conditions under which conversation occurs, and (c) their goals in achieving conversation with one another. The object of interest for researchers of both general conversation and the more specialized domain of classroom discourse is thus not the isolated utterance produced by the individual, but rather extended dyadic interaction mutually constructed (Gumperz, 1982; Levinson, 1983; Tannen, 1989). Taking this viewpoint, the study of teaching and learning, let alone dyadic teaching and learning, is often the study of conversational processes (Florio-Ruane, 1987).

Discourse analyses of teacher-student writing conferences have developed in part on the foundation of linguistic studies of discourse both in and outside school (see, especially, Florio-Ruane, 1986; Freedman & Katz, 1987; Freedman & Sperling, 1985; Sperling, 1988, 1990, 1991, 1992, in press; Ulichny & Watson-Gegeo, 1989; Walker & Elias, 1987). Research addresses questions about the structure and content of the writing conference, for example, or about implicit rule-systems governing teacher-student participation in conference interaction. While researchers from different theoretical and research backgrounds may differ in the goals they bring to writing conference study, many analyses focus on such structural concerns as raising and changing topics of conversation, interlocutor monitoring, asking and answering questions, and giving and following directions, as these impinge on such concerns about student text as engagement with its content, organization, or mechanics. In order to gain grounded insights into the ways in which such talk contributes to writing development for different students in different classrooms, research may also consider the place of the writing conference in the broader instructional context, as that context is shaped by the teacher and students in the classroom and located in the life of the school and the community—considering, say, other literacy activities that take place in the classroom, the teacher's and student's classroom goals, their objectives for a particular assignment, and student ability. In some writing conference research, discourse analysis of conference talk is one analytic tool employed in broader observational methodologies (see, e.g., Michaels, 1987; Sperling, 1988; Ulichny & Watson-Gegeo, 1989).

In sum, discourse analysis of writing conference talk is a mechanism for understanding how the writing conference is linguistically and sociolinguistically constituted, and how and why it is variously effective for students' writing development under different conditions of teaching. When analysis of writing conferences is informed by classroom particulars, that is, when researchers, aided by broader classroom study, can interpret how in the conference dyad "a set of individuals live together in the midst of the current moment, reacting to the moment just past and expecting the next moment to come" (Erickson, 1986, p. 129), the links they make between talk and student text, between talk and students' learning, and between talk and the development of students' writing processes, are less apt to be tenuous speculations than theoretically strong hypotheses. However, in order to be fully understood, the insights that can derive from such research must be seen from the perspectives of its methodological problems.

METHODOLOGICAL PROBLEMS

Problems develop throughout the research process. They are "caused" by a number of factors, including the classroom setting and the participants themselves, as well as the researcher's processes of recording writing conference activity, transcribing recorded data, gathering contextualizing information to inform conference discourse, and coding the data transcriptions. Undoubtedly, problems are caused by a number of other factors that will not be covered here. But usually the problems associated with the analysis of teacher-student writing conferences parallel those of research on general classroom discourse (see Cazden, 1986), and, since studying writing conference discourse often means making ongoing observations of the classrooms whose discourse we study, they also parallel the concerns of observational research in general. Delamont (1992), for example, in discussing what she calls the "pitfalls" of observational research methodology, presents as problem-ridden the processes of obtaining the setting, recording the action, and analyzing and theorizing about data. A focus on the study of writing conference discourse does not shift the location of these problems but imbues them with the particulars of the writing conference context.

Classroom Setting and Participants

Selecting a classroom in which to study writing conferences is, ideally, a process informed by the research questions and the research objectives. Obviously, the classrooms under study are those in which conferences are held. Depending on the research, writing conferences may preferably be frequently occurring events; it is also interesting to contrast classrooms in which conferences occur along with other interactions around writing, with those in which they constitute the only such interactions. In any case, no two classrooms that are of theoretical interest to a given research study will be alike,[2] and any number of factors can contribute to even one classroom's being different from one time to another. This variability, both between classrooms and within a given classroom, is an inherent problem in the research: Because classroom setting and participants shape the data, they also influence what the researcher can discover in the data at different times.

One English class that I recently selected for study demonstrates that *setting* and *participants* in even a single classroom are shifting variables. In this classroom, a teacher-intern, a graduate student from a nearby university, was present each day in addition to the regular teacher who taught the class. I understood when I selected the classroom that, though the intern would be present at the time of my observations, she would not be teaching the class. When the intern's timeline for assuming teaching responsibilities was modified by her university's graduate program, and she began to teach some of the class sessions during the last weeks of my observations, the classroom setting could not be regarded as the same as the one I had originally selected. And though I continued to record only the teacher-student writing conferences that occurred between the students and the regular teacher, even these may have been affected by the intern's emerging teaching presence. What I could discover in the regular teacher's writing conference data, then, was likely not what I would have discovered had the intern remained on the sidelines.

The story of the intern makes obvious the connection between classroom discourse and the internal shifting that inevitably occurs in classroom setting and participants. Such occurrences as the occasional presence of substitute teachers may have long-term effects on the dynamics of classroom discourse. And teachers' or students' own personal life-changes—in one classroom that I recently observed, the teacher was experiencing family changes and selling her house; in another the teacher's husband had died the year before; one student's stepmother had just "kicked him out" of the house—can affect teacher-student conversation in unmeasurable ways. To choose a setting in which to study the natural processes of teacher-student discourse about writing means to select an ever-changing phenomenon that constrains discourse accordingly.

Recording Writing Conference Activity

As teacher-student writing conferences, even when they occur in the midst of other classroom activity, are dyadic events, the researcher changes the discourse event the minute she sits in on it to record it. In a very immediate sense, when the researcher's hovering presence, albeit silent, expands the dyad to a triad, the researcher becomes part of what she studies,[3] even when the researcher sensibly absents herself bodily from the conference conversation and relies instead on the "impersonality" of recording equipment not only to act as stand-in observer but to pick up every spoken word in the order spoken, a feat that is beyond most human capability. Video equipment captures even more than words, allowing the researcher to supplement verbal with nonverbal data that can critically inform analysis. Even equipment intrudes, and its presence can potentially alter the nature of teacher-student interaction; video cameras are more intrusive than audio recorders. The following anecdote illustrates this problem.

Lisa, a student in Mr. Peterson's ninth-grade English class, told me in an interview what it was like to have her class recorded on camera every day for 6 weeks:

INTERVIEWER: Um . . . Lisa. We, as you know, did a lot of videotaping. /uh huh/ And we've all these videotapes that we're going to be looking at over the summer. And we were hoping that some of the kids that we talked to would help us look at the tapes and help us kind of give us a sense of what was going on in the class.

LISA: (Agreeably) Oh yeah. Sure.

INTERVIEWER: Would you be able to do that?

LISA: Yes.

INTERVIEWER: Great.

LISA: Because I don't think you will be able to find out what our classroom was, because . . . You know. Usually we'd, you'd be sitting there picking your teeth but the camera's there, and you don't, you know. Geraldine once wanted to blow her nose, but she didn't because she was embarrassed.

Whether Geraldine's self-consciousness carried over to her writing conferences, and whether her communication patterns during writing conferences, or Lisa's, or anyone else's in Mr. Peterson's class, were affected by such needs as maintaining face in front of a camera are questions that can probably never be answered. A researcher can only rely on the felt sense that participants in teacher-student conferences are not self-conscious during the research period if they appear comfortable, their conversations seem uninhibited, and they behave generally in ways that are perceived as natural. Yet, in the final analysis, the talk that gets analyzed is talk that has been witnessed in its unfolding by the presence of a machine.

There is another side to this coin, and it is one that I have not seen discussed in any of the research literature on classroom discourse. It is, ironically, the condition often expressed by research participants themselves of growing easy with the equipment. That such growing ease may be a hidden problem came home to me when, at the end of the time in which I collected data in Mrs. Vance's 11th-grade literature class, I was confronted with the apparent pervasiveness of this condition. Students wrote in class about what it was like to have researchers in the classroom every day for a semester. These writings were anonymous, and the responses most often centered on the audiotaping and videotaping. Many students—18 out of 32—wrote about experiencing a growing familiarity with being around recording equipment and being recorded on a daily basis. In their writing, their observations included the following:

"When you first brought the camera in I was worried or nervous about screwing up. After a while I got used to it."

"I guess at the beginning it was kind of weird because I always noticed the camera. But then it just kind of became part of classroom. Soon I forgot it was there."

"I had no real problem with the people being in the classroom filming/ recording and so on. It's certainly a distraction at first—an intruder in the classroom which takes a lot of attention and people tend to give a lot of attention to. But pretty soon I (and I think everyone) realized that the people were discreet and to give the people a lot of time was only going to defeat the purpose of their own learning or grade."

"After the first few days, I don't think anyone really even thought about the fact that we were part of anyone's study. These people, cameras, and micro-phones just became a fixed part of the classroom."

These reactions are different from Lisa's; but the issue, I suggest, is the same—that the use of recording equipment and the fact itself of taping can affect the kind of information obtained. That is, the familiar feeling that many students in Mrs. Vance's class expressed about our research team and our equipment may, in fact, have affected the ways in which their communi-cation patterns changed over time—the familiarity, they indicated, grew the longer we were there. When research questions about teacher-student con-ferences include such concerns as change in discourse over time or differ-ences in the discourse of different students, then how and when students variously grow familiar with the equipment is arguably problematic to teas-ing apart the variables behind interaction patterns—though many research-ers who gather taped data assert that, because students do become familiar with the equipment, especially if students have opportunities to work with the equipment themselves before or during data collection, equipment does not muddy up the research.

Regarding equipment, placement will probably always be a problem un-til technology advances such that cameras and microphones become virtu-ally invisible. In studying Mrs. Vance's classroom, for example, we at first hung an omnidirectional microphone from the classroom ceiling because, near the ceiling, it was at least out of direct line of sight, although nothing prevented roving eyes from focusing upward from time to time, especially during set-up time when a member of the research team had to climb up on a chair to get the microphone in place. Hanging the microphone from the ceiling, however, eventually caused it to slip from its mounting, and when that happened we had no other choice but to start placing it on the floor, on a tripod. It will never really be clear whether the location—and relocation—of the microphone affected interaction patterns between the teacher and her students, for not only did the microphone location finally affect the patterns of foot traffic in the room, but, like the video camera, the microphone became a constantly visible extension of the classroom "audience," extending, as well, the "audience" embodied in another auxiliary tape recorder that picked up more softly spoken writing conference conversation. These logistic concerns are not just nuisance issues. They are centrally implicated in the conversational process.

Transcribing Recorded Data

The problems of transcribing taped data, that is, deciding what conventions of transcription to follow, have been discussed at length (see, e.g., Chafe, 1982; Gumperz, 1982; Tannen, 1984). As with discourse analysis in general, the conventions that the researcher follows when transcribing writing conference talk will determine what can be said about the data. That is, the amount, level, and kind of detail that the researcher includes on a transcript determine what kinds of questions can be answered by analysis. I have purposely reversed what may be the more usual conception of the relationship between transcription and research questions, that the research questions themselves will determine the type of transcription used. This opposition of viewpoints highlights a central dilemma of the transcription process. On the one hand, transcription is dictated, often in large measure, by the research questions themselves. On the other hand, the more detail in the transcription, the more ways a researcher has to see the data and to wonder about it. This dilemma also points to the often evolving nature of research questions and, hence, the frequent difficulty of predicting beforehand the appropriate questions to ask of the data.

In transcribing Mr. Peterson's teacher-student writing conferences, I opted to capture all the major intonation contours ("idea units," as described by Chafe, 1982) of participants' speech, thus recreating to a certain extent the rhythms and emphases of the speakers' emerging thought. Each intonation contour or idea unit was given a line of transcription (after Chafe), and punctuation at the end of a line indicated the overall intonation quality of the idea unit (commas at the end of the line indicated rising intonation; periods indicated falling intonation, and so on). This procedure yielded a visual account of ideas emerging.[4] Yet transcribing at this level of precision was not always warranted by the type of analysis I was doing, which was concerned mostly with who in the conference dyad asked the questions or made initiating assertions, and who raised and changed topics of conference talk. I finally decided that the few times the transcribing of idea units helped in the analysis was worth the effort. For example, in the following illustration, in which transcribed talk is divided into idea units and punctuated according to intonation, the student, Misa, was telling Mr. Peterson about her friend Winifred, whom she wrote about in her essay.

MISA: Because like- it's it's like- after I know her for awhile you know,
            and *then* I know she has a sense of humor,
            about something similar to mine.
            Sometimes I- you don't have to go,
            into details of how or what's happening,
            she just knows what's going on.
TEACHER: She knows?

Transcribing at the level of idea units and gross intonation allowed me to see at what type of juncture in Misa's conversational turn Mr. Peterson took his turn. As the example demonstrates, Mr. Peterson spoke at the point where Misa finished an idea unit and, with falling intonation, indicated that her turn was over, a sociolinguistically appropriate juncture. Because speakers tend to take new turns or monitor their interlocutor's speech near the ends of idea units, adherence to or aberration from this pattern in the teacher-student writing conference yielded information about the flow and ease of the writing conferences for different students (see Gumperz, 1982), and this information, taken together with other discourse information, helped account for the relative efficacy of conference talk for different students (on this point, see Freedman & Katz, 1987; Freedman & Sperling, 1985).

Indeed, Mr. Peterson confirmed in interviews that talking to Misa was always pleasant and that he looked forward to their conversations. Without this notation system I could not have developed certain insights, either, about the sometimes long silences that filled some writing conference conversations, such as the following exchange between Mr. Peterson and Donald:

MR. PETERSON: You know of an example of that happening?
DONALD: (silence—the duration and timing of a synchronous conversational turn)
MR. PETERSON: Specific example of that happening?

When transcribed as discrete—albeit silent—conversational turns, Donald's silences could be seen to direct and shape Mr. Peterson's turns much as if they had been spoken words.

The problem that goes with the method is that no matter what conventions the researcher chooses, as soon as he has made a decision about transcription, he has set limits on the data. I did not employ transcription conventions that mark fine-grained features of spoken discourse such as pitch or stress, for example, and thus lost opportunities to discover discourse patterns related to issues of cross-cultural or cross-gender communication (as indicated, for example, in the work of Burnett, 1992; Erickson, 1975; Gumperz, 1982; Michaels, 1986; Tannen, 1990).

Another problem with transcription is that decisions about the conventions to follow may not be evident until data analysis is under way. Yet this is only a problem if the researcher does not accept the tenuous conditions of this kind of research and the ongoing and recursive processes of balancing scribal descisions with analytical insights. In one study of teacher-student writing conferences, for example, I began transcription by capturing speech characteristics such as stammers, false starts, and stutters. During analysis, some of these details got in the way of interpreting conference transcripts, while some of them were critical to the interpretation process. Thus, during the analysis phase, I added the step of eliminating transcription detail selectively, keeping those details that added theoretical insight to the picture that was emerging, and eliminating those that did not. The following example includes two transcribed false starts and one transcribed uncompleted thought along with the annotation "stutters" at a spot where the stuttering itself was not transcribed.

TEACHER: Well,
　　　　the (stutters)
　　　　You say- *[false start]* the thing is that- *[false start]* the thing you're making
　　　　about 'em is they react to other people,
　　　　and not- *[uncompleted thought]*,
　　　　right?
STUDENT: Yeah.

The false starts in this illustration show the teacher's shifting and reshifting of focus from student ("you say"), to generality ("the thing is that"), back to student ("the thing you're making about 'em . . . "). The uncompleted thought, which comes out as a single idea unit ("and not-,") followed by another idea unit ("right?"), indicates that because the student is on the teacher's wavelength, the teacher can make himself clear with a partially articulated utterance. Transcribing the stuttering did not seem to yield similarly relevant information, so all the stutters were eliminated and the word "stutters" inserted in their place.

As indicated above, which details are worth capturing in any given discourse analysis drives a critical decision that weds scribal work to language theory. It follows that the conventions that others have perfected in transcribing recorded data do not necessarily capture information important in one's own research.

Gathering Contextualizing Information
to Inform the Conference Discourse

If teacher-student writing conference talk is to be understood in context, it is desirable, indeed critical, to collect a variety of contextualizing information. Obvious and key are copies of the writing that the student and teacher hold conferences about, and copies of drafts that get produced subsequently. Supplementary material might include other student writing, written assignment sheets, grading scales, student artwork, teacher's handouts, copies of what gets written on the blackboard, and classroom logs. Problems associated with gathering some of these data have, in my experience, more nuisance value than theoretical interest: Not obtaining a handout that the teacher has run out of is a correctable nuisance, and whether to obtain the handout poses no real dilemma, just a decision driven by considerations of time and need. Dilemmas mostly occur when contextualizing information involves the participants whom one is studying. Interviews are a good example. (See Chin, this volume, for an extended discussion of interviews as a source of data.)

Interviews with teachers and students (or administrators, parents, others) can yield information such as teacher and student motives for giving or completing particular writing assignments, their reactions to certain classroom writing activities, their own histories as teachers and students of writing, and, not least, their reflections on particular writing conferences. Such information can figure in important ways throughout data analysis and interpretation, yet the timing of such interviews poses a central dilemma.

On the one hand, interviews held during the observation period potentially alter the classroom context just by bringing to participants' consciousness previously unexpressed or undiscovered ideas about the teaching and learning of writing, or by emphasizing ideas already in mind. When surfaced, such ideas may shape what subsequently gets talked about in class or in conference and how talk proceeds. Additionally, if one is studying the conferences of only a few selected students in the class, the teacher should not know who these students are during the observation period so as not to influence their classroom treatment. As it is often ethically desirable to wait until the teaching year is over before the classroom teacher knows which students were being studied, interviews with the teacher about her students often need to wait until that time.

On the other hand, as it is often desirable in interviews to obtain information about specific writing activities that have occurred on specific days and involved specific people, waiting for weeks, and sometimes months, to ask about the people and activities means retrieving information that is no longer fresh in participants' minds, or information that shrinks, or grows, in participants' memories, even when their memories are jogged by listening to or watching tapes of the activities in question. (See Greene & Higgins, this volume, for a discussion of the recency effect; and DiPardo, this volume, for an alternative perspective.)

What keeps this dilemma from having a completely ambiguous impact on the research is the fact that the imperfection of the interview data is itself data. That is, the way in which an interviewee remembers classroom writing events, what she forgets and what she clings to, are all valuable pieces of information. Thus, whether to interview early or late in the research period is a dilemma with a twist: Either way, the researcher gains insights determined solely by the timing of the interview. An interview that I had with Mrs. Vance about the students in her 11th-grade literature class illustrates my point.

Janine, a student in the class, had several writing conferences with Mrs. Vance on an essay that she wrote fall semester, when I observed Mrs. Vance's classroom. At the end of the school year, 7 months later, I held an interview with Mrs. Vance about her students. In this interview, she remembered her fall-semester conferences with Janine and offered, unasked, the following information:

> One day we were talking and she [Janine] wanted a specific word in a sentence, and I said, well, draw a blank line, go ahead, and come back to it. No, I want the word now. And she actually blocked herself and wouldn't go on until she had the word in there and she was frustrated with me because I couldn't get into her head and come out with the word she needed.

Later in our conversation, Mrs. Vance added more about Janine, remembering a group interview assignment that Janine did in which the interviewee was Janine's father and the topic of the interview was his experience during World War II:

Three of them [students in the class] had interviewed her dad and were talking about what that experience—as a freedom fighter in Hungary—was like, and umn, it struck me that umn, her father as a 12-year-old used to dodge Nazi tanks and run around. And one time he was playing tag with this tank, and the tank gunner officer turned the turret around and tried to shoot him, and blew up his barn. His parents were *furious* with him for playing tag with this tank. It was completely about the kind of life that he has led and he comes to this country and I'm sure he brought with him that very rigid (defying of the Nazis). So my approach to her [Janine] was thinking of probably what it was like in her home and how she had to survive there . . . and I have just assumed that that played itself out and her survival thing is *"No,* I want this word now!"

What I learned from this late-in-the-year interview with Mrs. Vance was not so much the information that Janine's father was a freedom fighter in Hungary, which Mrs. Vance could have told me at any time, or even the information that Mrs. Vance needed to think of Janine's father when she was holding writing conferences with Janine, something she could also have told me in an earlier interview. Rather, what I learned was that this information stayed in Mrs. Vance's mind in such a way that it was important to bring it up when she and I had our interview 7 months after the fact. When Mrs. Vance talked about Janine, her most vivid and salient memory was that one conference in which she confronted Janine's writing process, to which she attached a good deal of meaning, and to which I, too, could attach meaning based on this interview.

In sum, to believe that we can gain "perfect" or "definitive" interview data if only we knew the secret about how and when to interview participants is misleading, for what is learned from any interview is a function of the time the interview occurs, its proximity in time to the writing conferences the researcher is trying to learn more about, and the perspective that that particular timing gives to that particular interviewee. In this sense, no interview is perfect, yet all can be valuable.

Coding the Data Transcriptions

Perhaps more than any other problems in the research process, the problems of coding lay bare the intimate connection between researcher and study. Because coding, that is, labeling and categorizing parts of the conference discourse, is based on the researcher's interpretive framework, it reflects not so much what is "in the data" as it does the researcher's decisions about how to see what is there—yet the researcher's decisions can be constantly evolving hypotheses.

When analyzing writing conference discourse, I have followed an approach influenced by linguistic studies of conversation.[5] I have often coded speakers' turns for the ways in which they function in the discourse both to structure conversation (for example, as a series of questions and answers) and to raise and shift the writing-related topics that get discussed. This cut on conversational data derives from the notion that conversation is structured syntagmatically, adjacent speaker utterances or adjacency pairs (e.g., question-answer, offer-acceptance, request-compliance) working constructively to create something bigger than each part. By examining writing conference discourse syntagmatically, I can describe the kinds of initiative different participants take in helping the conversation along. To know who is asking the questions, making the offers, requesting information, and about what, for example, is to know something about who is doing the conversational steering and toward what writing end, and hence to know about different ways in which writing conferences work as teacher-student collaborations for different students or under different instructional circumstances. The following excerpt of coded writing conference conversation between Mrs. Vance and Kenneth is an example. It is also an example of how the coding process itself causes problems.

In the example, Mrs. Vance and Kenneth discuss a troubling paper that Kenneth has written, an argumentative essay about a novel that the class has just read. Each transcribed turn is followed by a code that describes the adjacency relationship of the conversational turns:

(1) MRS. VANCE: Now what can I do to help you make it clear? [INITIATING QUESTION]

(2) KENNETH: Actually=
[PARTIALLY ARTICULATED ANSWER]

(3) MRS. VANCE: You know what you did wrong? [FOLLOW-UP QUESTION]

(4) KENNETH: Yeah. Because I didn't state my thesis /yeah/ clearly.
[ANSWER]

(5) MRS. VANCE: If you don't have any- it's like- if you don't know where you're going, you can't possibly get there.
[OFFER OF INFORMATION]

(6) KENNETH: True. I guess that's it. (laughs)
[ACCEPTANCE OF OFFER]

When this excerpt of writing conference discourse is coded for adjacency pairs, the "steerer" in the conference is seen to be the teacher, and the coding confirms and helps to define the researcher's felt sense about the teacher-dominated tenor of this conversation. Yet, and here is the problem, a close look at this brief exchange between Kenneth and Mrs. Vance shows us that if we squint, that is, if we change perspective, what we read as the "first" and "second" elements of each adjacency pair can be otherwise construed. That is, Mrs. Vance's turn 1, "Now what can I do to help you make it clear," is indeed an initiating question, yet it is a question that is in effect a response to Kenneth's being present at the writing conference in the first place, to his presenting to her a paper to discuss, to his need as a student to learn something from her as a teacher, all in their own way initiating moves. In this regard, it can be read as the second element in another, implied, conversational turn pair, rather than the first element of the pair transcribed. And, on a more explicit level, one can argue that her turn 3, "You know what you did wrong," while indeed a question, is also a response, that is, an uptake, to Kenneth's tentatively spoken "Actually" in turn 2. And in its turn, "Actually" serves as both partial answer to Mrs. Vance's turn 1 and as prompt for turn 3. Kenneth's turn 4, "Yeah. Because I didn't state my thesis clearly," can be construed both as answer to Mrs. Vance's turn 3 and as an offer of new information that elicits Mrs. Vance's turn 5, "If you don't have any- it's like- if you don't know where you're going, you can't possibly get there."

Linguists have begun to pay close attention to the ways in which speakers' conversational turns pull double duty. Clark's work on conversations (e.g., Clark & Schaefer, 1989) examines this phenomenon from the perspective of the *contributions* both participants make in moving conversation along. Not surprisingly, coding discourse for characteristics that by their nature have fuzzy boundaries is a problem. Though with training coders can break down and name conversation according to a certain scheme, because the boundaries on conversation shift as the pragmatics of conversation shift, coding becomes a laborious and often confusing process, fraught with dilemmas that can only be resolved by artificial decisions (if it feels more like a question than an answer, call it a question). That the process is laborious and confusing, however, is a theoretically appealing problem, one that helps us to notice and to understand the complexity of the conversational process.

In sum, in discourse analysis, the researcher often imposes what come to be felt as unnatural boundaries on holistic events; yet this sense of unnatural imposition actually helps in interpreting results.

CONCLUSION

Discourse analysis of teacher-student writing conferences is a relatively new methodology, with disciplinary reference points dancing in the intersection where ethnomethodology meets linguistics. As its roots suggest, it is a methodology that depends almost entirely on elements that lie just outside the researcher's control, that is, teacher and students acting on particular days in time, talking about particular student papers with their own evolutions through classroom lessons both past and present, bringing to their conferences a range of goals dictated by the broader curriculum as well as by their own personal objectives. It is also a methodology comprised of routines that the researcher cannot fully control: the technology and logistics of recording classroom activity; the scribal decisions behind transferring to the static medium of print and paper the dynamic process of unfolding discourse; the capturing of context that is itself constrained and shifting; the naming of discourse elements that often refuse definitive naming.

I have tried to suggest throughout this chapter, however, that the methodology's imprecise and sometimes ambiguous nature is what constitutes its theoretical appeal, for the problems brought about by the methodology can often help us understand the human character of what we study. The imprecision and ambiguity can, in fact, help us understand the convergent nature of human discourse and the complex net woven by humans in interaction with one another. This net may entangle its participants, but it can also trace their points of connection.

In spite of the problems that inhere in the methodology, I believe that human beings have a capacious potential to understand themselves in all their complexity and that, furthermore, past research can beneficially inform future research. Researchers need simply be mindful of the messages in what present themselves as research problems. It seems reasonable to speculate that through its potentials and in light of its dilemmas, discourse analysis of teacher-student writing conferences can help researchers learn about students' writing processes and think about relationships between oral interaction and students' learning to write. I see potential in this methodology for researchers seeking tools for distinguishing the character of writing conference instruction from other classroom writing instruction, and for discovering the writing conference's value for different kinds of students and different kinds of teachers. There appears to be potential in this method, too, for theorists seeking to understand the social roots of writing and of text.

In sum, discourse analysis of teacher-student writing conferences holds promise for uncovering processes by which written language may develop in an instructional context, and in understanding one pedagogy that aims to serve its development. Ironically, the problems associated with studying writing conference conversations may be the very reasons to pursue their study.

NOTES

1. By teacher-student writing conferences I mean one-to-one conversations between a teacher and student about the student's writing or writing process. Such conversations can occur from elementary school through college; they can be held during class or in the teacher's private office; they can be spontaneous or scheduled. What they have in common are their concerns with writing and their dyadic structure.

2. For a related discussion of classroom selection in the study of peer response groups, see Freedman (1992); for an account of finding appropriate classrooms for study, see Freedman, with Greenleaf and Sperling (1987).

3. While I believe that whenever one conducts research one is part of the research picture, I do not intend here to hone a fine epistemological point. Rather, I make the more mundane observation that when recording a dyad, three's a crowd.

4. The system used by Hull, Rose, Fraser, and Castellano (1991) is similar to this one. Theirs is based on Gumperz's concept of information units, similar to Chafe's "idea units," and marks gradations of contextualization cues such as intonation, pitch, and audibility; it also times pauses in speaker turns in numbers of seconds elapsed.

5. This discussion of coding is based on my own experience of creating quantitative summaries of coded writing conference discourse. Such summaries allow the researcher to describe discourse on the basis of the patterns that counting reveals. Other approaches may emphasize or deemphasize quantitative techniques. It is useful here to cite Erickson (1977):

> Differences among approaches lie not in the presence or absence of quantification per se (if one thinks of quantification simply as a means of summarizing information) but in the underlying assumptions of method and proof. . . . What is essential to qualitative or naturalistic research is not that it avoids the use of frequency data, but that its primary concern is with deciding what makes sense to count. (Cazden, 1986, p. 458)

REFERENCES

Barnes, D. (1976). *From communication to curriculum*. New York: Penguin.

Burnett, R. (1992). *Conflict in the collaborative planning of coauthors: How substantive conflict, representation of task, and dominance relate to high-quality documents*. Unpublished paper.

Campbell, D. (1986). Developing mathematical literacy in a bilingual classroom. In J. Cook-Gumperz (Ed.), *The social construction of literacy*. Cambridge, UK: Cambridge University Press.

Cazden, C. B. (1986). Classroom discourse. In M. Wittrock (Ed.), *Handbook of research on teaching* (pp. 432-463). New York: Macmillan.

Cazden, C. B., John, V. P., & Hymes, D. (Eds.). (1972). *Functions of language in the classroom*. New York: Teachers College Press.

Chafe, W. (1982). Integration and involvement in speaking, writing, and oral literature. In D. Tannen (Ed.), *Spoken and written language: Exploring orality and literacy*. Norwood, NJ: Ablex.

Clark, H. H. (1992). *Arenas of language use*. Chicago: University of Chicago Press.

Clark, H. H., & Schaefer, E. F. (1989). Contributing to discourse. *Cognitive Science, 13*, 259-294.

Delamont, S. (1992). *Fieldwork in educational settings: Methods, pitfalls, and perspectives*. London: Falmer.

Erickson, F. (1975). Gatekeeping and the melting pot: Interaction in counseling encounters. *Harvard Educational Review, 45*(1), 44-70.

Erickson, F. (1977). Some approaches to inquiry in school/community ethnography. *Anthropology and Education Quarterly, 13*, 149-180.

Erickson, F. (1986). Qualitative methods in research on teaching. In M. Wittrock (Ed.), *Handbook of research on teaching* (pp. 119-161). New York: Macmillan.

Florio-Ruane, S. (1986, April). *Teaching as response: The problem of writing conferences*. Paper presented at the annual meeting of the American Educational Research Association, San Francisco.

Florio-Ruane, S. (1987). Sociolinguistics for educational researchers. *American Educational Research Journal, 24*(2), 185-197.

Freedman, S. W. (1992). Outside-in and inside-out: Peer response groups in two ninth-grade classes. *Research in the Teaching of English, 26*(1), 71-107.

Freedman, S. W., with Greenleaf, C., & Sperling, M. (1987). *Response to student writing*. (Research Report No. 23). Urbana, IL: National Council of Teachers of English.

Freedman, S. W., & Katz, A. (1987). Pedagogical interaction during the composing process: The writing conference. In A. Matsuhashi (Ed.), *Writing in real time: Modelling production processes*. New York: Longman.

Freedman, S. W., & Sperling, M. (1985). Teacher-student interaction in the writing conference: Response and teaching. In S. W. Freedman (Ed.), *The acquisition of written language: Revision and response*. Norwood, NJ: Ablex.

Graves, D. (1983). *Writing: Teachers and children at work*. Exeter, NH: Heinemann.

Green, J., & Wallat, C. (1981). Mapping instructional conversations: A sociolinguistic ethnography. In J. Green & C. Wallatt (Eds.), *Ethnography and language in educational settings*. Norwood, NJ: Ablex.

Gumperz, J. (1982). *Discourse strategies*. Cambridge, UK: Cambridge University Press.

Harris, M. (Ed.). (1982). *Tutoring writing: A sourcebook for writing labs*. Glenview, IL: Scott, Foresman.

Hull, G., Rose, M., Fraser, K. L., & Castellano, M. (1991). Remediation as social construct: Perspectives from an analysis of classroom discourse. *College Composition and Communication, 42*(3), 299-329.

Levinson, S. C. (1983). *Pragmatics*. Cambridge, UK: Cambridge University Press.

Mehan, H. (1979). *Learning lessons*. Cambridge, MA: Harvard University Press.

Michaels, S. (1986). Narrative presentations: An oral preparation for literacy with first graders. In J. Cook-Gumperz (Ed.), *The social construction of literacy*. Cambridge, UK: Cambridge University Press.

Michaels, S. (1987). Text and context: A new approach to the study of classroom writing. *Discourse Processes, 10,* 321-346.

Murray, D. (1979). The listening eye: Reflections on the writing conference. *College English, 41,* 13-18.

Rose, A. (1982). Spoken versus written criticism of student writing: Some advantages of the conference method. *College Composition and Communication, 33,* 326-330.

Sacks, H., Schegloff, E. A., & Jefferson, G. A. (1974). A simplest systematics for the organization of turn-taking in conversation. *Language, 50,* 696-735.

Sperling, M. (1988). *The writing conference as a collaborative literacy event: Discourse analysis and descriptive case studies of conversations between ninth grade writers and their teacher.* Unpublished doctoral dissertation.

Sperling, M. (1990). I want to talk to each of you: Collaboration and the teacher-student writing conference. *Research in the Teaching of English, 24*(3), 279-321.

Sperling, M. (1991). Dialogues of deliberation: Conversation in the teacher-student writing conference. *Written Communication, 8*(2), 131-162.

Sperling, M. (1992). In-class writing conferences: Fine-tuned duets in the classroom ensemble. *English Journal, 81*(4), 65-71.

Sperling, M. (in press). Speaking of writing: When teachers and students collaborate. In S. Reagan, T. Fox, & D. Bleich (Eds.), *New directions in collaborative teaching, learning, and research.* Albany: State University of New York Press.

Tannen, D. (1984). *Conversational style.* Norwood, NJ: Ablex.

Tannen, D. (1989). *Talking voices: Repetition, dialogue, and imagery in conversational discourse.* Cambridge, UK: Cambridge University Press.

Tannen, D. (1990). *You just don't understand.* New York: Morrow.

Ulichny, P., & Watson-Gegeo, K. A. (1989). Interactions and authority: The dominant interpretive framework in writing conferences. *Discourse Processes, 12,* 309-328.

Walker, C. P., & Elias, D. (1987). Writing conference talk: Factors associated with high- and low-rated writing conferences. *Research in the Teaching of English, 21,* 266-285.

Wells, G. (1981). Language as interaction. In G. Wells (Ed.), *Learning through Interaction: The study of language development* (Vol. 1). Cambridge, UK: Cambridge University Press.

Vygotsky, L. (1986). *Thought and language.* (A. Kozulin, Trans.). Cambridge: MIT Press.

10

What's All This Talk I Hear?
Using Sociolinguistic Analysis to Locate and Map Themes in Teacher/Student Talk About Writing

ELIZABETH HODGES

Fact: In most writing classrooms, talk predominates. In 1986, when I was in my ninth year as a teacher of writing and poised to begin my dissertation research, this fact was what I most wanted to investigate. Unsurprisingly, an extensive history of investigation into the nature of classroom interaction exists, offering observations ranging from descriptive and predictive (cf. Barnes, 1972; Bellack, Kliebard, Hyman, & Smith, 1966; Flanders, 1970; Medley & Mitzel, 1963; Mehan, 1974, 1979; Stubbs, 1986) to social and political (cf. Brodkey, 1986; Gilmore, 1983; Giroux, 1983). Most of these studies do not pertain to writing classrooms, however. To begin looking at how teachers and students actually go about talking about writing, and how that talk contributes to students' achievement of college-level literacy skills, I embarked on an ethnolinguistic study of a semester-long composition course and course-related activity. To make sense of this data, I developed (after much sampling of models for discourse analysis) an analytic system for coding verbal data in transcriptual form for the purposes of conversation analysis. I will discuss this system shortly, but before explaining that methodological development and the general usefulness of conversation analysis for educational research, I want to address a few whys and wherefores of the data collection.

A rationale for analyzing verbal data sociolinguistically, like a rationale for collecting verbal data ethnographically, assumes that discourse connects "the social and the cognitive" (Cazden, 1988, p. 86). It assumes, too, that language is social and that any theory of how language functions socially "must encompass the multiple relations between linguistic means and social meaning[s]" (Hymes, 1974, p. 31). The truth of these assumptions is straightforward, perhaps even obvious, but the reality of embracing them involves several enduring problems that may seem to compromise rationales for ethnolinguistic studies.

Often, efforts to collect data that represent multiple relations fully result in extensive data more suitable for book-length than journal-length research reports. For example, my study of the composition course generated approximately 90 hours of tapes. Thus, as is not uncommon to reports based on large verbal data samples, my reports from this study often present relatively small portions of data in detail, a fact that some critics of ethnolinguistic inquiry feel compromises attempts to represent contexts richly. The demands of educational research sometimes further complicate the issue of how much data can be presented in that educational research usually wants, and needs, implications or prescriptions for teaching; while the nature of ethnolinguistic research, with its roots in anthropology and sociolinguistics, is to work for description first, if not solely. Seeing in as much detail as possible how language works in context takes priority; to do so means determining both social and linguistic relationships and rules within a context.

There is little in this mode of inquiry that is efficient or neat or quick, a reality that can easily cause those of us who do such research to feel trapped between an institution we can usefully inform and a research method we have adopted for viable and belief-laden reasons. We work to find ways to show the usefulness of our work without forcing it to produce premature implications for teaching, and we work to generate assertions and observations, which, though often exemplified through small data samplings, are grounded in larger data analyses. The choice to share findings through the use of limited samples or case studies is epistemological: Detailed small samples illustrate the very depth of context we see as crucial to understanding teaching and learning.

Another challenge for ethnolinguistics involves the validity of interpretation and the nature of qualitative inquiry. Simply put, the ethnolinguist enters a context, altering it even if only by presence alone, and proceeds— with pen, tape, video—to record language use in that context through the filter of self she brings to that context. She may participate in the context to varying degrees. She may be familiar with that context to some extent. She brings along her own baggage, in my case about teaching, learning, writing, school. She focuses her pen, tape, video. Later she types up notes, transcribes tapes, logs videos. She revisits the people she has watched and asks them questions about what she has recorded them as having said or done. Together, the researcher and the subjects negotiate meanings, reconstructing them to document as accurately as possible what happened—to tell the most authentic story—a word I use very purposefully even though its implication of at least an element of fiction may be off-putting. The story, narrative, or anecdote is a valid and powerful device for creating a text that is rich and engaging (Brodkey, 1987; Herndl, 1991; Van Manen, 1990). While the fictive and the subjective are potential problems in ethnolinguistic reconstruction (if not all research), their impact is less problematic than often presumed. Ethnolinguistic accounts reduce language data according to linguistic principles, even though they acknowledge the extent to which the account is also subject to human selection and introspection. In the course of positioning oneself in the research, an ethnolinguist strives consciously for what might be called controlled subjectivity, that is, acknowledges that the analysis of data invariably exceeds explicit methods of analysis.

DATA COLLECTION

The study generating the analytic methods described here grew from a belief that systematic, careful listening to how the teaching and learning of writing play out in course discussions will improve us as teachers. The simple wisdom of this belief contrasted sharply with the complexity of acting it out. Stubbs' argument that the "social functions of language ought to be related explicitly to the linguistic forms that realize them" (1986, p. 244) suggested to me that attention to the cohesion of course conversations would improve understanding of the systemic nature of conversational interaction. To collect data, I observed and audiotaped all meetings of a fall composition course, and I did case studies of five randomly selected pairs of students as they worked through assignments at different points in the semester. When the class broke into groups, I followed the teacher or joined a particular group to observe a case study student. I taped spontaneous interviews, the teacher's conferences with the 10 case study subjects, protocols of the teacher grading those students' essays, and protocols of the students rereading their graded essays with the teacher's comments.

The 20 students in this course, mostly first year, had chosen a university to which students bring widely ranging school and language experiences. Composition courses like the one studied aim in part at familiarizing students with the discursive practices of the academy, challenging students to demonstrate more sophisticated levels of analytic ability and take greater responsibility for personal academic progress than ever before. In such a course, perhaps as nowhere else in the academy, one sees the extent to which language constructs social reality. Language is both topic and context. As producers and products of language, students and teachers negotiate, consciously or unconsciously, the fact that often their context is not benign.

Analytical Strategies in Theory

By the end of the semester I had collected enough talk to fill approximately 1,200 single-spaced typed pages, which I separated into classroom talk and course-related talk. To say that my analytical methods were influenced theoretically by various models for discourse analysis oversimplifies the evolution of those methods, for after several years of studying strikingly different models, and after a year seeking the best model with which to make sense of the data I was collecting, I gave in to the reality that there was no best model waiting in some source I'd not tapped. I doubt there ever is. Instead, I realized that I had become familiar with a wide range of linguists' individualistic ways of looking at talk, some more replicable than others, in which I could ground my fashioning of a suitable system for coding.

The linguists who shape the domain of discourse analysis differ according to what most concerns them and how they go about looking at talk. Speech act theorists, Austin (1962), Grice (1973), Searle (1969, 1979), propose rules or principles for how talk works and how conversations are organized, each offering his own concepts of the function of language and the uses of utterances. In *Pragmatics,* Levinson (1983) argues that conversation can be organized by units coming out of the work of ethnomethodologists (cf. Cicourel, 1980; Garfinkel & Sacks, 1970; Goffman, 1976, 1981; Sacks, 1972, 1974; Schegloff, 1968, 1979; Schegloff, Jefferson, & Sacks, 1974), who code the organization of actual or natural discourse for behaviors such as turn-taking, opening and closing, repair, adjacency pairs, and so on. Gumperz (1982a, 1982b), Gumperz and Herasimchuk (1975), Gumperz and Hymes (1972), and Hymes (1974) are concerned with what Hymes categorizes as "socially realistic" and "socially constituted" linguistics (1974, p. 195); their studies examine genres of speech events, the telling of stories, language rituals, formal negotiations, and so on as those events take place in natural contexts. Discussions of paralinguistic cues (cf. Birdwhistell, 1970; Cicourel, Jennings, Jennings, Leiter, Mackay, Mehan, & Roth, 1974; Erickson & Shultz, 1982; Gilmore, 1984; Goffman, 1961) call attention to the roles of eye motion, proxemics, posture, and the like in face-to-face encounters. Sociolinguists such as Bernstein (1971), Ervin-Tripp (1973), and Labov (1972, 1973) explore dialects and registers, personal and group styles. Halliday and Hasan (1976) examine syntactic issues of communication in ways that explain cohesiveness. Spradley (1979) calls attention to issues of topics and thematic unity.

These few representative linguists, however, though differing greatly at times in approach and concerns, do share a core strategy. Their work with verbal data involves searching for patterns, which is where I always start. Before formally analyzing transcripts, I study them for patterns. In the transcripts I refer to here, I looked for patterns that would help me describe and organize the overall semester's conversation. Those patterns that struck me as most relevant to the questions I was asking pertained to the features of articulations and to themes. To code the transcripts for these two kinds of patterns, I developed and combined two systems of classification, one to isolate lexical and structural patterns in the features of student/teacher statements, and a second, suggested to me by Spradley's (1979) domain analysis, to pinpoint recurring themes.

The first classification resulted in four categories of statements: Definition Statements (D), Rule Statements (R), Function Statements (F), and Nexus Statements (N).

Definition: "A first draft is not a final paper"—the teacher structures her point about a rough draft using the verb "to be"—definition by negation.

Rule: "You must not expect your first draft to be your final paper"—the teacher's statement, is structured in the imperative, using "you must not." One could argue that the verb "to be" makes this statement a definition, but I see an emphasis more directed at what students should not *do* than to what a rough draft *is*.

Function: "When writing your first draft, you should try to keep going and not worry about things like spelling and punctuation"—function statements explain a process, in this case, for how an aspect of drafting works.

Nexus: "If you try to make your first draft your final draft while worrying about things like spelling and punctuation when it's time to be developing your ideas, your paper probably won't be too successful"—this nexus statement contains two chronological relationships, one conditional relationship, and one causal relationship. Nexus statements, which connect concepts and

often contain numerous and varying relationships, accounted for half of all
statements made during the semester.

Spradley's domain analysis, which categorizes thematic content via cultural symbols, led me to reanalyze the transcripts for conversational themes
and to isolate four major categories: writing, reading, language, and world.
A second domain analysis examined how the statements that fell into each
category related to the other categories. This second analysis led to a subdi-
vision that resulted in the eight thematic categories I used for coding: Writing-in-Theory (A), Writing-in-Practice (B), Value-of-Writing (C), Reading/
Writing Connections (D), Reading/World Connections (E), Language Issues (F), Course Context (G), World Issues (H). To clarify this coding, let
me discuss four examples from the teacher's talk that fit into category C,
Value-of-Writing, a category accounting for those statements that address
evaluatively the quality of writing, the uses and usefulness of writing, practices for writing, and so on.

1. "A thesis is a very valuable guide for writers."
2. "Write those ideas down so you don't lose them!"
3. "Every successful paper I've written has gone through the prewriting process
   to find a thesis, then the drafting process where I develop my ideas, then the
   revising process where I make changes, then the editing process where I clean
   it up."
4. "If you dive right into an impromptu essay without planning, your essay isn't
   going to come out too well."

Taxonomically, all four statements fit under the topic of writing. Compo-
nentially, each addresses the value of something about writing: The first
values a thesis as a writer's guide; the second values writing for making
ideas tangible or retrievable; the third and fourth value a process approach
to writing.

These two systems for classification can highlight the frequency of statement structures or themes over the semester. Combined (see Table 10.1),
these classifications slow down teacher/student interaction and the processes embedded in it, showing the movement of talk thematically and the
shaping of it structurally.

Of the four value-of-writing examples above, the first is a Definition
Statement in Value-of-Writing (DC), the second a Rule Statement in Value-
of-Writing (RC), the third a Function Statement in Value-of-Writing (FC),
and the fourth a Nexus Statement in Value-of-Writing (NC).

TABLE 10.1

		A	B	C	D	E	F	G	H
Statement Typology	D	DA	DB	DC	DD	DE	DF	DG	DH
	R	RA	RB	RC	RD	RE	RF	RG	RH
	F	FA	FB	FC	FD	FE	FF	FG	FH
	N	NA	NB	NC	ND	NE	NF	NG	NH

Structural Classification Codes:

(D) Statements of Definition   (F) Statements of Function
(R) Statements of Rule   (N) Statements of Relationship

Thematic Categories:

(A) Writing-in-Theory   (E) Reading/World Connections
(B) Writing-in-Practice   (F) Language Issues
(C) Value-of-Writing   (G) Course Context
(D) Reading/Writing Connections   (H) World Issues

In various ways, this scheme for system helps me tell the stories of interaction embedded in teacher/student talk. The following application of the scheme serves several purposes. It shows moments in a particular student/ teacher story in ways that go beyond descriptive or even impressionistic narrative because the coding breaks the conversation into clear and manageable units. The thematic codes of these units make possible the mapping of themes as the conversation moves from talk about the world to talk about writing-in-theory to talk about reading/world connections and so forth. This coding scheme, particularly when used in conjunction with the noting of other varieties of discourse behaviors or moves, also illuminates how social realities are constructed in teacher/learner discourse. The particular analysis I offer here comments on two familiar pedagogical concerns—the student/ teacher conference and student ownership of text.

ANALYTICAL STRATEGIES IN PRACTICE

"What's the topic?"

Though relying mostly on transcriptual data, this analysis is informed also by descriptive notes taken during the conference. Transcripts can represent interactions very accurately, but they are twice removed from context. In fact, once transcribed, tapes become written texts and are stripped, aside from transcriptual notations or observational notes, of visual information, voice inflection, and speaking patterns. Transcript notation for providing some sense of these easily lost features can get quite complicated (cf. Gumperz, 1982a; Hull, Rose, Fraser, & Castellano, 1991; Ochs & Schieffelin, 1979), particularly for readers unfamiliar with such symbols. For this reason in part, I often strive to use minimal symbolic notation. I underline talk spoken loudly, use the symbol // to indicate when a speaker is interrupted; I note the length of pauses with bracketed numbers indicating seconds or with ellipses in which each point equals a second for pauses less than 5 seconds. I include partial words, repeated words, and at times spellings that reflect pronunciation. To give further context, I provide, in appropriate places, descriptions from my observation notes, at times sparingly using less than neutral words or phrases, which supply context more accurately than neutral language would. I emphasize this latter point so that readers might not feel manipulated by connotations when my sole intent is to replicate context.

With Strip 1, I demonstrate coding application in a pair of exchanges in which a teacher and her student, Glen, begin what will become a difficult negotiation over a paper topic. Each statement has been coded according to the scheme summarized in Table 10.1.

The teacher, Ms. Furness, has asked for an essay on some topic the students have expertise in. To help them find topics, she leads the class in a discussion of two sample student essays, one of which is a humorous paper on how students should go about selecting and getting into courses. She then offers several ideas for where students might have expertise (e.g., job, hobby, travel) and asks them to prewrite to find possible topics. When finished, some share topics with the class while Ms. Furness comments and makes general suggestions to the class based on various students' topics. Finally, she puts students in pairs to discuss their potential topics with a partner who will, in the next class, peer edit the resulting draft. Glen pairs with Elliot. Ms. Furness moves from duo to duo, entering discussions and commenting. She joins these two as they shift from Elliot's topic to Glen's.

Strip 1

MS. FURNESS: Okay, well I'd like to see what you're thinking about (NG). Test
     taking, have you written about this before (NB)? I know that's a popular topic

(DH). [Glen shakes his head no.] Oh I'd *love* to read about this (NE)! What do you think about these people [people who live on the Main Line] [1] (NH)? How would you describe them (NH)?

GLEN: They they there's lots of things (DH).

The coding in this brief strip locates the themes mostly in nexus (N) between the writer, the readers, and world issues. One use of locating the themes or topics of interactions is to gauge the extent to which individual or overall interactions focus on writing and related language issues. In the overall analysis of this semester of classroom discourse, for example, students' talk about potential topics is often located thematically in world issues (H), and it is clear that certain students get so lodged in world issues that they repeatedly have difficulty moving from world issues into writing-related themes.

Mapping thematic locations, then, might in one instance predict a pattern for a genre of interaction (e.g., finding topics will produce talk that has a high percentage of world issues themes), or thematic location might predict a pattern for certain writers (e.g., a sign of students who for some reason have trouble getting into writing might be that they do not move from talk about ideas to talk about representing those ideas in writing). The location of themes might also say something about the appropriateness or successfulness of a conversation. For example, an overall analysis of all the classroom interaction collected during the semester shows that approximately 70% of the themes can be categorized as A through D (Writing-in-Theory, Writing-in Practice, Value-of-Writing, Reading/Writing Connections). Though I have not generated any particular rule for how much talk about writing is necessary for a writing course to be "on task" or "on topic," this 70% suggests to me that Ms. Furness's course was very much so. Simply, my instincts suggest that 70% is a decent percentage while, say, 50% might indicate a lax focus. Another example: In small group talk, or in conference talk as we will see in the strips to follow, if the percentage of writing talk were particularly low, thematic location might shed light both on possible causes for degrees of interactional success and about ways to improve such interactions.

In Strip 1, the coding foreshadows a difficult interaction to come. Ms. Furness's first statement, a course-context nexus, establishes both her interest in Glen's and Elliot's conversation, thus a nexus, and her role of teacher, thus my thematic choice of course context. Her second statement, a question actually, is a writing-in-practice nexus; she wants to determine if Glen has a prior writing-in-practice relationship with this subject (i.e., she wants to know if he has already written this paper.) Her question risks confrontation as asked, implying distrust even though distrust may be only generally or genericly felt, if felt at all. Indeed, Glen seems startled. He turns his head quickly and looks directly at her with seeming confusion. Her next statement, a world issues definition, perhaps attempts a repair, that is, attempts to fix the potential damage done by her prior statement. It refocuses their interaction on the subject of test-taking instead of the student's relationship to the subject. But Glen answers her initial question silently, shaking his head no, and she refocuses again on his other topic, perhaps another repair.

I code this last statement as a reading/world connections nexus because she clarifies her relationship as a reader who would be interested in this subject. She then, in two world issues nexus, focuses fully on the subject of Main Liners and, uncited here, demonstrates her knowledge of that group by offering her own descriptors (e.g., Ms. Furness: "You know you're with a Main Liner when um they talk about friends named Muffy and Buffy."). Pretty clearly, Ms. Furness wants Glen to write about Main Liners, but after she moves on to the next duo, Elliot and Glen discuss the topic till Glen decides that it would cause him to stereotype people, which both he and Elliot agree is unacceptable. So Glen chooses test-taking as his topic just as Ms. Furness announces that she is inspired by Glen's idea of Main Liners for his topic and gives the class a sample paper in which people in malls are classified by their reasons for being there.

Glen meets Ms. Furness for a conference the next day. When she asks if he is going to write about "the Main Line people," he admits he has opted for test-taking in order to avoid stereotyping. She indicates that test-taking is okay, but suggests ways to get around stereotyping if he wants to write about Main Liners.

Strip 2

1 MS. FURNESS: All right, if you make it um you're honest about it and you say that these are certain types, exaggerated types (FB), probably it's okay to do that (DG). I mean, it's okay with me (DG).
2 GLEN: Well the thing is//
3 MS. FURNESS: It would have to be funny (RA).
4 GLEN: Right.
5 MS. FURNESS: The thing is?
6 GLEN: The thing is ah with say that essay that was written about mall people?
7 MS. FURNESS: Yeah?

8 GLEN: That was easier because people would have a general idea about mall people (DA) and when they go to the mall say, "Yeah, I do also," (NE) whereas Main Liners, not too many people know about them (NE).

9 MS. FURNESS: Hmm?

10 GLEN: It's not the same concept (DH). I mean, they really relate to those people (NE), and so . . . I thought maybe I could get myself into some trouble there (NE).

11 MS. FURNESS: Well what is your ah other topic (NB)?

12 GLEN: Guidelines for test-taking (DB). It's sort of gonna be funny (DA), what people should do as opposed to what they really get around to doing (DB).

13 MS. FURNESS: Well . . . you could do that (NA). I think I looked at your outline of the test paper (NB). But I don't want to discourage you about writing about the Main Liners if you want to (NG).

14 GLEN: If I found a way of getting around the stereotyping, maybe I could do it but. . . . (FA)

15 MS. FURNESS: Well but the whole point would be to stereotype, wouldn't it (DA)?

Thematic coding here indicates that the conference focuses on writing, usually in theory. In turn 1, Ms. Furness offers a writing-in-practice function for using exaggerated types. She follows this statement quickly with two that I code as course context definitions; their phrasing defines the potential paper as appropriate for the course. I am content with this coding decision, yet I can see how both statements might be coded as course context rules because they cancel a rule Ms. Furness established earlier in the semester: Papers that stereotype are unacceptable. These statements also work as repairs; they change course context to make it favorable for Glen to describe these people if he wants.

Glen begins to say something, but Ms. Furness interrupts with a writing-in-theory rule for the paper. Catching herself when he says "Right," perhaps because he says the word in a monotone which indicates "not right," she repairs again, repeating what he said before she interrupted, thus giving him back the turn she's taken. He takes the turn, changes the topic slightly and asks a question to reorient her focus; then, in turn 8, he offers a writing-in-theory definition in which he theoretically defines the comparative ease of writing the two papers, offering as warrant two reading/world connections nexus, in this case between readers and topics. He stops talking, but Ms. Furness does not take up the turn. With "Hmm?" she channels the burden of talk back to Glen, perhaps not understanding his point, perhaps refusing to engage with it.

To highlight the difficulty of this interaction, I supplement thematic and structural coding by noting repairs and turn negotiation. Thematic location here pertains to writing, though there is no clear movement from theory to practice, something one might expect in a conference the day before a rough draft is due. In fact, Ms Furness's response in turn 7 forces Glen's statements thematically away from writing and back out into the world. Structurally, the statements in this strip tend heavily towards definition. In the overall course analysis, definitions and rules were frequent only early in the semester and on the first days of new units, as if both kinds of statements pertained mostly to getting started.

In turn 12, Glen offers a writing-in-practice definition, naming his topic, and a writing-in-theory definition, saying the paper will be funny. He follows with a writing-in-practice definition about potential content. Interesting here is whether Glen had humor in mind before this conference or if he offers it now as a repair for the purposes of negotiation; he knows she wants him to write about the Main Line. At this point, Ms. Furness looks away, at the wall above her desk, and offers a writing-in-theory nexus, her voice rising in pitch as some people's do when speculating, saying "You could do that" in a manner which is clearly not offering a go ahead. Instead, she reintroduces the possibility of another topic by implying through her delivery *and you could do something else.* She makes two discourse moves and changes the topic back to the essay classifying Main Liners, then refers to a nonexistent outline. Still looking away, Ms. Furness does not notice that Glen looks surprised.

Speaking faster, she again sanctions the stereotyping of Main Liners as acceptable to the course with a course content nexus which is particularly interesting in how it positions her and Glen. She has not censored this particular paper topic, but her words suggest that she fears she has: "But I don't want to discourage you about writing about the Main Liners if you want to." In this statement she creates personas of a teacher who has somehow discouraged a student and is repairing that damage, and of a student who truly wants to write on a subject. Both characters are fictions, and I find it hard to believe Ms. Furness does not recognize that fact. Glen clearly wants to write about test-taking; she clearly does not want him to.

This round goes to Ms. Furness. Glen, his voice rising speculatively as does hers three statements before, his eyes focused on the floor, acquiesces, saying there may be some way to avoid the problem of stereotyping. Significantly though, he lets this sentence-turned-question trail off into a pause before Ms. Furness takes the floor and offers a writing-in-theory definition to sanction stereotyping by defining the paper as in that genre. In control of both the floor and the subject, she gives a writing lesson on using caricature for humor and to lessen the effects of stereotyping.

While writing this analysis, I have begun several times to apologize for this teacher, a subjective move I work to control. A difficulty of research deeply embedded in context is that people who allow themselves to be studied are very generous; any mention of something less than positive seems a personal critique, even though one is looking to describe interactions, not individuals. Work with verbal data highlights teachers' and students' less delightful communicative moments rather as magnifying mirrors highlight less delightful skin features. The fact is that few teachers, however careful and seasoned they may be, have not, at one time or another, found themselves pushing a student to write a paper or make a revision that goes against the student's wishes. Teacher interests can blur teacher awareness. Ms. Furness's initial reaction to the topic makes clear that this potential paper on Main Liners is one she very much wants to read; consciously or not, she is willing to fight for that opportunity. The bout continues; Glen speaks in a rush of short, structurally repetitive sentences and at one point even stutters. The interaction now moves thematically from writing to world issues.

"So you want me to write two papers?"

Strip 3

16 GLEN: Well, you see, Marie said that she's from the Main Line (NH) and that though there are people *like* that (DH), there are Main Liners who aren't (DH). And I'm from the Main Line myself (NH), and I'm not like (DH) that and she's Marie not like that (DH) and I I I think I got the feeling that if she read it she would be somewhat offended (NH) and so I was thinkin' if there was no way for me to classify a certain set of people, then I shouldn't write it (NB).

17 MS. FURNESS: Would the way to get around it . . . you don't want to offend people (DE), but the way to get around offending people is to do it in a humorous vein, in a real//(FB)

18 GLEN: I . . . that's what I was gonna try to do (NB), but it just seemed like it would be too difficult (DA) and maybe I wouldn't come across as well as I wanted (NE) and would end up maybe offending somebody (NE).

19 MS. FURNESS: Well you won't know until you try it (RB). You ought to give it a try (RB).

20 GLEN: Well maybe I'll write both (NB)?

21 MS. FURNESS: And bring them to class (RG).
22 GLEN: You think I should bring them both (NG)?
23 MS. FURNESS: Bring them both (RG). You have to bring them on Tuesday
    (RG), so why don't you bring both and we'll let your partner see if it's
    offensive (NE).

When Ms. Furness finishes explaining caricature, Glen is ready with another attempt to explain why he doesn't want to write this paper. In a series
of world issues nexus and definitions, he identifies a class member, Marie,
as a member of the group he would be stereotyping. He also categorizes
Main Liners as diverse, identifying himself as a Main Liner and establishing that neither he nor Marie fits the definition the stereotype would
perpetuate. With a reading/world connections nexus, he asserts that the
essay would insult Marie, and then he brings the conversation back to
writing, offering a writing-in-practice nexus for why he cannot write the
paper: Classifying is unavoidable. Ms. Furness, acknowledging his concern
in a reading/world connections nexus, offers a writing-in-practice function,
again suggesting humor as the approach to take. Glen again retreats from
the topic with four statements that move him from writing-in-practice to
writing-in-theory to reading/world connections. But with two writing-in-
practice rules, Ms. Furness compels him to try to write the paper. Finally,
Greg suggests that perhaps he should write both papers, raising his voice in
question after "both."

I classify his suggestion as a writing-in-practice nexus, but can see that it
might be a question about course context. For a student to sincerely offer to
write two papers is unique. His disbelief when she accepts his suggestion is
clear in step 22, a nexus of course context which seeks to clarify whether
she really expects two essays. It seems more likely that rather than offering
willingly to write two papers, Glen is testing the environment and its rules.
Course context, the nature of and rules for the setting, is a substantial part
of what students and teachers negotiate. In the overall course interaction,
course context accounted for 11.1% of the talk.

"Oh, well, Jonathan Swift offended people . . ."

The conference concludes; Glen has withdrawn. Face still, he gazes at the
desk surface. Ms. Furness—perhaps in victory, perhaps in repair of the
damage clearly done, perhaps a combination of both—moves the conversa-

tion thematically to world issues in a series of statements that explain her interest in the Main Line.

Strip 4

24 MS. FURNESS: I lived on the Main Line for a couple of years, in Narberth (NH). I just rented an apartment there (NH), but I know exactly what you are talking about (NH).
25 GLEN: Yeah but Narberth, you're not from there (DH).
(She claims Main Line experience; when she names the town she lived in, Glen defines it and her as not from the Main Line, but she deflects that rebuttal and refocuses on stereotyping another Philadelphia "type.")
26 MS. FURNESS: Well not really (DH). I only lived there for 2 years (NH), but there . . . anywhere you go there are some people who just stand out and there are certain Main Line types just like there are certain North Philly types (NH). Now nobody wants to say that everybody who lives in North Philly is like that ridiculous stereotype we think of (NH), but you could do a humorous sketch of that too (NB).
27 GLEN: [9 sec] All right (NG).

Ms. Furness seems to make a writing-in-practice suggestion that North Philadelphians would make a good subject too, and Glen, after a relatively long pause, says "All right." I classify this as a course content nexus because he seems to be giving in to her will. He is not engaging in the conversation. In fact, he says little as Ms. Furness goes on to sanction stereotyping again by mentioning several comedians who use stereotypes effectively. Thematically, most of Ms. Furness's statements are categorizable as world issues.

Strip 5

28 MS. FURNESS: Who's a good one at that (DH)? Whoopi Goldberg (DH). Now nobody gets up there and does what she does (NH). Did you ever see her (NH)?
29 GLEN: The Jamaican (DH).
30 MS. FURNESS: She does that Jamaican, but she also does in the beginning . . . I don't know that he has a name (NH). Whoever he is, she's calling everybody bla-bla-bla-bla-bla.
31 GLEN: Yeah, the addict (DH).

32 MS. FURNESS: The drug addict, right (DH). Well? . . . I mean that's a stereo-
      type (DH).
33 GLEN: True (DH).
34 MS. FURNESS: But people don't get offended when they see that (NH). Hmm?
      And or when Richard Pryor does it or Eddie Murphy or anybody makes a
      stereotype (NH). If you do it correctly and you do it humorously (FH).
35 GLEN: Well that's why at first I didn't think it would be a big deal until (DH),
      you know . . . some of the people read my outline and thought maybe it might
      be so . . . maybe I should just kind of abandon it unless I can (NB)//
36 MS. FURNESS: Oh well, Jonathan Swift offended people too (NE) and every-
      body reads him these days (NC).

Returning thematically to writing-in-practice, Glen tries one more time to
avoid writing the paper about Main Liners, invoking as authorities peers
who have read his outline and advised him against the topics. (Interestingly,
just as Ms. Furness earlier referred to a nonexistent outline for a paper on
taking tests, Glen now refers to a nonexistent outline for a paper on Main
Liners.) In step 36, Ms. Furness seems to relent, but not without invoking
an authority of her own, Jonathan Swift, whom she holds up in a reading/
world connections nexus as a model of one who offended audiences, but
whose writing is valued highly now (NC).

This last comment is intriguing. One must wonder if Glen knows who
Swift is and to what Ms. Furness is referring. No Swift has been read for
this course, nor is Swift a writer Glen has ever mentioned having read. Also,
Ms. Furness offers an odd notion—Swift offended people, but the fact the
he is read today somehow justifies his offensiveness—which seems counter
to what she usually advises students. Swift had writerly goals that involved
denigrating and angering some of his readers; Glen makes quite clear that
he does *not* have such goals. Glen is concerned with the image he presents
as a peer writing to his peers, and he is in no way concerned with the
possibility that his paper might be read widely by future readers.

METHODOLOGICAL APPLICATIONS CONSIDERED

Admittedly, most readers of the above strips might be able to tell a story
similar to the one I have told without what may appear to be the clutter of
the coding scheme. However, a coding scheme, whether the one described
here or another, enables systematic and articulate interpretations, the kind of

TABLE 10.2

	Strip	Writing ABC	Course Context G	World Issue H	Other DEF	Total
	1	1	1	4	1	7
	2	11	3	1	4	19
	3	7	4	7	4	22
	4	1	1	8	0	10
	5	2	0	10	1	16
Total		22	9	33	10	74

interpretations that are credible and lucid for those who read and use them. Tracing, as I have here, the interweaving of themes or the linguistic forms realizing themes can document many attributes of teacher/student interaction so that those attributes are recognizable, in our own teaching as well as in the teaching of others. We can see where talk fails because teacher goals with or for writing are not consistent with student goals. We can isolate moments when and ways in which interaction could have been more effective—when something said was taken wrong, when an assumption needed probing, when a question should have been asked. Such insights can help us monitor, interrogate, and adjust our habits for responding to students, leading us to both personal and general predictions about teacher/student interaction, which can enable us to move knowledgeably and carefully in our interactions.

What if, for example, Ms. Furness were frank with herself and students and at the start of a course told them that at times she may get so excited by some of their ideas that she gets pushy and that students should feel free to call her on that pushiness? What if Glen had then felt free to ask early on why she preferred one subject to another? What if Ms. Furness were tuned in to talk enough to note the thematic routing in interactions, recognizing when it strayed for too long or in unuseful ways from writing? In the five consecutive interactions between Glen and Ms. Furness offered here, the ratios of thematic categorizations to the total number of statements in each strip offer a telling pattern (see Table 10.2).

World issues, though certainly relevant to learning and teaching writing, account for 45% of the total statements in this interaction. Combined, the three categories that pertain directly to writing (A, B, and C) account for only 30%. Talk clearly pertaining to writing pretty much ceases after Strip

3, turn 20, and During Strip 3, talk about writing equals talk about world issues. Evident, too, in Strips 2 and 3 is negotiation of course context.

This mapping, by itself, merely summarizes the fact that talk about writing was short-lived during this conference, but analysis of specific strips and use of additional sociolinguistic coding concepts can illuminate interactions in detail. The coding scheme described here is unwieldy at first, but it is manageable and can be internalized conceptually. When teachers collect talk in their own settings, such a scheme can help them understand the content and nature of their interactions with students as well as students' interactions with each other. In one study, this method helped me determine that a student's problems with his writing had to do in part with his inability to make certain critical thinking moves, and in part with his inexperience with idiom, word choice, and connotative meaning. In my work with new teachers of writing, this coding scheme helps us talk in specific ways about the interaction of their classrooms, conferences, and tutorial sessions. Of course, this latter use often highlights for me the fact that coding decisions can vary from coder to coder, but the negotiation stimulated by such differences is a valuable part of using such a system to access talk meaningfully. In my research, I work for consensus through negotiation with those I have studied. In my work with teachers, similar negotiation occurs, and perhaps in this latter context more than others, the value of such coding becomes clear: Without obscuring data, this and other frameworks for discourse analysis employ specific attributes for describing and examining what we are doing when we teach and what our students are doing as our learners.

NOTE

1. "The Main Line" refers to a series of towns stretching perhaps 10 miles west, along Route 30, from the outskirts of Philadelphia. The towns are hubs for the surrounding suburban and rural region, which has a reputation for high-income brackets—horse country, private schools, country clubs, old estates.

REFERENCES

Austin, J. L. (1962). *How to do things with words*. Oxford: Oxford University Press.
Barnes, D. (1972). Language learning in the classroom. In Cashdan et al. (Eds.), *Language in education*. London: Routledge and Kegan Paul.

Bellack, A., Kliebard, H., Hyman, R. T., & Smith, F. L. (1966). *The language of the classroom.* New York: Teachers College Press.

Bernstein, B. (1971). *Class, codes, and social control.* London: Routledge and Kegan Paul.

Birdwhistell, R. L. (1970). *Kinesics and context.* Philadelphia: University of Pennsylvania Press.

Brodkey, L. (1986). Tropics of literacy. *Journal of Education, 168,* 47-54.

Brodkey, L. (1987). Writing ethnographic narratives. *Written Communication, 4*(1), 25-50.

Cazden, C. B. (1988). *Classroom discourse: The language of teaching and learning.* Portsmouth, NH: Heinemann.

Cicourel, A. V. (1980). Three models of discourse analysis: The role of social structure. *Discourse Analysis, 3,* 101-132.

Cicourel, A. V., Jennings, K. H., Jennings, S. H., Leiter, K. C., Mackay, R., Mehan, H., & Roth, D. R. (1974). *Language use and school performance.* New York: Academic Press.

Erickson, F., & Shultz, J. (1982). *The counselor as gatekeeper: Social interaction in interviews.* New York: Academic Press.

Ervin-Tripp, S. (1973). *Language acquisition and language choice.* Stanford, CA: Stanford University Press.

Flanders, N. (1970). *Analyzing teaching behavior.* New York: Addison-Wesley.

Garfinkel, H., & Sacks, H. (1970). On formal structures and practical actions. In J. C. McKinney & E. A. Tiryakian (Eds.), *Theoretical sociology.* New York: Appleton-Century-Crofts.

Gilmore, P. (1983). Spelling Mississippi: Recontextualizing a literacy-related speech event. *Anthropology and Education Quarterly, 14,* 235-256.

Gilmore, P. (1984). Silence and sulking: Emotional displays in the classroom. In M. Saville-Troike & D. Tannen (Eds.), *Perspectives on silence.* Norwood, NJ: Ablex.

Giroux, H. (1983). *Theory and resistance in education.* South Hadley, MA: Bergin and Garvey.

Goffman, E. (1961). *Encounters.* Indianapolis: Bobbs-Merrill.

Goffman, E. (1976). Replies and response. *Language in Society, 5,* 257-313.

Goffman, E. (1981). *Forms of talk.* Philadelphia: University of Pennsylvania Press.

Grice, H. P. (1973). Logic and conversations. In P. Cole & J. Morgan (Eds.), *Syntax and semantics* (Vol. 3). New York: Academic Press.

Gumperz, J. J. (1982a). *Discourse strategies.* New York: Cambridge University Press.

Gumperz, J. J. (1982b). *Language and social identity.* New York: Cambridge University Press.

Gumperz, J. J., & Herasimchuk, E. (1975). The conversational analysis of social meaning: A study of classroom interaction. In M. Sanches & B. Blount (Eds.), *Sociocultural dimensions and language use.* New York: Academic Press.

Gumperz, J. J., & Hymes, D. (Eds.). (1972). *Directions in sociolinguistics.* New York: Holt, Rinehart & Winston.

Halliday, M.A.K., & Hasan, R. (1976). *Cohesion in English.* London: Longman.

Herndl, C. (1991). Writing ethnography: Representation, rhetoric, and institutional practices. *College English, 53,* 320-332.

Hull, G., Rose, M., Fraser, K. L., & Castellano, M. (1991). Remediation as social construct: Perspectives from an analysis of classroom discourse. *College Composition and Communication, 42,* 299-329.

Hymes, D. (1974). *Foundations in sociolinguistics: An ethnographic approach.* Philadelphia: University of Pennsylvania Press.

Labov, W. (1972). *Sociolinguistic patterns.* Philadelphia: University of Pennsylvania Press.

Labov, W. (1973). *Language in the inner city.* Philadelphia: University of Pennsylvania Press.

Levinson, S. C. (1983). *Pragmatics*. Cambridge, UK: Cambridge University Press.

Medley, D., & Mitzel, H. (1963). Measuring classroom behavior by systematic observation. In N. Gage (Ed.), *Handbook of research on teaching*. Chicago: Rand MacNally.

Mehan, H. (1974). Accomplishing classroom lessons. In A. V. Cicourel, K. H. Jennings, S. H. Jennings, K. C. Leiter, R. Mackay, H. Mehan, & D. R. Roth, *Language use and school performance*. New York: Academic Press.

Mehan, H. (1979). *Learning lessons: Social organization in the classroom*. Cambridge, MA: Harvard University Press.

Ochs, E., & Schieffelin, B. B. (1979). Transcript notation. In E. Ochs & B. B. Schieffelin (Eds.), *Developmental pragmatics*. New York: Academic Press.

Sacks, H. (1972). An initial investigation of the usability of conversational materials for doing sociology. In D. N. Sudnow (Ed.), *Studies in social interaction*. New York: Free Press.

Sacks, H. (1974). An analysis of the course of a joke's telling in conversation. In R. Bauman & J. Sherzer (Eds.), *Explorations in the ethnography of schooling*. New York: Cambridge University Press.

Schegloff, E. A. (1968). Sequencing in conversational openings. *American Anthropologist, 70*, 1075-90.

Schegloff, E. A. (1979). The relevance of repair to syntax-for-conversation. In T. Givon (Ed.), *Syntax and semantics: Vol. 12. Discourse and Syntax*. New York: Academic Press.

Schegloff, E. A., Jefferson, G., & Sacks, H. (1974). A simplest systematics for the organization of turn-taking for conversation. *Language, 50*, 696-735.

Searle, J. R. (1969). *Speech acts*. Cambridge, UK: Cambridge University Press.

Searle, J. R. (1979). A taxonomy of illocutionary acts. In J. R. Searle (Ed.), *Expression and meaning: Studies in the theory of speech acts*. Cambridge, UK: Cambridge University Press.

Spradley, J. P. (1979). *The ethnographic interview*. New York: Holt, Rinehart & Winston.

Stubbs, M. (1986). *Educational linguistics*. Oxford: Basil Blackwell.

Van Manen, M. (1990). *Researching lived experience: Human science for an action sensitive pedagogy*. Albany: State University of New York Press.

Part IV
Interviews in the Field

11

Ethnographic Interviews and Writing Research
A Critical Examination of the Methodology

ELAINE CHIN

Interviewing has long been used by ethnographers to study cultural phenomena. However, it is only within the past several years that interviewing has become one of many methods composition researchers use in studying writing processes or the development of writing abilities. In large part, interest in interviewing has grown in proportion to interest in studying writing in naturalistic settings, of understanding how it is people write within particular contexts or situations. Although more research on writing now uses qualitative methods such as interviewing, little has been written about the ways in which the interview can be used in writing research, the specific questions that the use of such a method raises, or the difficulties researchers might encounter in using interviews as a means of gathering data.

In this chapter, I propose to take up these issues as a way to begin discussion around a much neglected topic. It may be that interviewing, and for that matter, all qualitative methods currently in vogue, have not been critically discussed in current literature on writing because these discussions have appeared in other forums, namely in articles on methodology or books on doing fieldwork written by sociologists and anthropologists (see e.g., Burgess, 1982; Ellen, 1984; Hahn, 1990; Kovar & Royston, 1990; Schegloff, 1990; Suchman & Jordan, 1990a, 1990b; Tourangeau, 1990). On the other hand, researchers of writing using qualitative methods may have felt the need to establish these methods as legitimate tools before subjecting them to the same kind of critical scrutiny applied to techniques that have been traditionally used in composition studies, techniques such as text analysis or the analysis of think-aloud protocols. Whatever the case may be,

a critical analysis of qualitative methods such as interviewing is long over-
due. To begin our discussion, let us first examine the issues raised by the
literature in sociology that looks at interviewing.

Many of the debates in sociology about interviewing have been concerned with making interviewing a more reliable form of data collection
(see e.g., Cicourel, 1982). In this case, reliability is achieved by standardizing questions and procedures for interviewing. Sociologists adopted the
standardization of such practices as a way to eliminate or at least minimize
researcher effects upon the respondents' answers. Standardized routines for
doing interviews reduce the possibility that respondents' answers will misinterpret the meaning of questions, thereby giving an answer that does not
reflect what they would have said had they known the true meaning of
the question. But, as Mishler (1986) and Suchman and Jordan (1990a) argue, the belief that standardization can improve the reliability of interview
data is based upon the mistaken assumption that interactions between interviewer and respondents can be stripped of their human elements.[1] Thus, the
responses elicited through an interview would reflect some "true" state of
affairs or some "true" set of beliefs held by the interviewee.

Attempts to improve reliability of interview data rely upon the assumption that researchers can ascertain a "truth" if standard scientific methods
are used, an assumption that has come under increasing attack by social
constructionists. Literature has begun to appear that challenges the traditional notion that standardized interviews can capture the true beliefs of
respondents. In addition, some sociologists (e.g., Mishler, 1986) have begun to argue that interviews themselves are a discursive practice, governed
by many of the rules of social interaction implicit in other activities in
which discourse plays a central role.

In composition research, protocol analysis came under a similar kind of
attack by researchers taking a social constructionist perspective. Social constructionists argue that generalizations made about cognitive processes rest
on the precarious claim that think-aloud protocols in some way reflect what
happens inside a writer's mind. It is not my aim to discuss the merits of
either side of this debate in this chapter. I do find it curious, however, that
the critical light shone on think-aloud protocols as a research methodology
has not been turned upon interviewing as well. A case can be made that
interview data are just as susceptible to being an inaccurate account of what
people do and think about in writing, that is, if accuracy is the goal we
strive to achieve. We may not be able to see how interviewing is problematic because there is still the tendency to read interview data as true reflections of people's thoughts and practices. After all, they are gathered in

naturalistic settings under naturalistic conditions. But the very "naturalness" of the conversations between researcher and participant masks the "unnaturalness" of the interview process. In other words, our theoretical understanding of the social constructionist nature of writing has not been applied to a critical examination of our own practices in doing research on writing. This seems especially to be the case for research practices that satisfy our desire to conduct more contextually rich studies of writing. The lack of self-consciousness in using interviews as a research method can best be demonstrated by a brief examination of the current state of this art.

CURRENT USES OF
INTERVIEWING FOR STUDYING WRITING

In making the following generalizations about the use of interviews in writing research, I reviewed research reports published during the past 6 years (1986-1991) in two major outlets for empirical research on composition, *Research on the Teaching of English (RTE)*, and *Written Communication (WC)*.[2] To establish some common ground upon which to compare the articles in these two journals, I first identified all articles reporting on empirical studies of writing done with human subjects.[3] I then identified all studies within this subset of the articles which explicitly stated, or from which could be inferred, that interviews are one of the data sources. The results from this initial tabulation of articles reporting the use of interviews are listed below.

As Table 11.1 shows, the percentage of articles on writing involving human subjects that included interviewing as one data source is approximately equal for both journals. These numbers seem to indicate that interviewing, as a methodology, plays a significant role in writing research. We need, then, to begin to question the ways in which interviewing is used if so many of our findings depend upon our analysis of the data gathered using this method.

To evaluate the use of interviewing, we must first establish what type of interviewing technique is used,[4] and how the interviews themselves are conducted. Although this is a simple approach to take, it tells us something about how carefully researchers have approached the use of interviews. In other words, the more researchers see a methodology as problematic and thus open to examination, the more likely they will be to report in some detail the procedures used. (Compare, for example, the extensiveness and

TABLE 11.1: Articles in *Research in the Teaching of English (RTE)* and *Written Communication (WC)* Using Interviewing to Investigate Writing: 1986–1991

	*RTE**	*WC*	*Total for Both Journals*
No. of Articles	113	119	232
No. of Studies on Writing Using Human Subjects	64	59	123
No. of Studies on Writing With Human Subjects That Used Interviewing	22	21	43
Percentage of All Studies on Writing With Human Subjects That Used Interviewing	34.3%	35.6%	35.0%

*The total number of articles includes the annotated bibliography of research that appears in every May and December issue of *RTE,* as well as special reviews or commentaries that appear (e.g., the commentaries appearing in the February 1988 issue by Stotsky, Hayes, Purves, and Hillocks's regarding Hillocks's (1986) meta-analysis of composition research).

detail given for intervention studies, ones involving quantitative comparisons, or those using protocol data.) The results from this initial analysis are reported in Table 11.2 below.

In general, few reports give adequate descriptions of the type of interview strategy used, the procedures followed in conducting interviews, or the questions asked. Of the 43 studies that used interviewing, only 16 of the articles explicitly identify the interview type, for example, whether they were open-ended, discourse-based, or text-based interviews (see e.g., Cross, 1990; Doheny-Farina, 1986; Prior, 1991; Redd-Boyde & Slater, 1989). Of the remaining 27, only 15 contain enough detail to allow me to infer the type. The 12 remaining studies could not be categorized because of lack of detail.

Other details about the interviews (specifically how many, with whom, how often, in what context) are also noticeably thin in many of the reports. Articles that include such details stand out because they are so scarce in the corpus I examined (see e.g., Cleary, 1991; Hilgers, 1986; Swanson-Owens, 1986). More serious than the missing description of procedures is the lack of information about the questions asked during the interviews. None of the reports include an interview schedule in their appendices, although one report (Duffy, Post, & Smith, 1987) states that the interview schedule ap-

TABLE 11.2: Types of Interviews Conducted in Research on Writing as Reported in *RTE* and *WC:* 1986–1991

	RTE	*WC*	*Total for Both Journals*
No. of Studies on Writing With Human Subjects That Used Interviewing	22	21	43
No. Explicitly Stating Type of Interview Used	8	8	16
No. Where Type Can Be Inferred From Textual Clues	7	8	15
No. Where Type Is *Not* Stated and *Cannot* Be Inferred	7	5	12

pears in an appendix, which is not included in the publication itself. Only 6 of the 43 studies report some or all of the questions supposedly asked of the participants, or contain a transcript that shows the interviewer interacting with his respondent (see North, 1986, for an example of a study showing the interaction between researcher and interviewee). The majority of the authors (24 out of the remaining 37) merely summarize, with varying degrees of specificity, the line of questioning followed.

Because so little information is typically provided about the methods used in gathering interview data, it is difficult for readers to assess a report's findings. This should be of concern to any researcher interested in using and reporting the results from qualitative studies (or for that matter, any study that utilizes interviewing as a methodology), for the subjects' responses bear the major burden of supporting the claims researchers make. Moreover, current practices in representing interviewing as a methodology leave researchers open to the charge that such research lacks rigor, a charge that is hard to refute, given the evidence from our reports.

I offer two possible and related explanations for the thinness of these procedural descriptions. First, qualitative research in writing is still a relatively new development in our field and one that is only now beginning to have an impact on how research is conducted and reported. Thus, few conventions exist for how to write such reports. The conventions that have traditionally guided report writing developed out of a positivistic paradigm for doing research, a paradigm alien to what many writing researchers now advocate.[5] Second, we know that writers of research articles operate under constraints imposed upon them by reviewers and editors of journals where their reports are published. Editors can seldom allot to writers the amount of space in the major forums for the kind of complete and detailed accounts we might wish to see. As a result, researchers often have to sacrifice details about the research process in order to give a full account of the findings. After all, we cannot afford to become so engrossed in the process of doing research that we ignore its basic aims—to further our knowledge about writing and the teaching of writing. However, a close connection exists between our research practices and the findings we report. If those practices seem at all questionable, then so too are the findings themselves. This point has been demonstrated by self-conscious and self-reflective accounts of the socially constructed nature of doing research (see e.g., Clark & Doheny-Farina, 1990; McCarthy & Fishman, 1991).

This chapter represents one attempt to bridge the gap between our theoretical understanding of the socially constructed nature of research and actual research practices by problematizing interviewing as a methodology for investigating writing. As someone who has extensively used interviewing in her work, I am particularly concerned that we begin to articulate some principles for conducting interviews, to explore and make explicit difficulties in collecting, analyzing, and representing interview data, and to examine our own taken-for-granted notions about what it means to use interviewing as a method for data collection. I begin from the position that interviewing is a meaning-constructive activity. I do not assume that researchers and their participants share similar understandings of what it means to engage in an interview. Nor do I assume that responses given in an interview transparently reflect a stable, unproblematic set of propositions. Analyzing interview data is more akin to the interpretation required in analyzing a literary text; we imbue statements with a special significance, determined in large part by the particular theoretical frame we impose upon our projects. (See, e.g., Mishler's [1991] reinterpretation of transcripts from three studies for a demonstration of how different theoretical frameworks shape the analysis of interview data.)

The remainder of this chapter is divided into four major sections that examine in more detail the problematic nature of conducting interviews. In the first section, I explore the ways in which the material conditions for interviewing affect and interact with the personal characteristics of interviewer and interviewees, an interaction that plays itself out in terms of power relationships that are tied to status, culture, and gender differences. The second section examines differences between one-on-one and group interviews, especially as these conditions affect the construction of responses to topics discussed. The third section discusses what the interview, as a kind of discourse activity, may mean for various participants. And the fourth section problematizes writing as a topic for discussion.

My examples are drawn from a year-long ethnographic study of graduate students learning to write the news (Chin, 1991). Although the problems I encountered are restricted to this study and the context in which it was done, the issues I confronted in dealing with these problems are ones facing all researchers who choose to use ethnographic interviews in their research.

Let me begin by distinguishing between interviews and informal talk. In the course of any research project, there are a number of times when researchers acquire important information through conversations with their participants. They take place over the phone, on brief walks, in any place and at any time the researcher is in the field. As important as these conversations may be in helping a researcher develop a thick understanding of what is going on, they are not interviews if we mean by interviews a planned process during which the researcher and participants have agreed to talk about specific issues. Interviews are a specific type of interaction between participants governed by an implicit set of rules. These rules establish, to some extent, the purposes for an interview, the kinds of activities that can take place, the various roles, the actions assigned to each participants' role, and the structure of the interaction.[6] To state in a report that interviews have been used, then, is to claim that a particular kind of interaction took place between researcher and participants that has fulfilled specific purposes established by the researcher, or jointly negotiated between interviewer and interviewee. In this chapter, the term *interview* is used to refer to the purposeful type of interaction described above.

CONDUCTING ETHNOGRAPHIC INTERVIEWS

No one definition can characterize the variety of approaches used in conducting ethnographic interviews. Some are more formal than others. Some require participants to do various tasks, such as sorting items, demonstrating procedures, or talking about an activity that the researcher has observed the participant do earlier. Questions may follow a schedule developed in advance by the researcher, they may arise during the course of the interview, or the two approaches may be combined. However, the common thread in ethnographic interviews is that the questions asked reflect the researcher's growing understanding of how the culture under study is organized and how people of that culture make sense of their experiences. Given this rather general understanding of ethnographic interviews, it is perhaps more fruitful to explore what happens during such interviews. We can begin to develop better ways of designing and using ethnographic interviews once we begin to identify those features of an interview situation that may shape the form and content of these interactions.

Conditions for Interviewing

Little attention is typically given to describing the specific conditions for the interviews themselves. We rarely read details about the setting for or time spent in interviews, who was present, what exactly was done during the interview, and how responses were recorded. These details are presented, if at all, as merely background information. Although these features may not be described in our formal reports, this background information tells us much about the interview itself. This is particularly true if we consider how context interacts with the roles and status researchers and their participants take on during a research project.

For example, I began my fieldwork as a graduate student in education. Having spent 4 years in graduate school, I felt comfortable working within an academic setting and confident about my knowledge of how to behave in such a setting. The chief participants in my study were faculty and graduate students of a Department of Communication and Mass Media Studies at a West Coast research university, which I call "Bayview University." My goal was to describe how graduate students in a one-year master's program learned to become journalists by learning to write news stories. I was careful to tell faculty and staff that my aim was to describe the students' learning processes and not to evaluate the program itself. I also made it clear to everyone involved that I was a graduate student and that I was doing this study for my dissertation. It was relatively easy to gain access to and acceptance within the program I wished to study. Both faculty and students were willing to let me sit in on classes, observe them while they worked, interview them, and collect samples of their writing. On the surface, I seemed to be very much a part of the journalism program.

However, as an outsider, I was not given, nor did I expect to be given, desk space anywhere in the department. Other than the time I was in the classrooms, most of my time was spent in the hallways, in the area containing the students carrels, or in a courtyard outside the building. This situation posed particular problems when I began to interview the faculty and students.

Interviews With Individual Faculty

With the faculty, the major difficulty involved scheduling time to meet in their offices. Given my own experiences as a student, I knew how much time and how many meetings I could reasonably expect faculty to give to this project. So, I scheduled no more than one 30-minute interview with each faculty member per term. Thirty minutes was about the amount of time the faculty typically gave to meetings with their own students. One meeting per term seemed a reasonable number of interviews to them since my focus was the students' learning, not their teaching. The faculty interviews were designed to help me understand what the professors were trying to communicate to students about journalism in their courses. That meant that my interviews with the faculty had to be quite focused. I went into these meetings with a list of major questions and a few possible follow-up queries. Given the aims of these interviews and the time constraints, I did not have the leisure to allow questions to emerge from the conversation itself.

In addition, because the interviews took place in the instructors' offices, these meetings tended to be more formal than my meetings with the students. The instructors always sat at their desks. I usually sat in a chair on the other side of the desk. The door to the office was shut during these conversations because the faculty sometimes told me information that they did not want made public. I was well aware that the faculty held the power in that situation and controlled, to a greater extent than the students did, the conduct of each interview. That is not to say that the faculty were in any way uncooperative or less than direct in their answers. However, it seemed to be the case that, in their eyes, I was a student rather than an independent researcher.

Faculty might also have been more likely to view me in a student role because I looked and dressed very much like the other students. I tended to dress casually and carried a backpack, a sure sign of studenthood. I made a conscious decision at the start of my fieldwork to present myself in ways that resembled the students rather than the faculty, in large part because I did not want the students to perceive me as being different from them. Moreover, the age difference between the faculty and myself was larger than that between the students and me. The majority of the faculty are male while the majority of the journalism students during the year of my study were female. About half of the journalism students belonged to a variety of ethnic groups. Superficially, I was not distinguishable from the rest of these students. My youthful appearance worked to my advantage in helping me establish rapport with the students and in presenting a nonthreatening, non-evaluative persona to the department at large.

Interviews With the Students

Interviews with the students developed a different set of dynamics from those with the faculty, in part tied to the material conditions in which these interviews were conducted. While the faculty had offices where information could be exchanged in private, students occupied open carrels, all located in a central location. Most lived in apartments or dorms with roommates or spouses. Moreover, I hesitated to ask students about interviewing them in their homes without having first been invited there for a social occasion. I felt it was important to maintain some separation between their public life at school, which they had permitted me to study, and their private life at home, which was not open to observation. Because there was no private place on campus that belonged to each student as such, I did most of the student interviews in various places around and off campus. Often we would talk over a meal or coffee. When the weather was nice, we would sit on benches, tables, planters, or on the lawn just outside the department. I needed to situate these interviews outside the department and in places where the students and I could see whether our conversations could be overheard by people in the department. Even though what students told me was not highly personal or confidential in nature, they did say things about the faculty, the program, and other students in the department that they did not want attributed to them. The open spaces, albeit public ones, then served the same function as the closed faculty office door in maintaining the confidentiality of their responses.

The general informality of the setting of my interviews with the students also contributed to the informality of the interview situation. Although I did formulate my questions in advance of these meetings, the topics discussed were open to negotiation. In general, my interviews with the students tended to be more loosely structured. I was also less likely to follow a strict interview schedule. These meetings tended to be longer in length (about 1 to 1.5 hours long) and more conversational in tone.

As I stated above, my resemblance to the students made it considerably easier for me to gain their trust and to convince them to participate. But there was another dimension to my involvement with some of the students that was not reported in my dissertation—my ethnicity and gender. I do not know to what extent my being a woman and an Asian-American might have affected any student's decision to participate. I do know, however, that in talking with some of the women and some of the minority students, topics were discussed that reflected our mutual concerns about what it means to be a woman in a male-dominated profession and what it means to be an ethnic minority in a field where such groups are so underrepresented (especially at Bayview, where the journalism faculty is predominantly Anglo and male). I based my decisions not to report on this aspect of my study and the ways these factors affected my data collection upon three central concerns.

Foremost was my concern that the participants of my study, especially my six key informants, remain anonymous in all subsequent reports. Given the uniqueness of Bayview's program and the possible visibility of these students later in their professional careers, I could not give so many details that any one individual could be identified. My understanding of professional ethics required me to do nothing that would fracture the agreement I forged with the students and faculty about maintaining their anonymity.

From a research standpoint, I downplayed individual differences among the students so that I could make larger claims about general tendencies in their learning and development as journalists. Focusing on individual differences was not in my research plan at that time, nor was it a part of the larger research question I had chosen to ask. Consequently, I did not systematically gather data about individual differences that were or were not related to gender or ethnicity. Any information I gleaned about these effects arose naturally, within the context of my involvement with specific students. Moreover, a discussion about the effects of gender and ethnicity on journalism learning would have required me to design a different study from the one I conducted.

Finally, the conventions of research report writing dictate that researchers should neither report on their personal attributes nor include much analysis about the ways in which these attributes affect work in the field. Although a number of accounts have been published documenting how researchers' personal background affected their fieldwork (see e.g., Powdermaker, 1966; Rabinow, 1977; Rosaldo, 1989; Whyte, 1955), these narratives usually appear in prefaces, appendices, or in monographs separate from the research report itself. As a novice researcher and one needing the approval of a dissertation committee, albeit one sympathetic to alternative forms of dissertation writing, it would not have served my ends to have included a discussion about gender and ethnicity not germane to my central thesis. That is not to say that I agree with the current practices for writing reports. But change comes slowly to the field of research, and by raising the issue here, I hope to at least make explicit some of the constraints all researchers work under.

Individual Versus Group Interviews

The dynamics of any interview situation change radically whenever more than one person is being interviewed, or whenever more than one person is conducting the interviews. There were three occasions when I was able to do group interviews. The first was a luncheon I hosted, to which all the students in the journalism program were invited. At this luncheon, I asked students to talk about their impressions and experiences during their first term at Bayview. Some of the topics addressed were ones raised in the questions asked; others evolved during the course of the conversation itself. During the second, I interviewed pairs of students about their experiences in reporting and writing about a single event they had all witnessed. During the third occasion, I met with one pair of informants, as well as a third student who was in the journalism program but not one of my principal informants. At this meeting, I asked students to do a sorting task and to explain their reasons for sorting news articles into particular categories.

The sorting task provides a good example for comparing how the dynamics of interviewing change when more than one person is interviewed, because the task was done under two conditions: In one of the conditions, the group condition, three men engaged in sorting and talking about their decisions, while in the other I did separate one-on-one interviews with two women. For the story sorting task, students were asked to read leads from 16 articles published in local papers and identify the type of news article each lead represented. I had retyped the leads onto a separate sheet of paper and removed any information that would identify where and when the article had been originally published, in what section it had appeared, and who the author was. Initially, I did not use terms such as *hard news, breaking news,* or *investigative piece* in identifying categories the students might use for classification. However, when each of the students asked me if I wanted them to talk about the articles as being representative of "hard" or "soft" news, I told them that that was one type of classification I would be interested in having them pursue. The transcripts below show my discussion with the three men and with each woman about one of the articles.

The article being discussed is part of a continuing series of short news reports about a proposal to extend a road connecting a freeway with a major street that runs through a number of the local communities. The lead from this article reads as follows:[7]

Two weeks ago, petitions signed by 2,700 local residents opposed to the extension of Vista View Road were delivered to city councils in Green Acres and Hillside. The petitions were being circulated about the time a package of unsigned leaflets were distributed in the Valley Green neighborhood west of Hillside.

The lead from this article appeared second in the list of leads the students read. I have put the transcripts side-by-side in Table 11.3, so that readers can see how each discussion proceeded. With the exception of my interview with Lisa, only that part of the transcript dealing with the Vista View Road article is included. I excerpted part of my interview with Lisa about the first article's lead, which is not shown here, so that the reader can see Lisa's segue into her comments about the Vista View Road issue. After making her short comment about Vista View, Lisa immediately turns to the next lead on the page. Katherine makes an identical move, going from her final comment about possibly being assigned to reporting on Vista to a remark about the next lead on the list. The transcripts reflect exactly what was said, including hesitations, misstarts, and pauses. I have not, however, provided the kind of fine-grained transcription that would show overlaps, interruptions, or para-linguistic features that are usually a part of verbal interactions.

Even though each of the three interviews elicited similar ideas from all five students, there are some obvious differences in how these responses were generated because of the nature of the interaction. In doing the follow-ing analysis, I am not interested in evaluating the content of each person's comment, nor did I see any of their comments as being wrong, incomplete, or inadequate. I could argue that the task and the text provided may have prevented the students from offering more detailed explanations. The goal of this discussion is to demonstrate how the construction of an interview response varies from individual to individual, as well as to show how inter-actional work done in a pair versus a group context shapes these responses.

Superficially, we see that Lisa's response is quite abbreviated compared to either Katherine's or the three men's comments. Lisa's classification seems based on two interrelated criteria: (a) where the event is located, and (b) who its likely audience would be—the community. She does not elabo-rate on this further. For Lisa, merely labeling the story as "community-oriented" and "local" seems to be adequate for accomplishing this task. In contrast, Katherine and the three men provide more elaboration of the par-ticular labels used to categorize the lead. For example, Katherine calls it "an ongoing news story," "very short hard news," "a wrap-up," an "up-to-date," or a "parenthetical story about what's going on." She eventually rejects the term *wrap-up* because she does not see the article as being the conclusion to a series of articles on the Vista View Road extension. In contrast, the men

TABLE 11.3: Group Versus Individual Interview Transcripts

Group Interview With John, Mike, and Stan	Individual Interview With Katherine (Kath)	Individual Interview With Lisa
JOHN: This one, obviously assumes, a degree of familiarity with uh, Vista View Road issue. Just from the lead, but, my problem is the second sentence says nothing to me.	ELAINE: Okay. Now for the second one. KATH: This is, this is the kind of horrible a story I only get assigned to. It's like, who cares? I would say, this is like, local, it's like a local issue that has been going on for forever, and they have to document every little twitch that happens about it. So it's like an on-going news story. I mean, this Vista View Road extension thing is endless. And this seems like, kind of cute, a very short hard news, sort of parenthetical story about what's going on, but very definitely like an up, keeping people up-to-date rather than breaking news. Because it's two weeks ago. It's sort of a wrap-up. It's not even a wrap-up. I think, it's just like they have to, maybe it's one of those things where they have to write about Vista View Road because they have something on it every single week.	ELAINE: What's spot news mean? LISA: It's a story that, that at the time you know is really timely because they just filed suit. For example, it wouldn't be good to do this a week later. I mean, you could, but it wouldn't be as fresh. And this is a, number 2 is about the extension of Vista View Road. It seems more of a community story about the extension and, because there's a lot of protest about it, it seems like a more community-oriented local story.
MIKE: Yeah, I know. I don't get it.		
JOHN: Um, but		
STAN: You don't know what the story is going to be about.		
JOHN: It probably, if you want to put it in a category, it's probably going to be about a classic development, community versus development, story.		
ELAINE: mm hmm		
STAN: It's kind of a news, I don't know, it wouldn't be, it would be news, but not hard news in terms of timeliness. It's gotta be something.		

260

MIKE: Yeah, two weeks ago, I mean I'm sure this is the *Green Acres Weekly*. But still that's two issues ago.

ELAINE: What makes you think so?

STAN: It might be an analysis of the uh, . . . well, I don't know what it's an analysis of.

MIKE: Well, I mean, I don't get it. A petition is being circulated about the time a package of unsigned leaflets was distributed in the Valley Green neighborhood?

STAN: What's happening there?

MIKE: I mean, the fact that those two, coincided at the same time, what does that mean? Y'know, what's the issue?

ELAINE: Okay. Let's go on to the third one.

ELAINE: Well, this is in the Green Acres Weekly.

KATH: Y'know, they have something on it every week, so any little twitch that happens regarding Vista View Road is going to go in there because everybody's all flipped out about it.

ELAINE: Do you guys cover that in the *Brookside Weekly?*

KATH: Yeah. I don't, but somebody does. I may have to.

wind up not even agreeing on a particular label. John offers one classification: "a classic development, community versus development, story," while Stan claims it is "news" rather than "analysis," but rejects the notion of its being "hard news." What is more important than the content of the remarks in this case, though, is the way in which the students arrive at their various classifications for the lead.

Katherine frames her remarks with references to the type of work she does as a reporter at her internship with the nearby *Brookside Weekly*. Notice how she begins by personalizing the article as "the kind of horrible story I only get assigned to." She ends her response to this article by answering my question about the weekly's coverage of this issue in terms of her own work load: "I don't [have to cover Vista View Road], but somebody does. I may have to." Her classification seems based, in part, upon her understanding of how local weeklies tend to cover community affairs, knowledge gained from her reading of one of *Brookside Weekly*'s competitors—the *Green Acres Weekly*—and from her own experience interning on a similarly organized weekly publication.

On the other hand, the men approach the task of classifying the story as one that requires them to untangle the confusion inherent in the second sentence of the lead. John begins the discussion by naming the issue, Vista View Road, and then introduces the "problem" with the second sentence, namely, that "it says nothing to [him]." Both Stan and Mike pick up on the idea of the problem. Stan extends John's initial idea about the "problem" in the second sentence by stating that readers cannot "know what the story is going to be about." So, not only does the second sentence present a problem in and of itself, but it can potentially create problems for the entire story. Mike contributes to the "problem" topic by providing details about what the problem is: "the fact that those two [the circulation of the petitions and the distribution of the leaflets] coincided at the same time, what does that mean? Y'know, what's the issue?" It is also striking that John's suggestion that the articles be categorized as a "community versus development story" gets dropped as a topic for further discussion on this article. What happens by the end of this brief interchange is that none of the possible categories named is fixed to the article itself. I also contribute to the nonresolution of the problem sentence and to the nonclassification of the article by closing down the discussion with my suggestion that we move on to the next story.

The differences in groupings is one way we can account for the differences between Katherine's and Lisa's interpretations and the men's interpretations of the task. That is, the men jointly constructed an interpretation of the sorting activity that turned it into, at one level, a problem-solving situation. They reinforce each other's notions of what problem exists and try out various explanations for why it is a problem. By reinforcing this common interpretation of the task, the men dismiss any possible classification, but seem to reach some sort of consensus about the article. In contrast, the women do not engage in a problem-solving task with me. I offer them no help or support for doing such a task. Thus, the task becomes one for Katherine and Lisa of searching for appropriate labels for the article that they can tell me, a definition for the task that I provided in my explanation to them of this activity.

There is one other distinction to note between group and pair interviews that is revealed in my analysis of these three transcripts. My job with the group of three men was to act as a facilitator for the discussion. I am not able to show the extent to which I kept the men focused on the task and moving through the various leads. However, I tended to interrupt and make statements such as, "let's go on to the next one," so that the three men would not spend too much time talking about any one article. If I had not done so, the men probably would not have completed the task before our time was up. However, I was not a facilitator of discussion in my interviews with the two women. Instead, I was their conversational partner. Both Katherine and Lisa decided when they had finished with a classification. They would spontaneously take up the next article without any prompting from me.

Gender differences in the interactional groupings may have also played a role in how these conversations functioned. We know from various linguistic studies that there are differences in conversational style linked to gender (Tannen, 1990). However, to account for effects from gender requires a more detailed and systematic analysis than can be offered here. Until such an analysis is done, I merely raise the issue as one we should seriously consider when creating and participating in interview situations.

It is no trivial matter to see how responses to any task change as a function of the number of participants involved, for it directly affects how we might analyze data collected under various conditions. For example, if we look solely at the content of what each student said in the group interview, we might interpret their remarks as evidence that only John understands or can categorize the story because he is the only one who offers a classificatory label without retracting it. Or we might assume that the category John states is one that both Stan and Mike agree with, when, in fact, we do not have evidence of their agreeing or disagreeing with this categorization. Or we might code this activity as being incomplete because they never arrive at a firm conclusion about the story, an interpretation that does not take into account the features of the news story they were able to attend to, such as timeliness, knowledge about the publication where it appeared, knowledge about the kinds of stories likely to appear in local weeklies, all of which play an important role in students' ability to distinguish among various types of news stories. Any analysis of interview data then needs to take into account what factors might have shaped the data we collect.

Thus far, I have described various factors that might affect interviewing without considering how the interview as a particular type of speech activity might be understood as such by the various participants (Mishler, 1986). The next section examines how the interview itself may mean something different for the interviewees than it does for the interviewer, that in fact, the interviewees' perception of what interviews are about and what happens may be tied to presuppositions they hold about interviews themselves.

HOW PARTICIPANTS CONCEIVE OF
INTERVIEWS AND ITS EFFECT ON DATA COLLECTION

Like ethnographers, reporters depend heavily upon interviewing as a method of gathering information for the stories they write. But unlike ethnographers, reporters seldom have the leisure or time to engage in numerous, extended interviews with their subjects. Nor would the subjects for their stories, mainly public officials and bureaucrats, submit to such intrusions on their time. Given my observations of reporters at work, I would say that reporters tend to rely on "blitzkrieg" interviewing strategies. They operate under severe time constraints and thus ask only a few key questions. This is particularly true in situations when they must compete against other reporters for a subject's attention, time, and energy. Their questions then narrowly focus on specific issues or topics closely related to the stories being produced. Reporters are less likely to engage their interviewees in the kind of "grand tour" questioning used by ethnographers (Spradley, 1979). As a result of the differences in working conditions, expectations about textual products, and their own interviewing practices, reporters perceive of the interviewing process as something akin to, but much different from, how researchers may understand it. Thus, before entering the field, researchers must first develop some sense of how interviewing as an activity might be interpreted by the participants. Specifically, what the journalists and journalism students I studied understood interviewing to be affected how I went about gathering and recording my data.

As experienced journalists themselves, the faculty had fairly specific ideas about what typically happened in an interview, ideas that they communicated to the students in the journalism courses. Because I observed these class meetings when such ideas were discussed, I was able to adjust my own interviewing style to match more closely those ideas described by the faculty. It was important to make these adjustments with the faculty in particular, because of the limited time I had for the interviews with them, a point I stated in an earlier section of this chapter. Besides asking more focused questions that covered a narrower range of topics, I knew that faculty looked askance at reporters who merely tape-recorded and did not handwrite notes during interviews. The point was made by several of the instructors that audiotaping was perhaps one of the worst practices reporters had picked up over the years. For them, there was no substitute for the winnowing of details and the highlighting of key points forced upon reporters when they were not able to transcribe a source's comments. So in interviewing the faculty, I made sure the faculty saw me writing notes even though I always audiotaped the interviews. It was a way of establishing and maintaining my credibility with the faculty, as well as ensuring that technical failures would not disrupt my data collection.

Note-taking was not the only area in which I had to adjust my behavior to conform to the participants' expectations for interviewing. Early in their careers, journalists learn the difference between on-the-record and off-the-record comments. Being able to distinguish between the two and act accordingly can spell the difference between a successful, long-term relationship with a key source and a disastrous, short-lived one. For reporters, cultivating the former while avoiding the latter as much as possible is one key to getting information that can lead to the next major, breaking story.[8] This is especially true in a profession where the fruits of one's labor and off-the-record comments may appear in the next day's newspaper.

Ethnographers have their equivalents of on-the-record and off-the-record comments. They suffer from the same dilemmas that reporters do in deciding whether to reveal the confidences their informants may have told them. Some ethnographers are able to justify their decision to publish off-the-record comments because so much time has passed between data collection and the publication of the final report. The greater passage of time might, in some cases, ameliorate any harm informants could suffer from having revealed this information to the researcher. Sometimes, what may be off-the-record during fieldwork may be acceptable or even necessary to report after the fieldwork and analysis have been completed. However, ethnographers should be aware that the decision one must make in reporting confidences is an ethical dilemma that cannot be dismissed by merely stating that research serves larger ends than those of a single news story. As a practical matter, better relationships are forged between researchers and their participants when researchers respect the wishes of their participants in the recording and reporting of confidential information.

Whenever the journalism faculty expressly stated that a certain comment was off-the-record, I behaved in ways that conformed to their expectations: I turned off the tape recorder and set down my pen. After such interviews, I wrote the gist of what was said and made a note of what was off-the record. My decision about whether to use this information depended on whether it was relevant to my analysis and whether the publication of these details would be more beneficial than harmful. More often than not, these comments did not appear in my dissertation, nor are they likely to appear in other reports, as they fail to fulfill either one of these criteria.

In working with the students, my methods for collecting interview data varied slightly. Although they had heard the admonition not to use tape recorders in their interviewing, they did not express negative feelings about my audiotaping their comments. In fact, note-taking during these interviews was a distraction. I tried writing notes during the first interview I conducted with each student, but soon found that students adjusted what and how much they said about any topic based upon how quickly or how much I was writing, even though I tried to write continuously throughout these interviews. Sometimes, the students would ask if they had given me the right answer after observing me write furiously in order to keep up with them. I had to give up note-taking in these interviews to prevent students from responding in this way.

Some field guides advise ethnographers to create situations for interviewing their informants that more closely resemble casual conversation. For many situations, this is good advice. However, with participants like the journalism faculty and students, people who knew how to and used interviewing in their own work, it would have been an insult for me to pretend that I was not interviewing them. Even though I became friends with some of the students and was made to feel accepted by everyone involved in the journalism program at Bayview, neither the students nor the faculty ever forgot why I was there or that they were the subjects of my research. To assume that I could disguise the true nature of interviewing as an activity would be to assume that my subjects were ignorant, an untenable position to hold.

I have attempted to question our assumptions about interviewing as an activity to make explicit how researchers' notions about interviewing may not match those of our interviewees. In a like manner, researchers too often assume that participants and researchers share a common understanding of the topics discussed in an interview. In the next section, I discuss how the term *writing* may or may not tap our participants' understanding of or ability to talk about their writing processes.

"WRITING" AS A PROBLEMATIC TOPIC FOR DISCUSSION

One of the primary goals of ethnographers is to try to translate the cultural meaning of key terms. But what if those terms are ones that we share in common with the culture we study, or if the culture we study is our own? Can we assume that we and our participants will share a common understanding of the term *writing*? This is a particularly vexing problem for composition researchers. We have a limited vocabulary to use in talking with people about writing. So the possibility always exists that researchers and their participants may not use "writing" to refer to the same phenomena. Let me illustrate how knotty a problem this can be when one works with highly literate individuals for whom writing is *the* central activity.

Typically, composition researchers use the term *writing* to refer to those processes and activities involved in the production of texts, as well as the texts themselves. Writing encompasses the moment when first attempts to construct meaning begin, continues through the process of transcribing language, and extends beyond the time writers dot the final i's and cross the final t's in their editing and proofreading. We ask writers to reflect upon what they have written and talk about the process, and by doing so we take them back through the process again.

Journalists, on the other hand, mean something quite different when they talk about writing. Three major things are meant by the term *writing*. First, they share the commonly held belief that writing is the physical act of setting letters on a page or characters upon a computer screen; that is, they see writing as the material transcription of thought into language. Second, writing refers to style, what reporters do that distinguishes graceful wordsmiths from competent hacks. It is much like what people mean when they say someone is a "good writer." Third, and perhaps the most controversial aspect of news work, writing is the subjective construction of a news story. For a profession that upholds objectivity as the ideal to which all journalists should strive, it is more than passing strange that reporters acknowledge, and sometimes even celebrate, the inherent subjectivity of all news work, whether such work results in a multipart investigative series or a 10-line news brief. But in fact, designating writing as the subjective aspect of news work allows reporters to live with the central paradox of all news work: that any news text be both simultaneously objective in its representation of reality and subjective in its construction of "the story" of news.

Journalists reconcile the paradox by dividing their work into two separate yet interconnected spheres of activity: reporting and writing. Reporting then refers to everything leading up to the actual event when reporters begin physically to write their stories. When they work as reporters, journalists gather information, interview news sources, read clips, and attend events. They say that they are being objective insofar as they try to gain as many perspectives as possible about any event or topic. When they write, journalists whittle down the unruly heap of information into a coherent, purportedly fair and objective (in that it represents more than one point of view) account of an issue or event. By dividing their labor into these two types of activities, and attaching a different label to each, reporters can hold two contradictory positions at the same time in their own minds.

For a researcher new to this field, one can imagine the difficulties that emerged as I tried to get reporters to talk about their writing. Every question asked about writing elicited responses that encapsulated one or all of the above meanings. As might be expected, few questions about writing ever got reporters to talk about their reporting, an aspect of their work that I considered to be part of the process of writing. Was it merely my inexperience as a researcher and general naiveté that got me into this quandary? In part, yes. But another explanation is that I had mistaken having a common terminology with shared understandings. We are all susceptible to falling into this trap as long as we continue to use terms such as *writing* in unreflective, uncritical ways. It is an easy pitfall to avoid if we can see how a participant's talk about writing may not necessarily reflect the researcher's expectations about what constitutes talk about writing.

CONCLUSION

There is more to be considered in designing and using interviewing for writing research than can possibly be covered in a single chapter on methodology. The topics I have chosen to discuss are ones that reflect my interest in the intersection among the personal, social, and cultural dimensions of doing research. Specifically, I have tried to show a few aspects of the complex and problematic nature of using interviewing as a methodology in writing research. However, there is still much work to be done in examining this subject. For example, I did not consider how the form, content, and interaction between researcher and interviewee around questions affect the responses given. I have not explored the issue of data analysis, a topic that is ripe for critical discussion. Nor have I examined how representation of interview transcripts, data analysis, or findings shapes our understanding of the findings reported in any account.[9] As a review of our own literature reveals, we are far from approaching interviews with the sophistication and critical awareness that have characterized discussions about other practices in writing research.

As I argued earlier in this chapter, a critical assessment of interviewing may not have taken place until now because we still operate under the belief that interview data can be read as transparent representations of people's thoughts and/or actions. Because interviews are seen as more naturalistic, the data gathered seem more real than data gathered using methods that seem more intrusive, such as interventions, or more artificial, such as protocols. But as this chapter has tried to show, interviews are as fraught with the perils of intrusiveness and artificiality as any other research methods; we remain ignorant of the problematic nature of interviewing because of its resemblance to naturally occurring conversations. Certainly, the experiences I describe here are familiar to anyone who has attempted to conduct interviews.

Finally, our published accounts have yet to capture or reflect the messiness and complexity of interviewing. However, if we are to add to knowledge about composing by using alternative methods for doing research, then these methods must be as open to scrutiny as any others we employ. In addition, we must begin to write reports on research using interviewing that meet the same stringent requirements for detailed reporting applied to other methodologies. Until such practices are adopted within our field, we cede our ability to critically assess research findings to the good intentions, honesty, and integrity of each individual researcher.

NOTES

1. Mishler (1986) contends that the drive toward standardization of practices comes out of a behaviorist view of human interaction. The interviewer's questions are seen as a

type of stimulus, and the interviewee's answer a response. Standardizing the stimulus results in answers that accurately reflect the interviewee's response to that particular stimulus (the meaning of the question) and not to extraneous features of the stimulus (e.g., the interviewer behaved in ways that the respondent found repugnant). See Smagorinsky, this volume, for a review of research on researcher-subject interactions.

2. Originally I had included in my analysis articles published in *College Composition and Communication* (*CCC*) as well, but it was difficult to determine which articles represented empirical studies using human subjects and which ones were descriptions of a teacher's or researcher's experiences that relied upon anecdotal evidence gathered from people. The form and content of the reports published in *CCC* differed so much from those found in *RTE* or *WC* that I decided not to include my analysis of *CCC*'s articles. To do so would have led me to make generalizations about noncomparable data.

3. I do not mean to imply here that empirical studies always include people as subjects of study, but rather an examination of interviewing as a research methodology requires us to review only those empirical studies where humans are subjects. Certainly, there is a long tradition of empiricism in composition studies. For example, research on the history of writing instruction such as Crowley (1989) or research based on the analysis of various kinds of texts such as Reeves (1990) are two examples of empirical research that do not involve human subjects.

4. There are two types of interviews typically used in social scientific research: structured and semistructured or unstructured interviews. Structured interviews are used most often in survey research. They may involve face-to-face interaction or communication that occurs at a distance (e.g., a phone call). The questions asked are fully formulated in advance. Interviewers are trained to follow the exact wording and sequencing of the questions. The questions are written in ways that supposedly eliminate the possibility of a respondent's wrong interpretation of the question's meaning.

Semistructured or unstructured interviews (sometimes called "open-ended" or "nondirective" forms of interviewing by writing researchers) may be guided by a set of questions developed in advance, but topics discussed are generally negotiated between the interviewer and interviewee(s). Researchers who use this method like to state that semistructured or unstructured interviews allow the participant to introduce topics that are significant or of interest to him or her, although whether this actually happens in interviews is not revealed in research reports. The discourse or text-based interview is a popular form of a semistructured interview used in composition research (see, e.g., Doheny-Farina, 1989).

As my colleague Martin Packer has argued, "structured" and "unstructured" are problematic adjectives to use in describing interview types because they imply that there is such a thing as unstructured social activity. All social interactions have some underlying structure. The terms *structured* and *unstructured* actually refer to the researchers' attempts to manage the interaction between themselves and their subjects. These terms do not describe the "actual" nature of the interaction itself.

5. See Bazerman (1987) for a provocative account of how the *Publication Manual of the American Psychological Association* reflects a particular epistemological stance.

6. Conversations, like interviews, are governed by a set of "rules." But these rules are different from those "controlling" interviews.

7. The names of places have been altered in the news lead to help eliminate the possibility that students could be identified by being linked to the locale mentioned in the lead itself.

8. Despite what reporters say about the independence of the press and their need to maintain a critical distance between themselves and their sources, a somewhat symbiotic relationship develops between reporters and the sources that must be continually fed and renewed (see, e.g., Roshco, 1975). News stories often result from tips, off-hand remarks, or consciously stated but unattributed comments (leaks) made by sources that reporters have cultivated over the years. The decision as to whether to publish a juicy off-the-record comment is often based more on the reporter's perception of that source's future utility than it is on a set of journalistic principles. I do not mean to imply that all journalists engage in such practices, but it is an unfortunate aspect of journalistic life (and perhaps in all areas where one depends upon others' willingness to "spill the beans") that opportunistic decisions like these need to be made.

9. See Ochs (1979) for one discussion about forms of representing transcript data.

REFERENCES

Bazerman, C. (1987). Codifying the social scientific style: The *APA Publication Manual* as a behaviorist rhetoric. In J. S. Nelson, A. Megill, & D. N. McCloskey (Eds.), *The rhetoric of the human sciences: Language and argument in scholarship and public affairs* (pp. 125-144). Madison, WI: University of Wisconsin.

Burgess. R. G. (Ed.). (1982). *Field research: A sourcebook and field manual.* London: Allen & Unwin.

Chin, E. (1991). *Learning to write the news.* Unpublished doctoral dissertation, Stanford University.

Cicourel, A. V. (1982). Interviews, surveys, and the problem of ecological validity. *American Sociologist, 17,* 11-20.

Clark, G., & Doheny-Farina, S. (1990). Public discourse and personal expression: A case study in theory-building. *Written Communication, 7*(4), 456-481.

Cleary, L. M. (1991). Affect and cognition in the writing processes of eleventh graders. *Written Communication, 8*(4), 473-507.

Cross, G. A. (1990). A Bakhtinian exploration of factors affecting the collaborative writing of an executive letter of an annual report. *Research in the Teaching of English, 24*(2), 173-203.

Crowley, S. (1989). Linguistics and composition instruction: 1950-1980. *Written Communication, 6*(4), 480-505.

Doheny-Farina, S. (1986). Writing in an emerging organization: An ethnographic study. *Written Communication, 3,* 158-185.

Doheny-Farina, S. (1989). A case study of one adult writing in academic and nonacademic discourse communities. In C. B. Matalene (Ed.), *Worlds of writing: Teaching and learning in discourse communities of work* (pp. 17-42). New York: Random House.

Duffy, T. M., Post, T., & Smith, G. (1987). Technical manual production: An examination of five systems. *Written Communication, 4*(4), 370-393.

Ellen, R. F. (Ed.). (1984). *Ethnographic research: A guide to general conduct.* London: Academic Press.

Hahn, R. A. (1990). [Comment on interactional troubles in face-to-face survey interviews]. *Journal of the American Statistical Association, 85*(409).

Hilgers, T. (1986). How children change as critical evaluators of writing: Four three-year case studies. *Research in the Teaching of English, 20*(1), 36-55.

Hillocks, G. (1986). *Research on written composition: New directions for teaching.* Urbana, IL: National Council of Teachers of English.

Kovar, M. G., & Royston, P. (1990). [Comment on interactional troubles in face-to-face survey interviews]. *Journal of the American Statistical Association, 85*(409).

McCarthy, L. P., & Fishman, S. M. (1991). Boundary conversations: Conflicting ways of knowing in philosophy and interdisciplinary research. *Research in the Teaching of English, 25*(4), 419-468.

Mishler, E. G. (1986). *Research interviewing: Context and narrative.* Cambridge, MA: Harvard University Press.

Mishler, E. G. (1991). Representing discourse: The rhetoric of transcription. *Journal of Narrative and Life History, 1*(4), 255-280.

North, S. M. (1986). Writing in a philosophy class: Three case studies. *Research in the Teaching of English, 20*(3), 225-262.

Ochs, E. (1979). Transcription as theory. In E. Ochs & B. B. Schieffelin (Eds.), *Developmental pragmatics* (pp. 43-72). New York: Academic Press.

Powdermaker, H. (1966). *Stranger and friend: The way of an anthropologist.* New York: Norton.

Prior, P. (1991). Contextualizing writing and response in a graduate seminar. *Written Communication, 8*(3), 267-310.

Rabinow, P. (1977). *Reflections on fieldwork in Morocco.* Berkeley: University of California.

Redd-Boyde, T. M., & Slater, W. H. (1989). The effects of audience specification on undergraduates' attitudes, strategies, and writing. *Research in the Teaching of English, 23*(1), 77-108.

Reeves, C. (1990). Establishing a phenomenon: The rhetoric of early medical reports on AIDS. *Written Communication, 7*(3), 383-416.

Rosaldo, R. (1989). *Culture and truth: The remaking of social analysis.* Boston: Beacon.

Roshco, B. (1975). *Newsmaking.* Chicago: University of Chicago Press.

Schegloff, E. A. (1990). [Comment on interactional troubles in face-to-face survey interviews]. *Journal of the American Statistical Association, 85*(409).

Spradley, J. P. (1979). *The ethnographic interview.* New York: Holt, Rinehart & Winston.

Suchman, L., & Jordan, B. (1990a). Interactional troubles in face-to-face survey interviews. *Journal of the American Statistical Association, 85*(409), 232-241.

Suchman, L., & Jordan, B. (1990b). [Rejoinder to comments on interactional troubles in face-to-face survey interviews]. *Journal of the American Statistical Association, 85*(409).

Swanson-Owens, D. (1986). Identifying natural sources of resistance: A case study of implementing writing across the curriculum. *Research in the Teaching of English, 20*(1), 69-97.

Tannen, D. (1990). *You just don't understand: Women and men in conversation.* New York: Morrow.

Tourangeau, R. (1990). [Comment on interactional troubles in face-to-face survey interviews]. *Journal of the American Statistical Association, 85*(409).

Whyte, W. F. (1955). *Street corner society.* Chicago: University of Chicago.

Part V
Counterpoint

12

Whither Wisdom?

DAVID N. DOBRIN

In any disciplinary discourse, some disciplinary acts are intrinsically related to the aims of the discourse and some are what one might call ritualistic. Since most disciplinary acts are statements, and since the aim of a
discourse is usually to get at the truth of the matter regarding the subject
matter of that discourse, the acts related to the aims are usually statements
that are attempts to get at the truth. They make claims, provide explanations, report observations, and so on. "Ritualistic" acts are gestures that turn
out to have little to do with getting at the truth.

Ritualistic acts do serve important purposes. Participation in a disciplinary discourse is a cooperative activity. It requires the goodwill and assent
of all. Making the appropriate gesture at the appropriate time indicates that
the person wishes to participate, knows the rules of participation, has gone
through rites of initiation, has a certain standing, can understand the statements of others, can be relied on to contribute where appropriate, and so on,
and so on.

This distinction between truth-seeking and ritualistic statements is independent of the actual truth of any discursive act. Many disciplinary discourses throughout history failed entirely to produce any statements that
were true, however earnest the participants and internally consistent the
discourse. (These discourses have been the delight of such commentators as
Kuhn and Foucault. See, for instance, Kuhn on phlogiston and Foucault on
the linguistics of Port Royal.) But even these discourses included ritualistic
elements, behaviors which did not further the aims of the discourse.

What acts are ritualistic and what truth-seeking? Often, the answer is not
clear, particularly to the participants. Often, as the discourse progresses,
certain behaviors regarded as intrinsic are seen as unnecessary and are
gradually perceived as ritualist and then discarded.

It is important in any discourse to be as clear as possible about the
difference, but it is also quite difficult. Living within an ocean of statements

often contradictory, tending to manifold purposes, contradicting, extending, deepening, distracting, one cannot easily discern which disciplinary practices have lost their meaning, which actually work against the prevailing tendency, which are merely irrelevant. It is much easier if you are not actually a participant in the discourse. You can stand outside the ocean and see the currents.

It is, however, quite rare for an outsider to conduct this kind of analysis on pages ostensibly devoted to the discipline he is criticizing. Most critics of a discourse are critics in hindsight; their remarks themselves constitute disciplinary discourse, gestures made to and understood by other members of their discourse community.

I find myself in that rare position. Some years ago I wrote a paper about protocols, mostly because the editor of *College English* asked me to. The article has been cited frequently (several times in this book) and criticized roundly by the community of researchers represented in this book. When Peter Smagorinsky decided to prepare a volume about the problems and pitfalls of research that collects verbal reports about writing, he decided I might be able to contribute a different point of view, mostly on the strength of that paper.

My aim in this chapter is to look at the current state of the discourse in this community from the stance of the outsider. I want to look at the totality of statements that constitute the discourse (I'll take the papers in the current volume as representing the current state) and identify those elements that are ritualistic: those that undercut or contradict or retard progress, those that are contradictory or retrograde, and those that are merely irrelevant. If you are familiar with Derrida you might say that I am trying to deconstruct the discourse, and in one sense that would be correct. But my purposes are not at all Derridean; I don't feel hostile or superior, so I don't feel any need to use that cloistered and inhospitable language.

Just so I do not do this incognito, let me identify the discourse community that I feel comfortable in. The crucial critical move within this community is to "bracket" (the word is Husserl's) the truth of statements and look at their internal structure as well. The community has roots in Levi-Strauss, by way of Foucault, but it also has roots in J. L. Austin by way of John Searle, and roots in Dewey and Heidegger by way of Richard Rorty. A central tenet of this community is that the truth of any statement is meaningful only within the context of the entire network of discursive statements; this idea is generally called "holism." Other holists influential in various parts of this community include Quine, Wittgenstein, Davidson, Putnam, and Kripke.

The aim of the discourse community I am looking at—let me call it the protocol community even though protocols are collected now by only a small percentage—is to explain writing behavior by asking people what they do when they write. Much energy has been spent in my community looking at the question of whether explanations of human behavior like those sought by the protocol community have any special structure or any special problems associated with them. Some holists (Davidson, Searle, Taylor, Dreyfus, even Rorty) conclude that there are, and throughout this chapter, I will be using some of their arguments. I will try to look at the current state of the community from the standpoint of a skeptical outsider, one whose perspective is no doubt unavailable to the participants who make up the community.

PROTOCOL DISCOURSE: A BRIEF HISTORY

Let me begin with a brief description of how protocol discourse evolved to its present state and what it is currently trying to do. About 1975 or so, a number of professionals in composition began to argue that current practice in teaching concentrated on what students produced, when it should in fact concentrate on the processes that they go through when they produce it. "Teach process, not product" the slogan ran. As happens so often in intellectual communities, influential people in the movement were borrowing heavily from a parallel movement in psychology called cognitive science.

At that time, research in cognitive science was taken up under many different ideological banners. For reasons of propinquity (I would guess) the banner most influential in composition was that of Herb Simon, a Nobel prize-winning computer scientist whose specialty was analyzing human problem-solving activity. Linda Flower and John R. Hayes, who were both at Simon's home institution, Carnegie-Mellon, decided to characterize writing as a problem-solving activity and study it in the way Simon did. Simon believed that the actual steps people go through when they solve problems could be determined simply by asking them to describe what was going on in their minds as they solved the problems. The procedure for doing this is called a "think-aloud protocol," as all of my readers already know.

Attached to the think-aloud protocol was a theory of cognitive processing developed by Simon and Newell, which Flower and Hayes tried to adhere to. Unfortunately, the theory never gained wide acceptance in the cognitive science community and it produced only indifferent explanations in writing research, for reasons described well in other chapters of this book. Simon developed the theory around the procedures undergone when solving well-formed problems. He was never as successful in characterizing tasks like writing, which were ill-defined or constantly being reconceptualized, and their followers ran into the same problem.

Collecting and analyzing protocols was an extremely time-consuming and expensive activity, and pursuing it with the rigor required to make any sense of the activity in terms of Newell and Simon's theory was simply impossible for the community at large. But even though the theoretical underpinnings were largely absent, the idea of teaching process and the notion that the processes could be analyzed by asking people what they were thinking had taken root.

It almost had to. To hear the process people tell it, writing teachers had been a combination of Mrs. Grundy and a small-time copy editor. Their primary activity was to "correct" writing. But students didn't seem to be helped by somebody going over their papers minutely and correcting their spelling. Basic writers and writers with writer's block were positively harmed by it; clearly, they needed intervention earlier.

Accordingly, process studies became common in the literature; process textbooks emerged; everybody characterized writing as a problem-solving activity, and in Maxine Hairston's words, we found ourselves in a "paradigm shift."

Once we decided to teach process, it became important to figure out what we should teach, and it also became important to find out how well we were doing. If we taught people that there were prewriting, writing, and editing phases to the writing process, did that make it easier for them to write? Did their writing improve? Did they actually use what we taught them? One simple way of answering these questions was to ask writers. And ask is what researchers did.

The original think-aloud protocols were a form of asking, a form done in highly controlled circumstances. The idea was to bring out actual traces of the actual mental processes that people went through as they wrote. As the interest in how people write expanded, people rewrote the rules of experimentation.

In this volume, for instance, there are still several think-aloud protocol experiments discussed, but there are also intervention protocols, in which the experimenter provides help while the writer is writing (see Swanson-Owens & Newell, this volume). Some experimenters abandon the think-aloud protocol entirely, preferring retrospective accounts (Greene & Higgins) and stimulated recall (DiPardo). In addition, more than the actual act of writing is observed. Sperling and Hodges observe entire writing classes for a long period of time; Sperling's focus is the writing conference and Hodges's is the conversation in the classroom. Both use interviews for gathering data, as well as analyzing videotapes or audiotapes of actual (non-laboratory) situations. Not surprisingly, as the range of experimental methods expands, so does the range of theoretical bases for the research. Chin and DiPardo do ethnography; Sperling does discourse analysis; even those people who do think-aloud protocols seem to have moved away from the original cognitive approach. Both Witte and Cherry and Bracewell and Breuleux, for instance, argue for a socio-cognitive approach.

There is nothing wrong or objectionable about pluralism. As any discourse develops, its assumptions, principles, theoretical ideas, experimental systems, and so on, and so on, are reexamined, modified, and discarded regularly. People will always go in different directions; different theoretical camps emerge. Very often, of course, disciplines simply break apart; and given the wide range of ideas about how experimentation should be done, one might have expected that here. In fact, it has not happened, and we might do well to ask why.

CONTRIBUTIONS TO
PROTOCOL DISCOURSE

How is it that such widely varying contributions can all count as contributions to protocol discourse? Evidently, each performs one or more qualifying acts, which lead others in the field to say that yes, they are members of this community. I would like to propose that at least the following may be qualifying acts.

- Each investigator studies the behavior of writers or students of writing while they are engaged in writing-related activities.
- Each investigator collects large amounts of information about that behavior.
- Each investigator spends significant resources in amassing this information, where resources may be time, money, or both.
- At least to some extent, the investigators ask the participants in the study about their personal experiences while performing the behavior studied.
- Each discusses prior attempts to gather information using similar or roughly similar methods.
- Each characterizes the information gathered about the behavior as data.

- Each attempts to reduce the data by "coding" the data, that is, by sorting it into groups.
- Each is concerned with the validity and reliability of the data coding.
- Each cautions us that the data gathered are difficult to manage and interpret.
- Each tells us that at least some of the data are susceptible to various interpretations.
- To the extent that conclusions are presented, each presents anecdotal information as support for the conclusions reached.

None of this is terribly surprising. What we have here is a discipline that aspires to a scientific style of empiricism but is unsure about how to do it. The qualifying acts are those that permit an investigator to get as close as possible to this kind of empiricism and still retain his or her integrity.

For this discipline to require genuine scientific empiricism as practiced in the twentieth century, there would have to be a few other qualifying actions.

- The entire discipline would have to have some kind of agreement about what phenomena it is studying, and the paper would have to show how it is situated in the community's investigation of those phenomena.
- The discipline would have to have some theory of why the phenomena are related and what mechanisms underly their behavior. In Newtonian physics, the phenomena include the interactions between matter, and the mechanisms are Newton's laws. The paper must either tacitly accept this theory or make a pronouncement about where it stands relative to the theory.
- In general, any paper purporting to contribute to the discipline would have some proposition, whose truth or falsity is unknown to the discipline, which it then proceeds to test.
- The paper reports the results of experiments designed to test this proposition (this is where the empiricism comes in) and then provides an analysis of these reports, which provides new information about the proposition.

One of the papers included in this volume (Stratman & Hamp-Lyons) does have these qualifying actions; it would probably be instructive for the reader to look at this paper before continuing.

The phenomena and the theory did exist in the discipline at one point, as mentioned earlier. Investigators were studying the problem-solving activities of writing as they occurred in short-term memory, the traces of which were made visible by think-aloud protocols. But only a few of these papers purport to study think-aloud protocols, and only one refers back to the ideas of the original theory. Instead, we have a modification of the theory (Witte & Cherry), a proposal about coding techniques whose relation to the theory is unclear (Bracewell & Breuleux), a couple of ethnographic studies (Chin; DiPardo), a discouse analysis study, and several studies (the stimulated recall studies) which, while interesting, appeal to no theory of cognitive functioning.

This is all to the investigators' credit. They choose to study writing conferences or what happens to student journalists or writing classes, and they would like to help us learn about them. An appeal to Simon's (or any other theory) of cognitive processing would be absurd, just as a study of the weather would be absurd if it appealed to Newton's laws.

As these papers show, empiricism does not necessarily require a theory. In fact, the first empiricist, Francis Bacon, felt that the really important thing was simply to collect data in an orderly fashion and then organize it. He felt that truths would emerge from this activity, as long as it was reported on diligently and honestly. Though physics shortly moved away from Bacon's empiricism—Sir Isaac Newton, for example, providing propositions, principles, and mechanisms, as well as observation—many other disciplines did not. Centuries after Bacon, you could still read in *The Proceedings of the Royal Society,* observations from rural priests about particularly large toads or particularly interesting roadside plants.

What marks these papers as examples of Baconian empiricism? First of all, the aim of most of these papers is not to determine whether some proposition is true or not. Here are some examples of what the investigators say they are trying to accomplish:

- increase our understanding of students' awareness of the rhetorical choices they make in a given situation (Greene & Higgins)
- use discourse analysis of writing conference talk as a mechanism for understanding how the writing conference is linguistically and sociologically constituted (Sperling)
- improve understanding of the systemic nature of conversational interaction (Hodges)
- use particular information provided by instructors to see how added scaffolding efforts might improve students' application of that information (Swanson-Owens & Newell)
- determine whether and (if so) how composing processes of college freshmen might differ for different types of writing tasks and for comparable writing tasks of the same type (Witte & Cherry)

With the first three, the aim is purely and simply to improve under-standing; there is no attempt to test propositions. The remaining two (both of which come more clearly from the Simon/Flower & Hayes tradition) express more specific goals. But the goals of both papers are really twofold: to see whether something happens (the proposition) and to see how. Neither proposition, however, could possibly be false, so neither is genuinely test-able. Surely instruction must affect "students' conceptualization of the task" (Swanson-Owens & Newell), at least for some students and to some extent; any paper that claimed that it didn't would be disbelieved within the dis-course community. And surely everyone believes that at least some compos-ing processes differ for different tasks (Witte & Cherry). Everyone knows that different writing assignments cause students more or less difficulty. The meat of each paper is really the "how," which makes these papers, too, a Baconian attempt to contribute descriptions.

Please don't get me wrong. Contributing to our understanding of the writing process is a worthy goal, and if you believe in the process paradigm and your job is to publish papers about writing, what these authors are trying to do is perfectly sensible. But in trying to reach that goal, they may be confusing—as I view the field from the outside—ritual gestures toward scientific empiricism with contribution to the understanding of writing.

DEALING WITH DATA

Almost every investigator, as I said before, worries about the "validity" of the empirical data gathered. Sperling is concerned that the microphone has been moved; Chin that she is Asian-American. Almost every author spends a lot of time and energy "coding" the data, explaining the coding method, and then presenting results in terms of the coding. It is these two acts, the discussion of validity and the coding, that I suspect are ritual. The two are related, of course; since the coding methods may be invalid, much time is spent justifying them or testing them.

Outsiders investigating discourse communities are always piqued by in-ternal contradictions, because they are often signs of some fissure in the discourse. So when an English teacher speaks about "questions about the validity of such data" (Swanson-Owens & Newell) or says that "the analy-sis of data invariably exceeds explicit methods of analysis," I prick up my ears. In English, strictly speaking, data cannot be valid; only propositions can. (Only statements can be true or false, not physical events in the world.)

Clearly, if English teachers come up with neologisms, there must be some discomfort over the procedures used for gathering data.

The reason for the discomfort is perfectly clear. In true scientific empiricism, experiments that gather data are supposed to be conducted under controlled conditions. All factors that might affect the results of the experiment (and thus the evidence for the truth or falsity of the proposition) are supposed to be held constant, except the factor being systematically varied. In any such experiments, of course, certain things are not held constant. A Nobel prize winner in chemistry conducts two experiments varying one factor, and between the two experiments, much has been changed. He has gotten older; his daughter has gotten pregnant; the earth has moved closer to the sun; the graduate student preparing the equipment has not had much sleep. But the assumption in the discipline of chemistry is that these factors will not affect the experiment, or will affect it randomly.

In empirical studies of literacy, it seems that almost any factor might have to be seriously considered as affecting the outcome. The sex, race, or smiling frequency of the interviewer or subject, the height of microphones, the very presence of the interviewer ("in a dyad, three's a crowd"), might all be a problem. Even where a need for controls might seem to be clearer, there is no real agreement on what controls might have to be imposed. We are told that cues or prompts need to be carefully controlled (Swanson-Owens & Newell; Chin), but we are also told that a stimulus that can't be well controlled is also very effective (DiPardo). Retrospective accounts, we are told, should be gathered as soon after the event as possible (Greene & Higgins), but they also actually benefit from the perspective that the passage of time gives (DiPardo). The discipline was founded on a theory that requires immediate, concurrent, unprompted expression of thoughts, but we are told that stimulus (Swanson-Owens & Newell; DiPardo) or even simply interviews (Sperling; Chin) are valuable additions, and, as it turns out, these immediate expressions distort the writing task in ways unexpected by the theoreticians (Stratman & Hamp-Lyons).

On the one hand, this disagreement (often called "pluralism") is generally approved of. The "socio-cognitive" middle ground is clearly the ground to grab for most commentators. On the other hand, Chin criticizes others quite harshly for being somewhat parsimonious in their descriptions of procedures, and almost everybody seems to prefer "rigor" in their experiments.

How can these contradictions exist, but not be felt as terribly important by most of the authors? It is because true scientific empiricism requires that the decisions about what to control be grounded in some theory. The phenomena being experimented on must be characterized in such a way as to make it possible to believe that certain factors are crucial to the behavior of the phenomena (and must be controlled) and other factors are taken to be irrelevant. As long as the purposes of the investigations are simply to investigate cognitive activity so as to provide a better understanding, then almost any kind of empirical investigation using almost any kind of method is allowed, and no method is any better or worse than any other.

If, however, any method is as good as any other, then rigor in carrying out a method is largely beside the point. And discursive acts whose purport is to establish or deny the rigor of a method or the "validity" of data are largely beside the point; they are ritualistic acts. Hodges, to pick an arbitrary example, may point out that an "ethnolinguist enters a context, altering [it] even if only by presence alone," but the discipline has no way of determining whether the presence of the ethnolinguist could produce an effect on Hodges's statements that would render them invalid, so her discussion is largely moot.

CODING METHODS

The participant in this discourse has usually collected an enormous amount of information, which must be reduced and digested before it can be reported on. In Baconian and scientific empiricism, one standard way of doing this is to put the information in categories, a process called "coding." Clearly, coding is a problem for these investigators. Bracewell and Breuleux are critical of a "proliferation of different coding schemes" that do not have a "principled basis." Instead, "coding categories arise largely in an ad hoc manner from the consideration of the protocol rather than from a rational analysis of the cognitive processes required for the task."

Certainly in this volume there are no fewer than five different coding schemes proposed, none of which has anything to do with the others (though admittedly they are all organizing different kinds of information). Each of these codings has one thing in common; it is difficult to apply consistently. "A laborious and confusing process, fraught with dilemmas that can only be resolved by artificial decisions," Sperling calls it.

The discourse is quite self-conscious about this. Bracewell and Breuleux talk about the "general ennui that accompanies the presentation and use of coding schemes for think-aloud protocols," an ennui surely due in part to the general lack of clarity of these schemes even in the examples the investigators supply. In one example that Hodges gives, for instance, she describes a comment as a "writing-in-practice nexus," which could also be described as a "question about course context." Greene and Higgins assign each sentence in a protocol to one of four categories: content, context, text structure, and language. They call "And then I went on in my paper" *content,* and they call "And they [five cognitive dimensions] lead to writer's block because they first lead to anxiety" *context.* They could be right, but I could just as easily see the two sentences being content and text structure.

One reason for coding is that the reduction to categories allows you to report on the information in statistical terms, something many investigators want to do. But not one of the investigators actually acknowledges the ambiguous nature of the coding in the statistical reporting. Several investigators (Sperling; Witte & Cherry; Greene & Higgins) do try to achieve some level of agreement (80% or 85%) among their coders, though in Greene and Higgins's case this was only achieved by allowing agreement if one coder put a statement in two categories and another put it into one of those two. But even if investigators can learn to agree on the handling of ambiguous cases, that doesn't erase the ambiguity. The statistical reporting should report the range of possible interpretations, not just the one that the coders finally came up with. Say, for instance, it is reasonable for me to code one third of Green and Higgins's data in a different way. Each of the percentages they report could be one third greater or one third less than they report if the ambiguous situations are handled in a different, reasonable way. The trouble is, though, that this level of uncertainty would make almost any statistical claims nugatory.

Witte and Cherry's paper is perhaps the best example to look at. Witte and Cherry would argue that their coding system has a principled basis, because they identify cognitive processes that the protocols are traces of. The coding is really an identification of the underlying cognitive process. Witte and Cherry argue at the end that the persuasive writer's tasks involve significantly more "memorial pre-text" than the expository writer's tasks. Apparently the persuasive writers spend more time reflecting on ideas that have not yet been written down, whereas the expository writers on sports subjects simply write a sentence and then use the written sentence to generate ideas. "Pre-text" is a concept proposed by Witte and one that he wishes to defend. Clearly, the difference between dealing with "memorial pre-text" and "generating ideas" is scarcely an obvious and tangible one, and in fact "failure to distinguish between generating ideas and translating pre-text" was one of three important categories of coding differences, all of which were eventually "resolved by mutual consent in conference." If, however, Witte and Cherry reported both the data after agreement had been reached and the data before agreement had been reached, one suspects (though one does not know) that most of the statistical significance claimed by them would be erased.

Of course, even if significance were reached unambiguously, many of the arguments applied to rigor and validity of information would apply here. Unless a change in the results would make a significant difference to the claims being made, rigor in the results (or accuracy of coding) scarcely matters. Indeed, as Sperling points out, the ambiguity of the data may be as illuminating as any consistency might be. Take Witte and Cherry's paper as an example. Anyone who has ever taught knows that the differing assignments given by Witte and Cherry are going to produce different styles of paper, which will require different organization of cognitive processes by the students, and anybody who has ever written knows that the amount of knowledge you have and your comfort with the rhetorical situation make a big difference to the way you go about it. For a discursive act in the paper to be truth-seeking, it must contribute something beyond what we all know.

Here is one such act in the paper:

> Compared to the "education" writers, the "sports" writers seemed to have available more individual pieces of information, but it was information that appeared not to be very well organized in memory, at least not well organized according to "the role of sports in American society." These apparent differences in the amount of available information and in the organization of that information appear to make composing a different task for the "sports" writers than it was for the "education" writers.

To gain this insight, Witte and Cherry went back to the protocols and described a pattern of writing activity. Their observation of this pattern is made entirely independently of the coding system they apply to the data. Their statistical data cannot describe the pattern (it is only concerned with frequency and is not that fine-grained), and the existence of the pattern would be the same even if their results had been vastly different from what they were. (Indeed, this insight makes so much sense that we would be inclined to suspect any numbers that did not accord with it.) This insight comes out not because of the coding, but alongside it.

One reason for this and similar problems with all the coding systems shown is that without a theory of the underlying processes, a coding system is hard-pressed to have explanatory value. A disciplinary discourse is trying to explain phenomena—the processes we go through when we write—in a way that allows us to get some control over them—for instance, to help writers whose processes are incomplete or poorly formed. Effectively, a coding system identifies processes that people go through. People themselves have explanations for any of these processes; these explanations are what think-aloud protocols are seeking. The farther the coding gets from the people's own explanations, the more remote the possibility that the investigator's explanation can genuinely identify salient characteristics of the behavior or allow people to get control of it.

Take, for instance, the question of whether a writer pays attention to the context, content, text structure, or language during planning. A division like this would have explanatory value if writers actually said to themselves, "Oh, I need to pay attention to the text structure now. What is my text structure? Is it adequate, and so on, and so on." But no one does this. They may pay attention to what Greene and Higgins would call text structure, but they would not recognize Greene and Higgins's term as part of what philosophers call a "reasoned explanation" for their acts. The same is true in spades for terms like "reviewing memorial pre-text" or "writing-in-practice nexus." It is, of course, possible that with enough explanation and review and teaching, the writer might accept these terms as descriptions of what happened. But that still doesn't mean that the writer actually thought, "Oh, I need to pay attention . . . " or that learning to think this way could ever give more control.

One reason for this problem is that any explanation, reasoned or not, of any behavior is extraordinarily complicated. Sperling's coding system is one that people might accept as embodying their own explanation of their behavior. People might well say that they are initiating a conversational change or responding to one. But, as Sperling points out, they could just as easily say that the initiation was in fact a response (to a pause, to a hesitation, to the sense that the previous subject had been exhausted). And they would be right in both cases. But where reasoned explanations multiply, then coding and statistical treatment of reasoned explanations, even accurate ones, are extremely problematic, since at this point in the discourse, people are coding things into only one category.

THE RHETORIC
OF PROTOCOL DISCOURSE

Reasoned explanation is attractive to philosophers partly because of parsimony. Insisting that explanations be reasoned limits the number of explanations to those that the subject would recognize and accept. As George Hillocks points out, when that constraint is removed, the number of possible explanations of any behavior multiplies apparently infinitely.

Natural, sensible, appropriate coding systems are, moreover, rhetorically powerful. People accept coding systems (explanations) that they find intuitive; accepting them, they adapt them to their own practice, do further research based on them, and even attempt to use them in their teaching. Coding systems that produce "ennui" are not only implausible; they endanger the discipline.

Clearly, the people in the discipline recognize the problem. Even though most of the space in papers that report results is devoted to discussion of coding systems and quantitative results, most of what is compelling in them is something entirely different, a narrative account. It seems to be tacitly accepted by the researchers that, as Smagorinsky says, "The particular strength of protocol data . . . is *their capacity for telling stories.*"

These stories often have little enough to do with the coding, and sometimes the point they make about teaching or learning seems to have little enough to do with the investigators' purposes. Nevertheless, to this outside observer, the stories are the thing, the sine qua non of the discipline. What is remarkable to me is that within the discipline, the stories are thought of as ancillary, and the coding is the sine qua non.

There seem to be two reasons for this. First, the existence of a coding scheme seems to lend the narrative descriptions a certain authority. Hodges admits, for instance, that:

> Most readers of the above strips might be able to tell a story similar to the one I have told without what may appear to be the clutter of the coding scheme. However, a coding scheme, whether the one described here or another, enables systematic and articulate interpretations, the kind of interpretations which are credible and lucid for those who read and use them.

Sperling argues that the "imprecise and sometimes ambiguous nature" of the coding schemes "can in fact help us to understand the human character of what we study." For DiPardo, whose ethnographic study seems to be the least susceptible to coding, the lack of systematic data limits the authority of what she has to say. "In terms of external validity, I aimed no farther than what has been called 'user' or 'reader' generalizability—that is, to provide others an opportunity to 'generalize personally to their own situations.'"

Second, and this is closely related to the first, it seems that mere stories do an injustice to the huge amount of work done by the researcher. One of the requisite discursive acts in this discourse is a statement of support. Somebody needs to have paid for the year or so of the researcher's time, the coders, the microphones or tape recorders, the transcriptions, and so on, and so on. Another virtually requisite act is a reference to the " 'labor intensive' character of the coding" (Bracewell & Breuleux). If a year of the researcher's time results only in a single account of a single student's experience, what was all the work for?

The existence of coding schemes, of a systematic approach to collecting data, of careful attention to previous research along the same lines seems to lend the research an air of rigor. Without that rigor, as Chin says, "we cede our ability to critically assess research findings to the good intentions, honesty, and integrity of each individual researcher." But, I would like to argue, unless the coding schemes actually make sense of the data, unless the systematic approach produces data or conclusions that are surprising, unless the careful attention leads the researcher to avoid earlier mistakes or to advance earlier conclusions, then discursive acts along these lines are merely ritualistic.

I may seem to be unduly harsh, but I do not mean to be. I happen to think that depending on good intentions, honesty, and integrity is not such a bad thing, and I happen to think that all are in bountiful supply in these papers. No dishonest conclusions are drawn; these papers are neither mendacious nor meretricious. It is precisely because the authors want to say something important that they include the narrations that I find interesting and valuable. Far from being harsh, I am merely suggesting something quite simple. People in the discipline can afford to abandon most of the activities that seem to be most difficult and fruitless, without abandoning the discipline.

It is possible, in other words, to do good research, to advance the aims of the discipline, and to answer important questions about writing simply by asking people how they write and by reporting on the answers. It is not necessary to ask huge numbers of questions of huge numbers of people and report on the answers quantitatively. It is only necessary to listen carefully, to see into the heart of the matter, and to tell the story simply and accurately.

13

Withered Wisdom
A Reply to Dobrin

ROBERT J. BRACEWELL

Dobrin calls our attention to the distinction in research between acts that advance knowledge in a discipline and those that do not but nonetheless allow people to participate in the disciplinary discourse. These latter he labels "ritualistic." He wishes to use this distinction to critique the chapters of this volume, with the objective of identifying activities associated with the analysis of verbal protocols that are ritualistic and consequently either irrelevant to disciplinary progress or in conflict with it. This would certainly be a worthwhile goal for a concluding interview, but unfortunately Dobrin is unable to attain it. His premises for discussion contain so many misconceptions about research in this area that his critique is almost a complete miss rather than the different perspective he promises in his introduction.

Let me list a number of Dobrin's misconceptions.[1] These can be divided into "errors of fact" (that is, misrepresentations of practice or belief within the scholarly community), and "errors of common sense" (the remedy of which requires no specialized knowledge). For each of these misconceptions I shall try to outline what the actual situation is.

With respect to the facts:

First, Herb Simon does not believe that you can determine "the actual steps that people go through when they solve problems" by asking them to think aloud. Simon and his colleagues have consistently said that think-alouds give one partial information about mental processes. In fact, Dobrin seems confused about Simon's position because later in the chapter he speaks of "actual traces of the actual mental processes." This confusion would be a minor matter, except that it bears directly on the issue of coding schemes. It is precisely because a think aloud provides only partial information that coding schemes are necessary in order to interpret the language of the think aloud and derive a model of the mental processes people use to do tasks. Information relevant to designing coding schemes usually comes from the researcher's prior knowledge of the nature of the task (commonly called a task analysis in such research). If a think aloud did yield the "actual steps," then there would be no need for coding systems.[2] Dobrin's failure to think this matter through has important consequences for the conclusion he draws about research using verbal protocols. These consequences are considered below.

Second, the Newell and Simon theory is a theory of problem solving, not cognitive processing, and it has gained a wide acceptance in the cognitive science community. The assumptions of the theory—that problem solving is knowledge driven, that people usually operate on the basis of limited knowledge and processing resources, that problem solving activity is in large part rule driven, and that people's goals determine their strategies— are accepted by all cognitive scientists. Sometimes the contributions of scholars become so much a part of the warp and woof of a discipline that they are not obvious to newcomers, and this appears to be the case with Dobrin. Doubters of the acceptance of the Newell and Simon approach should read, for example, the frontnotes of Miller, Galanter, and Pribram's *Plans and the Structure of Behavior* (1960), perhaps the most influential book in moving the information-processing approach from its origins in attention and memory research to the general study of learning and performance.

Third, as researchers we are not testing the truth or falsity of propositions. Positivist philosophy as an underpinning for empirical research was abandoned in the early 1970s, as the work in philosophy of science of Kuhn, Lakatos, Popper, and Toulmin became widely read, and in a related development as researchers gained a deeper insight into the epistemological implications of the inferential statistics used to accept or reject hypotheses (see, e.g., Lakatos & Musgrave, 1970). The discussion of the epistemological status of research findings is an ongoing one, as anyone who reads the American Educational Research Association's *Educational Researcher* is aware (see, e.g. Salomon, 1991).

Fourth, writers do pay attention to context, content, text structure, and language as they write. Dobrin denies that the following is characteristic of writers' think alouds: "Oh I need to pay attention to the text structure now. What is my text structure? Is it adequate?" But this is not correct, and one does not have to look far to find a counter-example. Consider the following transcription segments, taken from the journalist's protocol used to illustrate Breuleux's and my paper:

"Now that's not really said very well.
But u::h let's see:: *reads silently*
:h:: No doesn't work-, doesn't work.
Gotta rephrase that. *sighs*" (Protocol GM1, segments 167-170)

Of course this language does not have the same surface structure as
Dobrin's. It is highly elided, deictic, and pronominalized—exactly what
one would expect of language that is closely related to an ongoing task. And
in practice we would suspect that think-aloud verbalizations that had the
features of Dobrin's illustration would indicate that the writer was concentrating more on talking to an audience than doing a writing task. The coding
of this journalist's think aloud does require some sophistication in discourse
linguistics in order to specify his actions. And the think aloud must also be
coordinated with the written text. But all of what Dobrin denies is there: the
focus on language structure, the evaluation, and the goal setting.

With respect to common sense:

First, composition research in cognitive science was not based on
Simon's problem-solving approach for "reasons of propinquity." Dobrin's
statement is ridiculous if he means propinquity in the physical sense; researchers don't adopt a theoretical position because they have offices on
the same floor (actually, among academics, my experience is that physical
proximity more often leads to intellectual contempt). If Dobrin means propinquity in the more abstract sense of common interest, then he is undermining his own argument presented later in the chapter that there is little
relationship between research in this area and its declared theoretical base
in the cognition of problem solving.

Second, despite his knowledge of the research process, Dobrin is consistently confused about what is a theoretical matter and what is an empirical
matter, even for the simplest situation. Thus, in arguing against any substantive linkage of composition research with theories of cognition, by way of
illustration he claims that research on the weather would be absurd if it
appealed to Newtonian mechanics. However, as any high school student of
physical geography knows, the phenomena of weather and explanations for
them depend intimately on Newton's laws of force and motion. It would be
impossible to explain frontal systems, for example, without them. Later in
his chapter Dobrin claims that much of the terminology used by the authors
in this volume to describe writing processes would neither be recognized by
writers nor useful to them in composing. However, this is an empirical
matter that should simply be put to the test. The terminology may or may

not facilitate writing, but it is not worth arguing about in the absence of evidence.

Third, Dobrin favors coding systems and explanations that are "intuitive." Now Dobrin is free to be a true-believing member of the Flat Earth Society if that is what is right for him, but his advocacy of "intuitiveness" as a worthwhile criterion for evaluating coding systems and explanations can be rejected immediately. For one thing, people disagree about what is intuitively correct, and Dobrin presents no method for resolving these disagreements. For another, most of the interesting and powerful characterizations of phenomena involve constructs that counter intuition. Witness Newton's laws of motion and force, for example.

Fourth and by far most important, Dobrin concludes that good research can be done in this area "simply by asking people how they write and by reporting on the answers," and that "it is only necessary to listen carefully, to see into the heart of the matter, and to tell the story simply and accurately." This is altogether naive and inadequate prescription for research in this area. In part Dobrin's failure is due to a theoretical lacuna—he has missed the point that the partial information about mental processes produced in a think aloud (or any other verbal report) requires the use of a coding scheme as an instrument to infer the mental processes. But this failure is also one of common sense. If Dobrin's prescription were all that was necessary to develop theories of discourse processing and to solve problems of literacy development, then success would have been achieved long ago, and we would all be doing something different for gainful employment.

Unfortunately, the consequence of Dobrin's misconceptions is a critique that contains nothing that is contentious or challenging at any significant level. This outcome is regrettable, for there are issues to be considered. Two related ones that come to mind have to do with what may be called the ethics of treating data in this area, and with the instrumental value of coding systems for natural language.

The ethical issue concerns the responsibility of the researcher to deal with participants' data in a sophisticated and appropriate manner. As we move to investigations of performance in realistic tasks, where we assume (or at least hope) that participants are working at real problems, we ought to apply methods of coding that are sophisticated enough to pick up the complex nature of the task and participants' performance. To do less constitutes a sort of intellectual con game in which we expect participants to work seriously in order to provide us with data, but then fail to use methods of analysis that treat these data with the seriousness they merit.

The instrumental issue is the one that Dobrin does not address but should have. Ironically, the starting point for considering the instrumental value of coding systems is Dobrin's fatuous conclusion. We all realize that it is important to listen carefully to what one's writers say and to try to look into the heart of the matter. The real issue is *how* to listen carefully and *how* to look into the heart of the matter—an issue that is the underlying theme of all chapters in this volume. The methods presented in these chapters constitute ways of listening carefully. A critique of these methods that highlighted their similarities and differences, and assessed their potentials for revealing processes and knowledge that lie behind writing, would have advanced knowledge in the discipline. But Dobrin seems completely blind to this theme; his wisdom has failed him.

NOTES

1. This reply deals with the general as opposed to the specific misconceptions in Dobrin's critique. One anticipates that the other researchers who contributed to this volume (including Alain Breuleux and myself) would also have much to say about Dobrin's comments on particular aspects of their approaches.

2. I thank Michael L. Hoover for bringing this to my attention.

REFERENCES

Lakatos, I., & Musgrave, A. (Eds.). (1970). *Criticism and the growth of knowledge*. London: Cambridge University Press.

Miller, G. A., Galanter, E., & Pribram, C. (1960). *Plans and the structure of behavior*. New York: Holt.

Salomon, G. (1991). Transcending the qualitative-quantitative debate: The analytic and systemic approaches to educational research. *Educational Researcher, 20*(6), 10-18.

Author Index

Subject Index

About the Contributors

Robert J. Bracewell received his Ph.D. in Educational Theory from the Ontario Institute for Studies in Education. He is currently Associate Professor in the Department of Educational and Counselling Psychology and Director of the Laboratory of Applied Cognitive Science at McGill University. His research focuses on models of text production, the development of expertise in writing, and methods of discourse analysis.

Alain Breuleux received his Ph.D. in Psychology from Université de Montréal and is currently Assistant Professor in the Department of Educational and Counselling Psychology at McGill University. His research involves: (a) the acquisition of goal-directed problem-solving strategies by individuals as they develop expertise in task domains (e.g., instructional design, writing, computer programming); (b) development of models of technical writing and the design of computer environments to facilitate such writing; and (c) examination of learning in multimedia environments.

Roger D. Cherry is Associate Professor in the rhetoric program at The Ohio State University. His work focuses on rhetorical theory and the assessment of writing abilities, and he served as co-editor of *Written Communication* from 1989 to 1993. Among his recent publications are *A Brief Guide to Basic Writing* (with K. Halasek) and *A Rhetoric of Doing* (co-edited with S. Witte and N. Nakadate).

Elaine Chin is an Assistant Professor of Education in the Reading and Literacy Program at the University of Michigan. She teaches courses in social and historical foundations of literacy, writing research, and qualitative research methods. Her current research interests include examinations of the uses of literacy as a tool for learning in medical school, and forms of representation used by chemists on the job. She has published in the *National Reading Conference Yearbook* and was one of the recipients of the 1993 National Council of English Teachers Promising Researchers of the Year Award.

Anne DiPardo is Assistant Professor of English and Education at the University of Iowa. She is the author of *A Kind of Passport: A Basic Writing Adjunct Program and the Challenge of Student Diversity*; a 1992 recipient of the NCTE Promising Researcher Award; and a 1993 recipient of the Outstanding Scholarship Award from the National Writing Centers Association. Her current work focuses upon processes of teacher collaboration in varied school settings.

David N. Dobrin is the author of articles on writing research, technical writing, and computers in writing that have appeared in *College English, JTWC, Computers and Composition,* and many collections. His book, *Writing and Technique,* was published by NCTE. Direct responses to his chapter may be sent to dnd@qad.com.

Stuart Greene is Assistant Professor of English at the University of Wisconsin-Madison, where he directs freshman writing and teaches composition theory. His articles have appeared in *The Journal of Advanced Composition, Rhetoric Review, Written Communication, Research in the Teaching of English,* and *The Educational Psychologist.*

Liz Hamp-Lyons is an Associate Professor of English at the University of Colorado at Denver. Her research interests are in first and second language writing; language testing, especially writing assessment; the written discourse of minorities; and discourse analysis. Among her publications are *Assessing Second Language Writing in Academic Contexts* and *Portfolios and College Writing* (with Bill Condon). She has published in *College Composition and Communication, TESOL Quarterly, Language Learning,* and other journals and scholarly collections.

Lorraine Higgins has a Ph.D. in rhetoric and composition from Carnegie-Mellon. She has worked as a writing researcher at the National Center for the Study of Writing and Literacy for the past 6 years. She is also Director of The Community Literacy Center of Pittsburgh, an innovative educational center that studies and supports literate practices in urban communities. Dr. Higgins has written on the subjects of argumentation, literacy, and collaborative writing, and her work has appeared in a number of professional journals and books. Her chapter, "Reading to Argue: Helping Students Transform Source Texts," recently appeared in *Hearing Ourselves Think,* a research-to-teaching textbook published by Oxford University Press.

George Hillocks, Jr., received his B.A. in English from The College of Wooster, a Diploma in English Studies from The University of Edinburgh (Scotland), and his M.A. and Ph.D. from Case Western Reserve University. He taught secondary school English in Euclid, Ohio, where he was Director of the Project English Demonstration Center from 1963 to 1965. He taught English at Bowling Green State University, where he served as Director of Freshman English Programs. Since 1971 he has been at The University of Chicago, where he is currently Professor in the Department of Education and the Department of English Language and Literature, and continues to serve as Director of the Master of Arts in Teaching/English and as advisor to the graduate program in English Education. His articles have appeared in the *American Journal of Education, Research in the Teaching of English, American Educational Research Journal, English Journal, English Education, College English,* and other journals. He is the author or co-author of several books and monographs, including *Research on Written Composition: New Directions for Teaching,* published by the National Conference on Research in English. He is currently working on a book that attempts to pull together the various theories implicated in the teaching of writing, tentatively titled *Teaching Writing, Integrating Theories.*

Elizabeth Hodges is an Assistant Professor of English at Virginia Commonwealth University, where she teaches essay writing workshops, freshman to graduate, and graduate courses in composition theory, research, and pedagogy. She contributes to writing program administration as the Associate Director of Composition and Rhetoric, the Director of the Writing Center, the Co-Director of the Capital Writing Project, and the co-director of a State Council of Higher Education in Virginia Grant, which is addressing the improvement of student writing through composition faculty development. In part, this grant targets concerns of adjunct faculty and provides rewarded opportunities for adjunct teachers to explore current issues in composition studies and develop skills as teacher-researchers. Currently, her research and writing focuses on the sociolinguistics of teachers' and students' interactions about writing, with special attention to conversations ongoing in the margins of essays. She received her Ph.D. from the University of Pennsylvania.

George E. Newell is Associate Professor and program coordinator of English Education in the College of Education, The Ohio State University. After teaching high school English for several years, he received his Ph.D. from Stanford University. He was recognized for his *Promising Research in the*

Teaching of English from the National Council of Teachers of English. He has authored numerous articles exploring the interrelationship of writing and learning, in journals such as *Research in the Teaching of English, Written Communication, Journal of Reading Behavior,* and *Review of Educational Research,* and recently co-edited (with Russel Durst) *Exploring Texts: The Role of Discussion and Writing in the Teaching and Learning of Literature.* His current research examines how school and departmental contexts shape how English teachers construct classroom literature curriculum.

Peter Smagorinsky is an Assistant Professor in the College of Education at the University of Oklahoma, where he teaches in the English Education program. His research interests focus on classroom literacy. To that end he has recently used protocol analysis to study high school writers as they compose across the curriculum; stimulated recall to analyze alternative school students' artistic responses to literature; discourse analysis to study high school students discussing literature in teacher-led and small-group settings; and interviews to study teachers' and students' conceptions of the purpose of writing in a variety of disciplines. His work has appeared in *Research in the Teaching of English, Written Communication, Communication Education, English Education, The Social Studies, Journal of Advanced Composition,* and *English Journal.*

Melanie Sperling is Assistant Professor of Education at Stanford University. She studies writing and the teaching and learning of writing, with particular interests in the social contexts of written language acquisition and development in the secondary school. Her current research focuses on the social dimensions of writing and responding to writing, exploring the roles writers and readers enact in these processes. She teaches courses covering writing and literacy theory and research, as well as teacher preparation in the English language arts. She is a recent National Academy of Education Spencer Fellow and received the National Council of Teachers of English Promising Researcher award for her studies of teacher-student writing conferences. Her work has appeared in journals and books, including *Research in the Teaching of English, Written Communication,* and *English Journal.*

James F. Stratman is Assistant Professor and Director of Graduate Studies in the Department of English at the University of Colorado at Denver, where he teaches courses in technical communication and legal reasoning and writing. He received his Ph.D. in Rhetoric from Carnegie-Mellon University. His current research interests include real-time study of legal argument reading and interpretation processes in experts and novices; strengths, limits, and innovative uses of think-aloud protocol methodology; and rhetorical analyses of scientific and risk communication controversies. He is an active reviewer for several rhetoric and composition journals, and has published articles in *College English, Review of Educational Research, Discourse Processes, Journal of Business and Technical Communication, Management Communication Quarterly, Industrial Relations Law Journal,* and *Legal Writing,* among others.

Deborah Swanson-Owens received her Ph.D. from Stanford University and teaches at San Francisco State University. She has previously published her research in *Research in the Teaching of English* and frequently makes presentations at national conferences.

Stephen P. Witte is Knight Professor of Composition Theory at Kent State University. He is the co-founder (with J. Daly) of *Written Communication,* and he has served as one of its co-editors since its founding in 1954. Over the past 15 years, his articles and chapters have appeared in a number of journals and book collections. Among his recent publications are *A Rhetoric of Doing* (co-edited with N. Nakadate and R. Cherry). He is currently working on a book on writing assessment and one on situated writing from a constructivist semiotic perspective.